A Decision-centred View of Environmental Planning

by

ANDREAS FALUDI

University of Amsterdam, The Netherlands

PERGAMON PRESS

OXFORD · NEW YORK · BEIJING · FRANKFURT
SÃO PAULO · SYDNEY · TOKYO · TORONTO

U.K.	Pergamon Press, Headington Hill Hall, Oxford OX3 0BW, England
U.S.A.	Pergamon Press, Maxwell House, Fairview Park, Elmsford, New York 10523, U.S.A.
PEOPLE'S REPUBLIC OF CHINA	Pergamon Press, Room 4037, Qianmen Hotel, Beijing, People's Republic of China
FEDERAL REPUBLIC OF GERMANY	Pergamon Press, Hammerweg 6, D-6242 Kronberg, Federal Republic of Germany
BRAZIL	Pergamon Editora, Rua Eça de Queiros, 346, CEP 04011, Paraiso, São Paulo, Brazil
AUSTRALIA	Pergamon Press Australia, P.O. Box 544, Potts Point, N.S.W. 2011, Australia
JAPAN	Pergamon Press, 8th Floor, Matsuoka Central Building, 1-7-1 Nishishinjuku, Shinjuku-ku, Tokyo 160, Japan
CANADA	Pergamon Press Canada, Suite No. 271, 253 College Street, Toronto, Ontario, Canada M5T 1R5

First edition 1987

Library of Congress Cataloging-in-Publication Data
Faludi, Andreas.
A decision-centred view of environmental planning.
(Urban and regional planning series; v. 38)
Bibliography: p.
Includes index.
1. Environmental policy—Decision making. I. Title. II. Series.
HC79.E5F28 1987   333.7   87-10414

British Library Cataloguing in Publication Data
Faludi, Andreas.
A decision-centred view of environmental planning.
(Urban and regional planning series, ISSN 0305-5582; v. 38).
1. City planning 2. Regional planning
I. Title II. Series
711 HT166

ISBN 0-08-032698-6 Hardcover
ISBN 0-08-034983-8 Flexicover

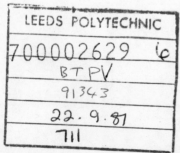
Printed in Great Britain by A. Wheaton & Co. Ltd., Exeter

To the memory of

PETER DE RUIJTER

scholar and friend

PREFACE

My aim in this work is to reconstruct planning theory around a view of planning that sees its main purpose as helping us in taking decisions. The readership which I have in mind is students and their teachers, with whom I have been engaged in many debates in the past. I also address practitioners: their grievances against planning theorists are sometimes legitimate. What I can offer, though, is not less theory, but theory that takes planning practice as its starting point. For this readership I seek to clarify the position I take, and to demonstrate its value to real-life decision-making and planning.

This book is a sequel to *Planning Theory* (Faludi, 1984, 1st edition 1973). It distinguishes itself from that work by (a) the fact that it has been preceded by much research on planning practice (some of it of a comparative nature, see Thomas *et al.*, 1983); (b) the influence exerted on me by the "IOR School" (named after the Institute for Operational Research, see Chapter 6); (c) proposing a "decision-centred view of planning" which is a synthesis of the pragmatic approach of this school with the "rational planning model" so prominent in the American literature of the sixties; (d) going beyond my previous "generic" approach, so that this work culminates in a new look at environmental planning-an umbrella term used to refer to the planning of all forms of environmental intervention.

There are three main messages, one in each part of this book.

Part One relates to the sense of crisis in planning thought. Often the rational planning model is seen as the culprit. It is said to be ill-adapted to uncertainty and conflict. But the proponents of rational planning were fully aware of these from the start, and the development of planning thought has been more continuous and cumulative than many are willing to grant. The major break in it concerns not the rational planning model as such, but its application. Traditionally, that application has been to the making of plans. But the widespread failure in getting plans implemented raises important questions about their role. Part One shows that a cogent, if modest, view on this can be formulated by starting, not with plan-making but with those concrete decisions which have a real impact on our lives. Sometimes they require the making of a plan, but it is these decisions-and the question whether they are rational-which we should start with.

Part Two applies this pragmatic view to environmental planning. Often it is argued that environmental planning requires a theory of its own. Indeed, account must be taken of the nature of that with which environmental planning is concerned. Part Two seeks to show that its object is the sum of decisions which authorities take with respect to the environment. Drawing up coherent schemes for these decisions is what environmental planning is about. Part Two then analyses typical approaches to environmental planning, and shows how it copes with the need for flexibility.

Part Three summarises the argument and points out where current debates concerning the role of the state touch upon continuing concerns in planning. Perhaps the most important idea to be relegated to the dustbin is that planning is wedded to a strong role of the state. In the main, this link is made because a strong state promises opportunities for bringing superior wisdom to bear on societal decision-making. But planning does *not* necessarily represent superior wisdom. It merely adds some-albeit important-considerations to such decision-making as is going on already. Sometimes these considerations should override ongoing concerns, but sometimes not. Also, a strong role for state agencies may not be the only, let alone the best, way of making sure that planning considerations are in fact taken account of. A cool look is needed, therefore, at the ideological affiliations of planning. The same is true for the working of planning in practice. Part Three gives an agenda for research. Not the least important item on it is the comprehensive evaluation of environmental planning, its institutions and its practices.

My sympathy for practitioners of planning notwithstanding, this work is neither a "how-to-do-it" book, nor is it about planning method. Rather, it seeks to point out what the fundamentals of a practicable approach to planning are. It is hoped that this will instill a new-albeit realistic-sense of purpose in planning-theoretical debates.

References

Faludi, A. (1984; 1st published 1973) *Planning Theory*, Pergamon Press, Oxford.
Thomas, H. D., Minett, J. M., Hopkins, S., Hamnett, S. L., Faludi, A. and Barrell, D. (1983) *Flexibility and Commitment in Planning*, Martinus Nijhoff, The Hague, Boston and London.

ACKNOWLEDGEMENTS

ANY work that summarises thinking developed over more than a decade owes much to other people. It is impossible to acknowledge all of them, let alone do so briefly. I can do no more than indicate the major sources of inspiration, most of them fellow academics and students, whose paths crossed mine at various times.

Undoubtedly, the major factor in my life since publishing my previous works on planning theory has been my taking up academic appointments in The Netherlands. Dr Steve Hamnett joined me for a number of years. His distinguished career since has taken him back to Britain and on to Australia. I shall never forget the inspiration which I drew from our joint work. That was when the idea of a decision-centred view of planning arose.

It was during these years, too, that my acquaintance from earlier days with John Friend and Allen Hickling (both of them associated with the development of what I like to call the "IOR School", about which more in this book) developed into friendship. That I owe much to our discussions will be evident to the reader from the content of Chapter 6. The reason I embarked on a programme aimed at introducing their strategic choice in The Netherlands relates to work done with students. Two of them, Roel Hartmann and Hans Meester, continued to work with me as researchers, applying their skills to the production of much useful material. They are now successful planners, using strategic choice with consummate skill.

Others joined me in my explorations of the implications of strategic choice for Dutch planning practice. None worked with me for as long and as intensively as Dr Hans Mastop, whose fundamental study on Dutch provincial planning took him far beyond strategic choice to the dizzy heights of legal doctrine and the depths of the philosophy of science. Much in this work bears his stamp. Chapter 6, in particular, owes a great deal to a joint paper published in *Environment and Planning B* in 1982.

Writing this book was made possible by the University of Amsterdam granting me sabbatical leave during 1984/85. The main part of that year was spent as a Fulbright Scholar at the University of California at Berkeley, enjoying the facilities and privileges of a Visiting Scholar at Professor Melvin Webber's distinguished Institute of Urban and Regional Development. The award of an Australian-European Fellowship by the Commonwealth of Australia made it possible to include some material on Australian planning.

Many people have read and commented upon parts of the manuscript of this book. This is especially true of Chapter 2 on the Chicago School, which

I submitted to the scrutiny of all the Chicago faculty and graduates who were available. Professors Edward C. Banfield, Melville C. Branch, John Friedmann, Britton Harris, Richard Meier and Ira M. Robinson all gave their time willingly.

Professor Melvin Webber read a substantial part of the manuscript. I remember our lively discussion with gratitude. Professor Donald Miller helped with clarifying my ideas and gave me access to valuable sources. Professor Judith de Neufville and Dr Karen Christensen gave of their time as well. On my travels, I developed a very fruitful relationship, too, with Dr Doug Cocks and his staff at Canberra in Australia. Our discussions concerned the basic ideas underlying Part Two on the application of the decision-centred view of planning to environmental matters. An early version of my views were published in the journal *Landscape Planning* in 1985, and I owe my thanks to the editor, Professor Peter Jacobs, as well as to the three referees for their comments on drafts of that paper. Chapters 12 and 13 contain material that was published for the first time in 1985 in the *Australian Planner* and in 1986 in *Environment and Planning B: Planning and Design*.

Through personal meetings and correspondence, Professor George Lefcoe has provided much stimulation. His knowledge of United States planning, acquired in his dual capacity of academic and Planning Commissioner of Los Angeles County, gives his writings a special flavour.

Dutch scholars have also commented upon parts of this manuscript. Dr Hans van der Cammen, Dr Hans Mastop, Dr Barrie Needham, Arnold van der Valk, and my new colleague and friend at the University of Amsterdam, Professor Jaap Buit, are those whom I can remember-with the usual apologies to those whom I have forgotten.

This book bears a close relationship with another one published in 1986: *Critical Rationalism and Planning Methodology*. Cross-references have been included at the appropriate places throughout the text. Another work to which I refer throughout this book is the joint product of a number of my former colleagues at the Oxford Polytechnic, Dr Hamnett and myself: *Flexibility and Commitment in Planning*. I think that writing a book between six of us was no mean achievement. Thanks are due to all the co-authors, of what I refer to in the text as the "Leiden-Oxford study", for the stimulating time which we had together; but I suppose particular thanks are due to David Thomas, who has taken on the thankless task of editing the whole work so that it could come out in a volume that I am still proud to have contributed to.

In the Foreword of *Planning Theory* I invited critics "to pour scorn on the flaws in my argument", at the same time expressing the hope that "I may achieve the academic requirement of impartiality when reviewing their counter-arguments" (1984, 1st published 1973, p. x). There have been many occasions since to do the latter, including the writing of the Foreword to the 1984 reprint. Chapter 5 draws on it, and on a number of other papers as well. The reader must judge for himself whether I have lived up to the standard which I set myself fourteen years ago.

Typing this work has been a wholly private affair, as all my major work is, these days, between my dear wife, our word processor, and myself. Many a marriage seems to have been threatened by the introduction of the personal computer into the home. During the more than three years that we have shared ours with one, our marriage has gone from strength to strength. Of course, it is not the word processor that I credit with this achievement, but my wife. She has accepted our new companion, and the way of life and the chores that go with it, contributing her major share, as cheerfully as ever.

References

Faludi, A. (1984; 1st published 1973) *Planning Theory*, Pergamon Press, Oxford.

Faludi, A. (1985) "Flexibility in zoning: the Australian case", *Australian Planner*, **23**, 19-24.

Faludi, A. (1985) "A decision-centred view of environmental planning", *Landscape Planning*, **12**, 239-56.

Faludi, A. (1986) *Critical Rationalism and Planning Methodology*, Pion Press, London.

Faludi, A. (1986) "Flexibility and US zoning: a European perspective", *Environment and Planning B: Planning and Design*, **13**, 255-78.

Faludi, A. and Hamnett, S. L. (1976) "Flexibility in Dutch local planning", Working Papers No. 28, Oxford Polytechnic, Department of Town Planning, Oxford.

Faludi, A. and Mastop, J. M. (1982) "The I. O. R. School: the development of a planning methodology", *Environment and Planning B*, **9**, 241-56.

Thomas, H. D., Minett, J. M., Hopkins, S., Hamnett, S. L., Faludi, A. and Barrell, D. (1983) *Flexibility and Commitment in Planning*, Martinus Nijhoff, The Hague, Boston, London.

CONTENTS

PART ONE

Towards a Decision-centred View of Planning

MAN'S world is built from decision. We might discuss whether choice is illusory. But in everyday life we do assume that it exists, that the consequences of decisions are a matter of concern, and that those who take them must be answerable for them. Thus, when my neighbour decides to raise chickens which wake me up, I hold him responsible. Likewise, when I build an extension to my house and apply for the necessary permits, the authorities have a genuine choice in the matter and are held responsible for the consequences. As I shall explain later, it is the purpose of planning to help with the taking of such decisions.

We live not only with decisions on which we must take action; there are potential decisions also. My daily journey to work is 50 miles, but we do not move house. One day we might. We bear this possibility in mind when considering whether to have the house painted, the roof repaired, a boiler installed, and so forth. When I went on a sabbatical to write this book, we contemplated whether to sell up and move closer to my work after my return, thus saving us the worry of letting our home. So far, we have always decided against leaving charming Delft, but the possibility is there, making us realise the conditional nature of everyday actions.

Many contingencies result from the interrelatedness of decisions. The lease of our department expires in a few years' time. It might move to somewhere farther away from Amsterdam Central Station, thus prolonging my journey to work. But if the department does move, then where it goes determines where we should move within the Amsterdam region-if at all. After all, shorter working weeks might make a journey to work which is longer still seem acceptable. We decide to hang on after all. In other words, the outcome of planning can be no action at all. The example demonstrates also that planning has everything to do with such contingencies as we try to come to terms with, either by removing uncertainty, or by taking account of it. Planning relates to (a) those decisions which we take, either because the situation forces them on us, or because we want to change that situation deliberately into something

1

more in tune with our wishes; and (b) those taken by others which affect us (thus becoming part of the context in which we take our decisions). In planning we relate all these decisions to each other, thereby trying to make sense out of our choices.

But not all decisions require planning. The dustbin goes outside to be emptied by the refuse collectors every Wednesday. Carrying the bin outside is ordinary routine, but this isn't so with all maintenance work. I am not a do-it-yourselfer: maintenance work costs me money. Whenever we have a problem of water seeping through, we call the plumber as automatically as we carry out the dustbin. But paint work can wait, and whether or not to have it done this year is a matter of deliberation. Such a decision becomes the object of planning. The reason for this is that it relates to other expenditure: that car that needs replacing, or that vacation to wherever it is.

Having planned my expenditure does not mean to say that I follow the plan slavishly. There are emergencies and unforeseen opportunities. When, in a drive to stimulate employment, the Dutch government offered subsidies for paint work, we put in an application, committing ourselves to paying our share immediately, spending plan or no spending plan.

If all this sounds very much like common sense, then so be it! It is one of the characteristics of this book that it does not draw a line between planning and everyday life. Often, planning is glorified out of all proportion. As in other walks of life, planners have their heroes, celebrated for their courage and drive. Their achievements are the New Towns, rehabilitation schemes, roads, and so on. Often they have reached their objectives against opposition from short-sighted people concerned with their own, rather than the common, good. (There are tragic planning heroes also, whose warnings go unheeded. Undaunted by disappointment, they go on propagating their visions.) But in any case, planners' heroes are men of action, men of war almost. But many planners overlook one basic fact of life in planning: it is not about the designing of a better world from scratch. It can hardly ever be compared to building a new house. Rather, it is coordinating what is going to happen anyway, as I do in decisions about paintwork and whether to call the plumber. It is making things happen *without* designing them from scratch, and often without carrying out the work involved oneself. Its essence lies in improving what is being done, and in this sense, of course, a better world is being sought. But this is done *indirectly*.

My planning hero looks like Jonathan Barnett, therefore, who writes about designing cities without designing individual buildings (Barnett, 1978, 1982). Like so very few designers, he accepts that he is not creating the good city but helping the many actors who shape the urban fabric to pursue their own plans, whilst at the same time trying to avoid unwanted side-effects, and to achieve some good for the community.

How does planning thought relate to this form of planning? That is what Part One is about. Now, planning thought is afflicted by a curious problem.

Nobody dares say anything positive about it. Rather, it is said to be "in the doldrums" (de Neufville, 1983, p. 35). The old "paradigm"-identified either with comprehensive land-use planning (Galloway and Mahayni, 1977) or with the "rational model" (Alexander, 1984)-is said to be obsolete, but there is no replacement. The model "remains in force because no competitive set of ideas has attracted sufficient support to supplant it" (Hemmens, 1980, p. 259). Indeed, a survey by Klosterman (1981) showed that half of the planning programmes still set Davidoff and Reiner (1962; see Section 3.1) as required reading. Research by Vasu (1979, pp. 42-8, 198-80), and the prominence given to the rational planning model in the International City Managers' Association's *The Practice of Local Government Planning* (So *et. al.*, 1979) show its continuing use by practitioners.

Still, the obsolescence of this rational model is one of the dogmas most frequently heard. It is said to be based on the assumption of certainty (Christensen, 1985, p. 66), on a consensus view of society (Thomas, 1979, in Paris, 1982, pp. 24-5), on a technocratic view of the role of the planner (Friedmann, 1973, p. 68), and the like. But does the "rational planning model" really suffer from all these shortcomings? What form has that model taken, since Meyerson and Banfield (see Section 2.3) introduced it into the planning literature in 1955? In this book I show that the "rational planning model", attacked in this way, is a straw man. The original formulation anticipates practically all the criticisms which have been voiced against that model ever since; its critics have been unable to add much to its original formulation. Alternatives, like Simon's "satisficing", Etzioni's "mixed scanning" (see Section 3.4) and Dror's addition of extra-rational elements (see Dror, 1968), are but extensions of the basic model.

Only three real advances have been made. The "IOR School", to be discussed in Chapter 6, has introduced the notion of strategic choice. It refers to the taking of decisions in the light of their wider context. The distinction results between ordinary decisions and decisions relating to groups, or clusters, of other decisions defining that context. Chapter 8-presenting my decision-centred view of planning-identifies these as *operational* and *planning decisions.*

The literature, up to and including Christensen (1985), identifies planning with problem-solving. However, we now see that not all problem-solving is planning. The distinctive characteristic of planning is, rather, that it relates to clusters of interrelated decisions. In other words, the problem which planning addresses is coordination. It is *problem-solving*, not of the first, but *of the second order*, so to speak.

The second addition I claim some credit for. It relates to the distinction drawn above between operational and planning decisions. Traditionally, the rational model is being applied to plan-making. Operational decisions are supposed to implement the rational plan formulated in so doing. But the "IOR School" puts the emphasis on operational decisions. Plans are mere aids to taking them rationally, that is with full awareness of their consequences. This

DCV–B

means that the primary concern must be not with rationality in plan-making, but in operational decision-making.

The third innovation relates to the function of the rational model. *Planning Theory* presented the rational planning model, not as a prescription for how to act in planning, but as a *rule for testing decisions* (see Chapter 4). This notion is central also to the parallel work on *Critical Rationalism and Planning Methodology* (Faludi, 1986). Indeed, it permeates my whole thinking and is clearly present in this work, too, where it criticises leading planning writers for conceiving of rationality as a behavioural, rather than as a methodological rule.

With this, the basic idea has been given of Part One. Before outlining it in more detail, a comment is needed on the context of the developments described in this book. The context is that of the Anglo-American academic network, a major force in planning thought. Even Dutch planning bears the marks of its influence. But it is wrong to think that this network makes for uniformity. There are distinct and shifting emphases which it is important to understand. Thus the concern for a methodical approach in planning, commensurate with the canons of science, in which the rational planning model is rooted, originated in the America of the fifties and sixties. British planning writers started following the example in the late sixties and seventies at a point in time at which American enthusiasm for such approaches was almost over.

My earlier work, discussed in Chapter 4, was written whilst teaching at the Oxford Polytechnic. The aim, in particular of *A Reader in Planning Theory* (Faludi, 1973), was to make American literature accessible to British planning students. *Planning Theory*, too, draws heavily on American sources. Before me, McLoughlin (1969) and Chadwick (1978, 1st edition 1970) had successfully turned American ideas into a distinct "systems approach". The fact that I criticise it in Section 3.3. should not detract from their achievement, which was to synthesise ideas and to relate them firmly to the, at that time seemingly very challenging, tasks of town and country planning.

The "IOR School", too, has its roots in American thinking. It also presents a distinctively British contribution, bearing the mark of its time, characterised by more optimism as regards public planning than current fashion permits. With its emphasis on uncertainty, on a step-by-step approach and learning, it proves, however, remarkably adaptable to the present chilling climate. Despite the fact that it has never received much recognition in the United States, many parallels exist in the recent American literature. The reason for this is its recognition, without this being rooted in deep reflection on the theory of knowledge and of science, of the tentative and value-laden character of all human insights. This is what attracted me in the work of the "IOR School" when I started referring to it in earnest whilst working on my first major empirical research, the Leiden-Oxford Study (Thomas *et al.*, 1983). With this, and because I had returned to the Continent of Europe after almost 7 years of immersion into British planning, a new element came to the fore in my thinking. The study focused on the tension between flexibility and commitment, particularly evident in The Netherlands, where the emphasis on order in development is strong. The impossibility of early commitment to the implementation of detailed schemes seemed evident, though, even in that Dutch context. The "decision-centred view of planning", in which Part One culminates, takes account of this.

The basic skeleton of Part One is formed by Chapters 2, 4, 6 and 8. Chapter 2 introduces the rational planning model as developed by the "Chicago School" and is thus distinctively American; Chapter 4 discusses *Planning Theory*, based on American literature, but relating also to the British context; Chapter 6 introduces the British "IOR School"; and Chapter 8 the decision-centred view of planning which draws on the Dutch-British comparison.

The other chapters provide supportive arguments: Chapter 1 identifies classic planning thought on both sides of the Atlantic as falling short on planning method. This provides the background for an appreciation of the "Chicago School" whose achievement is to have formulated the methodical approach to planning evolving around the rational planning model which I advocate. Chapter 3 marks high points and diversions in its development during the sixties, mainly in the United States. The "proceduralist" versus "substantivist" controversy resulting from the proposal, in *Planning Theory* and many other works, that planning thought should concentrate on the planning process and planning organisation, is the topic of Chapter 5. That debate has been more prominent in Britain, although North American scholars, some of them Marxist-inspired like Scott and Roweis, have also participated. (Even then, British planning journals-the various *Environment and Planning* series-provided their main medium of expression.) Chapter 7 documents parallels in the (mostly American) academic literature to the "IOR School". They have in common with that school that they-wrongly, to my mind-dismiss the rational planning model. That model is implied in what they say, which is one of the things I show in Part One.

References

Alexander, E. R. (1984) "After rationality, what?: review of responses to paradigm breakdown", *Journal of the American Planning Association,* **50**, 62-9.

Barnett, J. (1974) *Urban Design as Public Policy: Practical Methods for Improving Cities,* Architectural Record, McGraw-Hill, New York.

Barnett, J. (1982) *An Introduction to Urban Design,* Harper & Row, New York.

Chadwick, G. A. (1978; 1st edition 1970) *A Systems View of Planning,* Pergamon Press, Oxford.

Christensen, K. S. (1985) "Coping with uncertainty in planning", *Journal of the American Planning Association,* **51**, 63-73.

*Davidoff, P. and Reiner, T. A. (1962) "A choice theory of planning", *Journal of the American Institute of Planners,* **28**, 108-15.

Dror, Y. (1968) *Public Policymaking Reexamined,* Chandler, Chicago.

Faludi, A. (1973) *A Reader in Planning Theory,* Pergamon Press, Oxford.

Faludi, A. (1986) *Critical Rationalism and Planning Methodology,* Pion Press, London.

Friedmann, J. (1973) *Retracking America: A Theory of Transactive Planning,* Doubleday Anchor, Garden City, New York.

Galloway, T. D. and Mahayni, R. G. (1977) "Planning theory in retrospect: the process of paradigm change", *Journal of the American Institute of Planners,* **43,** 62-71.

Hemmens, G. C. (1980) "New directions in planning theory", *Journal of the American Planning Association,* **46,** 259-60.

Klosterman, R. E. (1981) "Contemporary planning theory education: results of a course survey", *Journal of Planning Education and Research*, **1,** 1-11.

McLoughlin, J. B. (1969) *Urban and Regional Planning: A System Approach,* Faber & Faber, London.

Meyerson, M. M. and Banfield, E. C. (1955) *Politics, Planning and the Public Interest: The Case of Public Housing at Chicago*, Free Press, New York.

Neufville, J. I. de (1983) "The doldrums of planning theory", *Journal of Planning Education and Research,* **3,** 35-45.

Paris, C. (1982) "Introduction by the editor, Part One: A critique of pure planning", in: *Critical Readings in Planning Theory,* (ed. C. Paris), Pergamon Press, Oxford, pp. 3-11.

So, F. S., Stollman, I., Beal, F. and Arnold, D. S. (eds) (1979) *The Practice of Local Government Planning,* International City Management Association, Washington, D C.

Thomas, M. J. (1979) "The procedural planning theory of A. Faludi", *Planning Outlook,* **22,** 72-6; see also C. Paris (ed.) (1982) *Critical Readings in Planning Theory,* Pergamon Press, Oxford, pp. 13-25.

Thomas, H. D., Minett, J. M., Hopkins, S., Hamnett, S. L., Faludi, A., and Barrell, D. (1983) *Flexibility and Commitment in Planning,* Martinus Nijhoff, The Hague, Boston and London.

Vasu, M. L. (1979) *Politics and Planning: National Study of American Planners,* University of North Carolina Press, Chapel Hill, NC.

* Included in Faludi, A. (ed.) *A Reader in Planning Theory*, Pergamon Press, Oxford.

CHAPTER 1

Without Method

CLASSIC planning thought pays little attention to method. Though seemingly the empitome of a systematic approach, the doctrine of the Scottish biologist-cum-sociologist and town planner Patrick Geddes (1854-932) of *survey before plan* does not fill this void. Emphasising research before a plan is made, if anything, deflects attention away from the vital step of translating knowledge into action. But knowledge does not do what a naïve view of science expects of it: provide an unambiguous guide for action; so this step does warrant special attention. The purpose of planning method is to make this step explicit. As we shall see, it was not until Meyerson and Banfield (1955), in a work to be discussed in Section 2.3, that the literature in environmental planning paid attention to it. Since bridging the gap between knowledge and action is what planning is all about, it is no exaggeration to say that that is when planning thought really started.

"Survey before plan" is indeed no better than the ideology of the *creative leap*, holding that insights suddenly gel into an intuitive understanding of the nature of whatever one is concerned with. This has disturbing consequences for democratic decision-making. It replaces public argument, leading from accepted premises to conclusions reached by reference to mystical faculties of the individual mind.

Geddes is a father figure in planning but, clearly, we have surpassed him. Contemporary social scientists have a low esteem for surveys (see Abrams, 1968) and reject the role of handmaiden to the master-designer into which "survey before plan" casts them. So why flog a dead horse? The reason is that, albeit in modified form, the idea of knowledge forming a rock-solid base for action persists. The idea of "comprehensive planning" leading to a master plan (see Section 3.2) was based on it. For a while the systems planners and model-builders (discussed in Section 3.3) entertained it too. In pretending that their research reveals its "true nature" as reflecting the contradictions of capitalism, some of those engaged in materialist analyses of planning (see Section 5.3) are not entirely free from it either.

The first section discusses *the Geddesian approach*, claiming that it is both mistaken and undemocratic. *Noble intentions, noble plans* extends this critique to classic American authors and examples. *Why method?* emphasises the

7

importance of rendering thought processes explicit so that they can be shared. It stresses that human knowledge is fallible, but capable of improvement.

1.1 The Geddesian approach

What is wrong about "survey before plan"? Does it not make sense that one should acquaint oneself with the situation before starting to tamper with it?

My aim in discussing the Geddesian approach is to show that this doctrine disregards the conditional nature of knowledge and the need to render explicit such value judgements as are implied even in the simplest survey. It also disregards the fact that the step from knowledge to action involves choices.

The next section shows this basic principle to be violated not only by Geddes but by planning pioneers generally. It is a feature of classic planning thought as such.

Geddes is firmly rooted in nineteenth-century positivism. That philosophy put great trust in the power of "positive" knowledge (knowledge uncontaminated by religious-today we would say ideological-belief) as held by experts to guide us in action. As his biographer Boardman (1978, pp. 33-5) relates, Geddes was fascinated by Auguste Comte, the founder of this philosophy (see also Fletcher, 1971, pp. 832-9). In his later years he saw himself as updating it (Boardman, 1978, pp. 408-9).

Geddes is credited with much vision (Goist, 1974). There are those also who think of him as somewhat confused. For instance, Hall (1982) says that Mumford's greatest achievement was to "take Geddes' visionary ramblings and to make them not merely sense, which certainly Geddes never did, but also the inspiration that Geddes so passionately felt but could not adequately convey" (p. 217). Boardman (1978), too, gives the impression that there was not only profusion of ideas but also confusion in his manner of working. As regards the prime example of a survey-that concerning Edinburgh-contemporary witnesses do convey a chaotic impression. It was the force of his personality which brought it to life when Geddes took people through the exhibition devoted to it. Fletcher (1971), on the other hand, credits the sociographers, including Geddes, with a thorough understanding of methods.

Taylor (1980) raises a different point. He criticises "survey before plan" as representing the inductive method:

this method of gaining knowledge, whereby one begins with empirical observations and then derives the facts of the situation from that survey, is essentially similar to the traditionally accepted method of gaining knowledge. This traditional theory of science has it that the scientist begins the process of scientific discovery by first making observations of phenomena in the world, and then, where these observations repeatedly reveal regularities ... he generalises his observations to arrive at some universal empirical or scientific theory which describes and explains the appearance and behaviour of the phenomena under question (p. 165).

But the issue here is not whether Geddes conducted surveys systematically. It is not even whether his method was "inductive"-that is, whether Geddes argued from the particular to the general. The issue is the use to which Geddes put surveys. Here we find a great void. Nowhere does Geddes reveal how that step should be taken. We must infer his method from his writings and doings. (More from the former than from the latter, because, very much to his chagrin, he received few planning commisions, most of them in India.)

One of the examples on which we can draw is the plan for Dunfermline submitted as part of a competition (see Geddes, 1904a). It shows a lack of attention to the step which leads from knowledge to action. His proposals are simply presented as flowing from his survey.

Boardman's description of the "Outlook Tower"-where he kept a permanent exhibition on Edinburgh-shows that this lack of attention for planning method was no accident. Rather, Geddes regarded the step from insights to action as a personal affair. Apparently, the museum contained a bare room, the Inlook Tower, in which the visitor was invited to ponder the implications for action in splendid isolation, much as designers do (see Boardman, 1978, p. 141).

It is the faithful collaborator and co-author of a number of books by Geddes, the first Secretary to the Sociological Association in Britain, who describes this "method" of proceeding, which they call "civics", in more explicit terms:

Having made his civic survey, the student retires, let us say, into his meditative cell. He takes with him a carefully built up store of mental imagery ... of the given city and its inhabitants as evolving towards definite ideals or degenerating towards their negation. ... (Then) the student of sociology re-emerges into the world as civic statesman. ... The man of action is getting ready with a programme and policy (Branford, 1914, p. 393).

"Definite ideals" and their "negation" indicate an evolutionary view of social development which is not at issue here. What is at issue is the imagery of the emergence of the "sociologist" as civic statesman. It represents a personalised view of what we would presently call the planning process, and underlines the importance attached to knowledge as a basis for action, as well as of the expert possessing such knowledge as being predestined to prescribe it. It is a "method" fit for working with the enlightened maharajas who gave Geddes planning commissions, but not for democratic planning. But, then, Geddes did not have much patience for representative democracy anyway, saying that it "fails to yield all that its inventors hoped of it, simply because it is so tolerantly representative of its majorities; and there is great truth in the common consolation that our municipal governments, like larger ones, are seldom much worse than we deserve" (Geddes, 1904b, p. 113). There is more than a faint resemblance here with the "conservative reform movement" in the United States, with which planning will be shown, below, to be linked.

This may be thought to contradict the emphasis on what, today, we would call participation. Geddes was involved in extramural studies at various universities and also organised many exhibitions to educate the public in civic matters. But that is the whole point: like planners in the sixties keen to use public participation to sell their plans (see Broady, 1968), he was seeking to educate citizens to recognise Truth as it had revealed itself to him. There was no notion in this of uncertainty, no idea that his insights were conditioned by his values. Today we recognise that every survey of, for instance, housing conditions is based on certain assumptions: that poor housing is a social problem which should be remedied, and so forth. We recognise also that the views of the researcher may colour his findings.

The planning "method" of Geddes suited architects in planning. It complemented their approach to design, where it is standard practice to do site visits and collect information on the requirements which a building must meet. This is why the doctrine of survey before plan was accepted eagerly, and architects called upon social scientists to render their service. A division of work and a functional hierarchy emerged which was to dominate British planning, in any case, for many decades to come.

The effectiveness of surveys in guiding action has been questioned. Planning agencies "are the repositories of many unutilized surveys", as Davidoff and Reiner (1962, in Faludi, 1973, p. 29) complain, in a paper to be discussed in Section 3.1. Indeed, one of the reasons why social scientists in British planning accepted American approaches like model-building and systems analysis so eagerly in the late sixties (ironically at a time when they started being questioned in the United States; see Batty, 1982; Breheny, 1983, Hall, 1983) was the promise of a social-scientific planning expertise beyond surveys which would liberate them from the architectural yoke (see Faludi, 1978; see also Section 3.3). (Dutch planning was in turn strongly influenced by the British systems approach to planning.)

Survey research is by no means unique to planning. Harvey (1969) refers to geography being caught up in the same nineteenth-century view of science. His *bête noire* is the view, represented by Hartshorne (1959 1977; 1st published 1939), that geography is an exception amongst the sciences in that, rather than searching for generalities, it deals with unique phenomena. As in history, an "idiographic method" (description) is said to be more adequate than the standard model of explanation.

Hartshorne is aware of the fact, though, that one cannot observe everything. So the question arises of how to choose what to observe and what to leave aside. This

is sometimes called the "problem of significance". In practice geographers do not study *everything* in spatial context, but limit considerations to a selection of phenomena. The question arises as to the grounds for this selection. Hartshorne (1959, chapter 5) examines this bothersome problem but the only criterion of significance he could establish was that the phenomena should be "significant to man" (Harvey, 1969, p. 74).

Harvey's complaint is that this criterion "can be applied to all knowledge, however, and without further refinement it remains empty of any meaning" (*ibid.*). Another complaint might be that it relies on the personal appreciation of the researcher. Where this is not made explicit, there this view comes close to the design doctrine of the "creative leap".

What is underlying is a misconceived idea, in the first instance about knowledge; and in the second about its relation to action. This misconception has a long tradition and conforms to popular beliefs about science and the role of experts:

The doctrine, deriving no doubt from the faith of the French Enlightenment in the perfectability of man and society, contends that wise leaders can know enough about what goes on to say what is right and wrong about it. It holds too that those wise leaders are capable of inventing a better social order than the present one, then of rationally designing a sequence of actions to induce that order (Webber, 1983, p. 93).

But knowledge simply does not show us what we must do, and experts must not seek to play a leading role. As one of the authors to be discussed below (Davidoff, 1965) puts it, in a flamboyant statement on planning in a pluralist society: "The right course of action is always a matter of choice, never of fact" (p. 279). Experts should know better than to deny this.

This touches upon a discussion that has raged for a number of years: the charge against planning as being "technocratic". Technocracy is a natural corollary to the belief in the role of knowledge as an unambiguous guide to action. After all, he who has the knowledge which can guide us seems predestined to show the way into a better future. In this sense classic planning though is, indeed, technocratic. This does not necessarily apply to contemporary planning thought which is imbued with the awareness of the element of choice in planning.

1.2   Noble intentions-Noble plans

Whatever Americans have brought to planning in terms of a social and political science input, Europeans think that the idea is theirs. Was Ebenezer Howard, the father of the New Towns, not an Englishman? Has the only American pioneer whose works are widely read in Europe, Lewis Mumford, not been influenced by Geddes? The reader of the monumental history of *American City Planning* since 1890 (Scott, 1969) gains a different perspective, and recent research confirms this impression. The tradition of United States planning, though often inspired by Europe, is very impressive. According to a survey by Nolan, one of the planning pioneers, no less than 176 comprehensive planning reports had already been produced by 1926 (see Krueckeberg, 1982a, p. 14).

American planning is generally said to originate in the "City Beautiful" movement-later to be superseded by the "City Practical" (Krueckeberg, *op. cit.*). It emphasised beautification by way of private initiatives aimed at large-scale public projects (see Gerckens, 1979, p. 34). Public control over private development as a tool for implementing plans came later.

What this section is concerned with, though, is the planning method advocated, and the underlying ideas concerning the role of experts. So I elaborate upon the theme that classic planning thought adhered to a view which we would nowadays describe as technocratic. (The section that follows shows why methods are needed in planning; the more so the more democratic the intention.)

The first pioneer discussed is an exponent of the all-important landscape architecture movement, Frederick Law Olmsted. Krueckeberg (1982a, p. 22) says he

fathered a profession that was highly synthetic. On the one hand were the tools of science: the empirical knowledge of plants and materials, the systematic analysis of land forms and site characteristics. On the other hand was the art of design; the power of the creative idea and the process of developing a concept into a plan. These processes of scientific investigation and artistic design were moulded into a professional service for clients whose problems ranged, in the words of Charles W. Eliot, 2nd, "from the backyard garden to the whole USA". This method, passed on through Eliot's sons and his students, permeated the study of landscape architecture at Harvard, through which a whole generation of students graduated, and then went to dominate American colleges and universities in the teaching of American planners.

This method is a natural outgrowth of architectural practice. Like "survey before plan", it pays respect to such "scientific" data as can be assembled, but leaves planning as such to the imagination of the master-designer.

The case of Reading, Pennsylvania, related by Hancock (1982, p. 37) in his biographical sketch of John Nolan is a good illustration. In 1908 a group of prominent men had formed a non-political Civic Association for promoting better physical development. Their aim was to influence local power groups by making a survey of existing problems. Their first act "was to seek the advice of an 'expert' who, coming from outside the city, could analyze its physical problems, forecast future needs, and then 'form a general programme of city making' " (p. 37).

This was no isolated incidence. The history of American city planning by Scott (1969), the autobiography of Edward M. Bassett (see Krueckeberg, 1982b), and biographical essays on Alfred Bettman (Gerckens, 1982) and Benjamin C. Marsh (Kantor, 1982) show the involvement of planning pioneers in civic initiatives, independent commissions and fund-raising for expert studies. They had the support of what is called the progressive reform movement, which distrusted existing political "machines" and their practices. (On machines see Meyerson and Banfield, 1955; to be discussed in Section 2.3.) For a considerable time this movement had nurtured ideas not only of "clean", but also of "scientific", administration and government. The political scientist Frank P. Pichard had stated as early as 1892 that this required what today we would describe as an interdisciplinary approach, "a thorough knowledge, obtained by careful study of past and existing facts" (Scott, 1969, p. 41).

In this tradition, when Marsh succeeded in getting congestion on the political agenda in New York in 1910, the *New York Times* "urged the Aldermen to stay off the Commission and appoint only qualified experts" (Kantor, 1982, p. 64).

The scope of this type of work was broad. At the first National Conference on City Planning in 1909 Nolan asked: "What is needed in American city planning?", giving the answer himself: "Everything". In terms reminiscent of Geddes, he continued:

We should no longer be content with mere increase in population and wealth. We should insist upon asking, How do the people live, where do they work, what do they plan ... there is a close relation between moral reform and material progress. A more honest, economical and wiser expenditure is indeed sorely needed, and, ultimately the change of (civic) policy would lead there.... The main source of this new wealth ... is in a wiser husbanding of our aesthetic and human as well as our national resources, in the promoting of physical health, legislation that meets more successfully the needs of twentieth century city life, in doing things at the right time ... in the right way, using to our advantage science, art, skill, and experience (quoted after Hancock, 1982, p. 51).

Nolan was also interested in education as a way of achieving civic reform. Indeed, he had spent many years as director of an extramural university department-a surprising parallel with Geddes.

Interest in putting planning on a scientific basis increased with the drive towards efficiency in municipal government generally. Charles Dyer Norton, spiritual father of *The Regional Plan for New York and its Environs* (to be discussed shortly) had been involved in the setting up of a bureau of research as a permanent centre for efficiency studies in Washington before becoming involved in city planning (Kantor, 1982, p. 181). The same source claims that the research leading to the enactment in New York of the first comprehensive zoning ordinance in the United States was performed by a Bureau of Municipal Research set up in 1906 as a result of the impulse toward greater efficiency and management. Lastly, Alfred Bettman, one of the fathers of American zoning, built on his experiences as city solicitor at Cincinnati when a mayor elected on a ticket of fiscal reform "undertook a comprehensive topographic survey of the city to serve as the basis of future capital investment decisions" (Gerckens, 1982, p. 122).

The scale was different, but as far as planning method was concerned, *The Regional Plan for New York and Its Environs*-completed under the direction of the Scottish town planner Thomas Adams-was no different. It was "the greatest assemblage of planning studies ever focused on an American city" (Krueckeberg, 1982a, p. 19), filling ten volumes of research and recommendations. It applied the "scientific techniques of surveying and data gathering" (Kantor, 1982, p. 179). When it came to planning, though, the region was simply divided up into sub-areas, and consultants commissioned to design plans, with "uneven" attention being paid to the surveys (Johnson, 1985). In the end, Adams synthesised their proposals, smoothing out any problems remaining. On an even larger scale, the National Resources Planning Board during the New Deal repeated the same pattern by engaging in this type of "comprehensive planning" on a national scale (see Gerckens, 1979, p. 40).

This method has been spelled out early on by Marsh, social worker, critic of overcrowding, and author of the first American textbook on city planning. The steps necessary to a meaningful city plan were: survey, publicity, and legislation (Kantor, 1982, p. 70; see also Scott, 1969, p. 99). His friend, the architect George B. Ford, was even more outspoken in advocating surveys which he saw as the way of turning city planning from a "rather capricious procedure into that highly respectable thing known as an exact science" (quoted after Scott, 1969, p. 121). He held that determining the best plan was solely a matter of proceeding logically-of gathering facts, analysing them, and discovering the logical and convincing solution of the problem involved" (*ibid.*).

In this tradition, Bettman wrote surveys into the standard state enabling acts for planning and zoning on which United States local planning is based. Since then, the comprehensive plans which underpin zoning must be based on scientific analyses-surveys. After World War II the conditions under which the federal government provided grants for housing to local authorities (the "701" comprehensive planning assistance provision of the US Housing Act of 1954; see Gerckens, 1982, p. 143) spawned an urban consultancy industry based on the same idea.

"Survey before plan" soon found its way into standard texts. An influential book was the one compiled on behalf of the International City Managers' Association by Segoe (1941). Segoe had been responsible for the pioneering planning work at Cincinnati (see Krueckeberg, 1982b). In this book he claims:

Any active planning agency has for its primary job the making of a comprehensive land-use, economic, and social survey. It finds out what sort of houses people live in, when they were built, their size and condition, how many people live in each house, where they work and how they get to work; as well as what industries there are, how many workers they employ, and why they move away leaving jobless men behind them. With such knowledge to draw on, the department of welfare can intelligently determine where best to apply what funds it has at its disposal.

Most modern communities are faced with serious problems of traffic congestion. ... It is the job of a planning agency to study the traffic situation ... and find out where the worst congestion occurs. On the basis of this knowledge, the least wasteful and most efficient methods for correcting the situation can be more easily and quickly determined (p. 16).

But under "making and giving effect to plans", there is a mere half-page, mainly on the need for coordination. Elsewhere the study says about the master plan and its preparation merely that it "requires the collection, analyses and interpretation of a large body of facts about the past and present, and careful inquiries into the future" (p. 44). Nothing is said about the process of formulating the master plan itself. Follow-up volumes to this reputable work (Goodman and Freund, 1968; So, *et al.*, 1979) pay much more attention, too, to methods of analysis than of planning.

The first edition of Chapin, *Urban Land Use Planning* (1957), represents the high point in this development. It bears the mark of decades of accumulated survey experience. Sometimes it has a decidedly modern ring about it. Thus it emphasises the planning process rather than the plan, stresses its cyclical, or iterative, character, and puts goals and objectives first. However, it is still weak as regards the decisive "design" phase. (In fact, as regards the approach taken, it shows remarkable similarities to the Segoe volume in which Chapin-at that time with the Tennessee Valley Authority-is listed as among the advisers.)

Chapin bases himself on the so-called *progressive planning approach* developed by the National Resources Planning Board at the beginning of World War II (see Public Administration Service, 1943). It consists of a six-point sequence, beginning with a "first estimate of existing conditions and significant trends in the urban area" and proceeding to the determination of "the principal and most pressing problems and needs", the formulation of "a detailed program indicating priorities for undertaking component studies of comprehensive plan", the carrying out of "detailed plan studies according to program and priority" and the integration of various plan studies into the comprehensive plan. The approach recommends also the revision of plans as conditions alter their applicability (see pp. 271-2).

Forming part of the comprehensive plan, a special land-use plan study consists of: statement of objectives; existing conditions and future trends, proposals and implementation. It is presented in the form of a report. About its formulation Chapin merely says:

Once the land use requirements have been presented, the section of the report devoted to the plan itself follows naturally. Here, in accord with objectives, the limitations of the existing pattern of uses, and the principles and requirements previously established, the basic features of the plan's design are presented (p. 282).

Elsewhere the treatment of plan-making is no more detailed. After delineating the study area, the planning area and planning districts within it, the surveys ("tooling-up studies") aim to obtain the following information: current and forecast urban area *population*-total and by school age groups; current and forecast urban area manufacturing, wholesale and office-related *employment*; map and tabular summary of *existing land use* by planning district; map and tabular summary of *vacant and renewal land* characteristics by planning district; summary of current *stock of dwelling units* by structure type and by planning district; summary of currently *substandard dwelling units* by structure type and by planning district (p. 287). On this basis future land requirements are estimated, after which the land use plan is designed. This phase is discussed on slightly more than half a page, where we learn that plan-making "involves the collation of preliminary proposals as to location and distribution of various types of land use as developed in the preceding phase of the work and the preparation of the preliminary land use plan in firmed-up form" (p. 289). By this time a preliminary thoroughfare plan, visual surveys, cost-revenue, land value and attitude studies should be available.

With all this information at hand, then begins a "cut and fill" process, a process or ironing out conflicts in location. These are of two orders: conflicts between the land use pattern and the thoroughfare scheme, and conflicts between the different land uses. Each land use category is reviewed for the economic feasibility of development in the locations indicated, considering the fiscal ability and legal authority of the one or more municipalities and counties which may be involved for realizing the plan in the planning period.

Once location conflicts are brought into harmony, space requirements are reexamined as necessary and the space needed for each use is brought into overall balance. The final result is the best practical, most economical, and attractive design for all uses, fitted to the topography and the existing land use pattern and articulated with the circulation system (p. 289).

This is fleshed out in subsequent chapters by discussing standards and planning principles like the neighbourhood concept. In the introduction to the final chapter on "The land use plan", Chapin makes another revealing statement:

Up to this point in the land use planning process, the city planner has been drawing primarily on the science of planning, with only secondary attention to the art of planning. He has been assembling, collating, and analyzing facts within the framework of a prescribed methodological approach to problem solving. ...

The city planner is now ready to apply himself to what is primarily the design phase of land use planning. His task is to translate these previously derived requirements into a well-articulated scheme for land development in the urban area which . . . reconciles conflicts. . . . He now examines all the individual use requirements as an interrelated group of requirements. . . . In addition . . . he seeks a synthesis of the land use with the circulatory requirements so that the preliminary land use and transportation plans which subsequently emerge are mutually compatible (pp. 371-2).

Maybe Chapin is dissatisfied with the science-design distinction to explain planning. He has another go at describing plan preparation, but concludes in exasperation that the "creative aspects of this final synthesizing process of design are not readily described in words, but it may assist in picturing the rudiments of this process to summarize briefly its mechanics and the form in which the results are presented" (p. 377). But what we are told is merely that overlays are used to test solutions to each problem.

Thus each problem is studied individually and finally in combination until a scheme emerges with all elements in balance and harmony. With a decision reached on a scheme, the final task of the operation is the recapitulation of the summary of space allocation adjusted to this final version of the preliminary land use plan (p. 378).

So, since Geddes and Branford, little progress has been made as regards planning method. True, the master-designer must look at more data. Even here, design theorists like Jacobs (1985) question the amount of attention being given to research results, advocating the acquisition of personal "feel" instead. In any case, plans still "emerge"-are the result of a "creative leap".

There has been tension all the way between the elitist practice of planning, drawing directly from moral, rather than political, authority, and the need to translate noble intentions into proposals for the exercise of public control and the spending of funds. Section 1.1 has shown Geddes to be troubled by this. The way out to many seemed to reform municipal administration to make it more suitable for pursuing grand designs and orderly development. This reform movement occurred on a large scale during the first decades of this century, and planning had a major share in it. The planning function in the United States was taken "outside politics" in many localities, and independent city planning commissions were formed, consisting of respected community leaders and set up to prepare truly objective plans. A unique way was found to relate these plans to the exercise of control over private development by requiring that zoning provisions must be "in conformance with the comprehensive plan" (see Chapters 12 and 13). This abdication of public responsibility for formulating the substantive basis for the exercise of police power has been widely attacked, ever since Walker (1950, 1st edition 1941) advocated that planning should be a staff function of local government (see Fagin, 1959; Nash and Durden, 1964; Beckman, 1964; for the continuing advocacy of planning boards see the comments on Nash and Durden by Bacon, 1964, and Howard, (1964). Up until today, planning boards persist. Bolan (1967, p. 12) points out that the form of planning organisation is a function of the "decision-making environment, with smaller non-partisan communities being particularly prone to maintaining planning boards". Such planning is not only "beyond politics", it is also prone to take a less methodical approach.

1.3 Why method?

Why is it good to be methodical? What problems do methods address anyway? The aim of discussing these issues is to relate methods squarely to the view of human knowledge as fallible. This was spelled out early on. In an editorial in the journal *City Planning* in 1926, a reply was given to claims by architects for the sole responsibility for designing cities, towns and villages and other groups of buildings. The answer was that city planning "is cooperation-cooperation of fallible humans each contributing what he can" (quoted after Krueckeberg, 1982a, p. 23).

In principle, all human knowledge is uncertain. Thus no form of human knowledge can escape criticism. For planning, this view entails an argumentative approach which encourages outside actors (each of them fallible, of course) to engage in dialogue with planners, thereby improving the chances of finding correct answers. Methods are ways of structuring this dialogue; no more and no less.

If truth were self-evident and solutions to problems were obvious (at least to him who has taken the trouble of doing surveys), then we would need no planning methods. Neither is the case, and we need to argue things out. We must talk about whether a proposition represents a true account, a good solution to the problem before us, a correct decision in the situation which we face. In all these debates we take steps from the statements which-for sake of argument anyway-we accept to the conclusions which we try to convince ourselves (and others) should be drawn. *Method* refers to established ways of inferring conclusions from assumptions and evidence. It conveys legitimacy, therefore, on the outcomes of arguments, be it in research, or in planning.

Methods make no sense, where there is no argument; and argument makes no sense where no methods are used. So talk about methods in human pursuits rests on a view that debates are necessary, and the opinions of others are resources for the resolution of problems. In debates on matters of truth and the correctness of decisions there is always, albeit implicit, reliance on methods. They are "not of private origin and possession" (Dewey, 1950, quoted after Hoch, 1984, p. 337). They are responsible, furthermore, for the social character of thinking.

That all this applies also to planning would hardly bear emphasis if it were not for the fact that that other powerful tradition exists which holds that good solutions do *not* bear arguing about. Quality either exists, and then you can feel it, or it does not. Where it does, it springs from a creative mind which has undergone the necessary training. This same tradition holds that satisfactory environments are not designed by debating solutions, by having regard to manifold inputs. This is expressed nicely by the saying, popular in environmental design circles, that the camel is a horse designed by a committee. It betrays not only the patently wrong view that design must ultimately be seen as the work of one individual human mind, but at the same time a singularly Western disregard for the special qualities and gracefulness of camels.

The ideology of the creative leap is opposed to democratic values, and is fundamentally ineffective. This does not, of course, mean that there is no role for intuition in planning. The manner in which ideas are generated is often far from systematic, and "creative leap" a good way of describing it. But alleged creativity can never be sufficient ground for accepting ideas. Such acceptance requires adducing arguments and, therefore, invoking methods.

Now, it is true, a methodological approach to planning is also being associated with experts arrogating decision-making to themselves-what is being described as *technocracy*. No doubt method can be, and has been, used in this way; but as we have seen, to plan without method means courting the same danger. It leads to decision-making by men whose wisdom seems to entitle them to a superior role. On the other hand, the proper use of planning method can reduce this danger. Minimally, a well-designed methodical approach helps in distinguishing facts and values, a precondition, if anything, of holding experts at bay.

There is nothing that inherently contradicts freedom of choice in this view of method. Methods are not constraints, but they assist with coming to resolutions in arguments, as we have seen. They are not sacrosanct either, but open to criticism; and the legitimacy which they convey is conditioned upon recognition of their validity. It is more the everyday view of scientific method, endowing it with too much authority, which needs to be attacked, than the use of methods as such. They are tools for decision-making. They do not take the human element away from decisions. On the contrary! The critical application of method in arguments around planning issues makes the value judgements involved the more evident.

Conclusions

Despite the veneer of a social-scientific foundation which "survey before plan" conveyed on planning, classic authors failed to appreciate planning method. They encouraged planners to rely on their understanding of the subject matter of planning instead, and paid no attention to how such understanding leads to recommendations. So those concerned committed the double sin of positivism and technocracy.

Classic planning thought, with its exclusive reliance on the intuitive understanding of well-meaning experts, has come to a dead end. The next chapter introduces its alternative: the rational planning model. It indicates the type of methods needed in order to make planning decisions accessible. We owe it to the "Chicago School". Initially however, as we shall see, contemporary planning thought, the beginnings of which are at Chicago, applied a methodical approach exclusively to the making of plans. Implementation was thought to follow. It is an achievement of the "IOR School" (see Chapter 6), and parallel schools of thought discussed in Chapter 7, to have focused on implementation (conceiving of it as an ongoing stream of decisions in their own right) and to have redefined the role of plans as aids to these decisions rather than as the mainspring of action.

References

Abrams, P. (1968) *The Origins of British Sociology,* University of Chicago Press, Chicago and London.

Bacon, E. N. (1964) "Comment on A task-force approach to replace the planning board", *Journal of the American Institute of Planners,* **30,** 25-6.

Batty, M. (1982) "Planning systems and systems planning", *Built Environment,* **8,** 252-7.

*Beckman, N. (1964) "The planner as a bureaucrat", *Journal of the American Institute of Planners,* **30,** 325-7.

Boardman, P. (1978) *The Worlds of Patrick Geddes: Biologist, Town Planner, Re-educator, Peacewarrior,* Routledge & Kegan Paul, London, Henley and Boston.

Bolan, R. S. (1967) "Emerging views of planning", *Journal of the American Institute of Planners,* **33,** 233-45.

Branford, V. V. (1914) *Interpretations and Forecasts,* Duckworth, London.

Breheny, M. J. (1983) "A practical review of planning theory", *Environment and Planning B,* **10,** 101-15.

Broady, M. (1968) *Planning for People,* The Bedford Square Press, London.

Chapin, F. S. (1957) *Urban Land Use Planning,* Harper, New York.

*Davidoff, P. (1965) "Advocacy and pluralism in planning", *Journal of the American Institute of Planners,* **31,** 331-8.

*Davidoff, P. and Reiner, T. A. (1962) "A choice theory of planning", *Journal of the American Institute of Planners,* **28,** 108-15.

Dewey, J. (1950) "Liberalism and social action", in: *Pragmatism and American Culture,* (ed. G. Kennedy), D. C. Heath, Boston.

Fagin, H. (1959) "Organizing and carrying out planning activities within urban government", *Journal of the American Institute of Planners,* **25,** 109-14.

Faludi, A. (1973) *A Reader in Planning Theory,* Pergamon Press, Oxford.

Faludi, A. (1978) *Essays in Planning Theory and Education,* Pergamon Press, Oxford.

Fletcher, R. (1971) *The Making of Sociology: Developments,* Nelson, London.

Geddes, P. (1904a) *City Development: A Report to the Carnegie Dunfermline Trust,* Birmingham.

Geddes, P. (1904b) "Civics: as applied sociology", *Sociological Papers,* pp. 101-18.

Gerckens, L. C. (1979) "Historical development of American city planning", in: *The Practice of Local Government Planning,* (eds F. S. So, I. Stollman, F. Beal and D. S. Arnold), International City Managers' Association Washington, DC, pp. 21-57.

Gerckens, L. C. (1982) 'Bettmann of Cincinnati', in: *The American Planner: Biographies and Recollections,* (ed. D. A. Krueckeberg), Methuen, New York and London, pp. 120-48.

Goist, P. D. (1974) "Patrick Geddes and the city", *Journal of the American Institute of Planners,* **40,** 31-7.

Goodman, W. I. and Freund, E. C. (1968) *Principles and Practice of Urban Planning,* International City Managers' Association, Washington, DC.

Hall, P. (1982) "The neotechnic vision", *Built Environment,* **8,** 217-18.

Hall, P. (1983) "The Anglo-American connection: rival rationalities in planning theory and practice, 1955-1980", *Environment and Planning B,* **10,** 41-6.

Hancock, J. (1982) "John Nolen: the background of a pioneer planner", in: *The American Planner: Biographies and Recollections,* (ed. D. A. Krueckeberg), Methuen, New York and London, 37-57.

Hartshorne, R. (1959) *Perspectives on the Nature of Geography,* Rand McNally, Chicago.

Hartshorne, R. (1977; 1st published 1939), *The Nature of Geography: a Critical Survey of Current Thoughts in the Light of the Past,* Greenwood Press, Westport, Conn.

Harvey, D. (1969) *Explanation in Geography,* Edward Arnold, London.

Hoch, C. J. (1984) "Doing good and being right", *Journal of the American Planning Association,* **50,** 335-45.

Howard, J. T. (1951) "In defence of planning commissions", *Journal of the American Institute of Planners*, **17**, 46-9.

Howard, J. T. (1964) "Comment on: 'A task-force approach to replace the planning board'", *Journal of the American Institute of Planners*, **30**, 24-5.

Jacobs, A. B. (1985) *Looking at Cities*, Harvard University Press, Cambridge, Mass.

Johnson, D. A. (1985) "Seventy-five years of metropolitan planning in the N. Y.-N. J.-Connecticut Urban Region: a retrospective assessment". Paper presented at the Annual Meeting of the Association of Collegiate Schools of Planning, 19 October, 1984, New York, NY.

Kantor, H. A. (1982) "Benjamin C. Marsh and the fight over population congestion", in: *The American Planner: Biographies and Recollections*, (ed. D. A. Krueckeberg), Methuen, New York and London, pp. 58-74.

Krueckeberg, D. A. (1982a) "Introduction to the American planner", in: *The American Planner: Biographies and Recollections*, (ed. D. A. Krueckeberg), Methuen, New York and London, pp. 1-34.

Krueckeberg, D. A. (1982b) "From the autobiography of Edward M. Bassett", in: *The American Planner: Biographies and Recollections*, (ed. D. A. Krueckeberg), Methuen, New York and London, pp. 100-19.

Meyerson, M. M. and Banfield, E. C. (1955) *Politics, Planning and the Public Interests: The Case of Public Housing at Chicago*, Free Press, New York.

Nash, P. H. and Durden, D. (1964) "A task-force approach to replace the planning board", *Journal of the American Institute of Planners*, **30**, 10-12.

Public Administration Service (1943) *Action for Cities: A Guide for Community Planning*, published under the sponsorship of the AMA, ASPO and ICMA, Chicago, Ill.

Scott, M. (1969) *American City Planning since 1890*, University of California Press, Berkeley and Los Angeles.

Segoe, L. (1941) *Local Planning Administration*, The International City Managers' Association, Chicago, Ill.

So, F. S., Stollman, I., Beal, F. and Arnold, D. S. (eds) (1979) *The Practice of Local Government Planning*, International City Managers' Association, Washington, DC.

Taylor, N. (1980) "Planning theory and the philosophy of planning", *Urban Studies*, **17**, 159-72.

Walker, R. A. (1950) *The Planning Function in Urban Government*, University of Chicago Press, Chicago.

Webber, M. M. (1983) "The myth of rationality: development planning reconsidered", *Environment and Planning B: Planning and Design*, **10**, 89-99.

* Included in Faludi, A. (ed.) (1973) *A Reader in Planning Theory*, Pergamon Press, Oxford.

CHAPTER 2

The "Chicago School"

THE "Chicago School" laid the foundations of contemporary planning thought, in particular as regards the "rational planning model".

"Chicago School" refers to a graduate programme known as the Program of Education and Research in Planning offered at the Social Science Division of the University of Chicago in the forties and fifties-the first ever to be offered in such an environment. It was the meeting ground of those interested in the application of the social sciences to practical problems on the one hand, and city and regional planners concerned with broadening the foundations of their professional expertise on the other.

Contemporary planning thought refers to ideas developed in the United States, in particular since World War II-although its origins have been traced back to institutionalist economics of earlier decades by Gellen (1985). The emphasis is on scientific rigor and the assimilation of the social sciences into planning. Its hard core is the rational planning model, the most durable contribution of the "Chicago School".

Why was it in the United States, rather than in Britain with its well-developed planning system, that contemporary planning thought originated, and why did it take Britain two decades to catch up? In no small part this must have something to do with the massive growth of American social sciences. Some social scientists-like Tugwell, Perloff and Banfield discussed in this chapter-found their way into planning a long time before the same movement started in Britain. (There, many of the earlier social-science analyses of planning-see for instance Foley, 1960-were written by United States scholars whilst on sabbatical leave in Britain.) The very fact that town and country planning had been successfully institutionalised in Britain may have contributed as well. Glass (1959, in Faludi, 1973, p. 64) argues that it made it less receptive to critical inquiry.

The chapter starts with *The context, the personalities, the message.* Then comes the testimony of somebody involved in a key capacity, Perloff (1957), *Education for Planning: City, State & Regional.* The chapter ends with a discussion of the seminal work of the "Chicago School", *Politics, Planning and the Public Interest-The Case of Public Housing at Chicago* (Meyerson, and Banfield, 1955) which introduces the rational planning model.

2.1 The context, the personalities, the message

In which context did the "Chicago School" thrive? Who was involved? Why is it still relevant to remind ourselves of an experiment of several decades ago? Answering these questions helps us to realise the continuity of ideas in planning.

Perloff's book, and an autobiographic chapter in a collection of his works (Burns and Friedmann, 1985) apart, the only, albeit short, scholarly work on the "Chicago School" (Sarbib, 1983) describes its roots in the New Deal, when the foundations were laid for an interventionist role for the federal government in the United States, and interest grew in the more efficient discharge of local government functions. World War II demonstrated further the need for planners in public as well as in private corporations. Some of that rubbed off on post-war reconstruction, when there was a distinct fear of another recession.

In this environment, Louis Wirth-the famous Chicago sociologist-suggested a new training programme to fill staff functions in agencies like the Tennessee Valley Authority-the proudest achievement of the New Deal. Among his peers, Wirth "had probably the longest and most intimate association with metropolitan planning (having) made a major contribution to the report of the National Resources Committee on the role of cities in the national economy" (Friedmann and Weaver, 1979, pp. 56-7). Also, the Social Science Division of the University of Chicago enjoyed much fame. Urban ecology had emerged there, and the names of Thorstein Veblen and John Dewey are associated with it. (On the importance of their work see Friedmann and Weaver, 1979, pp. 25-7; on Dewey's influence in particular see also Hoch, 1984; Blanco, 1985; Gellen, 1985.)

Among the sponsors of the programme was Charles Merrian. As against Wirth, who saw planning as an applied social science thriving on substantive research, Perloff (Burns and Friedmann, 1985) describes Merrian's view of planning as that of a staff function in government. This is not surprising. Merrian had been promoting the study by Walker (1950, 1st edition 1941) mentioned in Chapter 1 for its criticism of planning commissions, and arguing for planning as a staff function in local government rather than a task for independent commissions. (For a discussion see: Howard, 1951, 1964; Nash and Durden, 1964; Bacon, 1964).

Another sponsor was Walter Blucher, Executive Director of the American Society of Planning Officials (ASPO; now merged with the American Institute of Planners to form the American Planning Association). He perceived a need for high-level planners. With Wirth he promoted links between the Social Science Division and the architectural and engineering capacity of the Illinois Institute of Technology. Perloff (Burns and Friedmann, 1985) relates, though, that this was made impossible-"in fact, ludicrous"-by Hilbersheimer's exclusive interest in developing the model of the high-rise linear city for which he has become famous (see Hilbersheimer, 1944).

Wirth succeeded in interesting Rexford G. Tugwell, ex-governor of Puerto Rico, in chairing the programme. Tugwell represented the progressive reform movement. He was one of the institutionalist economists. These believed

that a market-oriented economy was giving way to an administered system dominated by large enterprises. They viewed this as an inevitable development-the product of the application of science and technology. ... They perceived that a system of private planning had emerged. ... These developments led New Dealers to the conclusion that.... economic abundance could only be attained by fostering cooperation between all the "functional" groupings and classes in the economy-consumers, farmers and laborers. To achieve this, there had to be some type of public interest control over private economic planning (Gellen, 1984, p. 76).

Tugwell had been the first chairman also of the New York City Planning Commission-where, according to Gelfland (1985, p. 159) he had succeeded in antagonising everybody, thereby dealing "the idea of comprehensive planning a blow from which it never recovered". He had been instrumental also in setting up the Greenbelt Towns. Like institutionalist economists generally (see Gellen, 1984, p. 83), he had a vision of "people of science contributing to guide societal choices and to curb the irrational decisions of politicians" (Sarbib, 1983, p. 79). He is most famous, though, for the institutional set-up which he proposed for planning as a "fourth power" of government. This is characteristic of the more radical wing of institutionalist economists whom Tugwell represents-and who were eventually set aside by a more moderate group during the New Deal (see Gellen, 1985, p. 75). As regards the reliance on expert knowledge, there are clear parallels with classic planning thought. It is on this point that Friedmann (1973, p. 7; see also Section 7.2) distances himself from his teacher Tugwell.

Tugwell's views anticipated the work of authors propounding cybernetic thinking (Deutsch, 1966; Buckley, 1967; Etzioni, 1968; Beer, 1966). He conceived of society "as a complex organism and of planning as a central function-similar to the brain and central nervous system in the human body-specifically concerned with co-ordinating its diverse elements for the benefit of the whole" (Friedmann, 1973, p.46).

Soon, Melville C. Branch (the first Ph.D. from Harvard), Harvey S. Perloff, Julius Margolis, Richard Meier, Martin Meyerson and Edward C. Banfield joined in various capacities. Herbert A. Simon was close by. Thus, Chicago became the

pioneering locus of the use of social science techniques for the analysis of and attempt to solve planning problems. And the war and the immediate post-war period were fertile in technical advances. ... These advances encouraged a kind of scientific optimism which became the hallmark of the rational planner (Sarbib, 1983, P. 79).

The programme started in the fall of 1947. At the beginning the faculty, with Tugwell, saw planning as *really reflective decision-making*. Also with Tugwell, it searched for planning as a separate discipline. The uniqueness of planning was defined as "the process by which a team of planners was able to assemble and to reduce to reciprocal relatedness the materials furnished by the ordinary techniques of political science, economics, sociology, anthropology, engineering, and architecture, and by which it could project a composite future". It was applying the "methods and results of science in order to achieve group or social purposes". Planners were not to make social decisions, but they could "help verify values, and to make purposes definite". Decision-makers confronted with "inescapable facts or trends" would be "much less likely to act on the basis of caprice" (Sarbib, 1983, p. 79).

In this conception, planners came close to representing the *free-floating* intelligentia which played such an important role in Karl Mannheim's writings. Their social science training would establish a basis of a scientific kind of politics, but their personal qualities ... would prevent them from usurping the traditional decision-making functions in a democracy on the basis of technical expertise (Sarbib, 1983, p. 80).

Gellen's study of the intellectual origins of planning in the United States in institutionalist economics makes this understandable. Institutionalist economics harbours ideas concerning a sort of technological imperative for planning and the role of experts therein. More important institutionalists

conceived of planning generically as the application of scientific knowledge to problems of social organization and control. Planning by this definition was not solely a governmental function. Planning could be practiced by business, individuals, cities and nations alike (Gellen, 1985, p. 83).

Thus, the foundation was laid for generic planning theory (see Chapters 4 and 5). At the same time it was perhaps unfortunate that Tugwell favoured not only planning, but also central control, something which not all institutionalists shared. Indeed, as early as 1929 the mentor of many institutionalists, John Dewey, had rejected central planning, claiming that

the attempt to plan social organisation and association without the freest possible way of intelligence contradicts the very idea of *social planning*. For the latter is an operative method of activity, not a predetermined set of final truths (Dewey, 1929, pp. 431-2; quoted after Hoch, 1984, p. 336).

The tensions which this caused were also evident at Chicago. Perloff-himself steeped in the institutionalist tradition-rejected the "fourth power" concept as being neither theoretically sound nor practically feasible (Burns and Friedmann, 1985). Friedmann (1973, p. 46) comments that there "was no chance whatever that such a central body could come into being in the United States". Chicago followed Dewey's concept of planning instead. Friedmann regrets that, as a result, Tugwell's writings on the planning process have been forgotten. He relates the disenchantment also of students with Tugwell's organismic metaphors and his aloof, patrician manner, contrasting his teaching with the persuasiveness of Banfield applying "the method of Socratic dialogue with consummate skill" (p. 3).

After having taught planning theory jointly, Tugwell's and Banfield's interests diverged. Banfield took over the course and turned it into a rigorous testing ground of the intellectual stamina of students. Next to his method of teaching, what Perloff (Burns and Friedmann, 1985) describes as Banfield's idiosyncratic attitude to planning was responsible for this. Still, Friedmann has fond memories of this course:

Banfield's early flirtations with planning eventually gave way to a deep pessimism about man's condition and the ability of society to deal with its problems through purposeful intervention by central authorities. Nevertheless, his openness to the ideas of his students, and the rigor he demanded of their presentations, contributed to making his seminars among the most memorable in the program and the study of planning worthy of the student's best efforts (pp. 3-4).

Perloff himself reports having felt more comfortable with a more pragmatic approach than either Tugwell's or Banfield's (on whose rational planning model more in Section 2.3 below). When assuming leadership he brought a wide variety of experiences to it. Having studied economics and government, at, amongst other places, the London School of Economics where he had been exposed to Hayek and worked for Laski, and at Harvard, where Schumpeter and Leontieff taught, he had written his Ph.D. on the national budget. It was to set him on a course which would lead him to develop "the outlines of what came eventually to be known as the Planning-Programming-Budgeting System. His emphasis on 'strategic' or policies planning had a profound influence on the thinking of his students" (Friedmann, 1973, p. 4). He had worked on early plans for postwar recovery, in particular for river basin development and urban redevelopment. After the war he had worked in Puerto Rico, which is where Tugwell had met him and invited him to come to Chicago.

Responding to the challenges of others in the Social Science Division arguing that, if planning was identical to wisdom, then everybody could have a share in it, the definition of planning was turned down under Perloff to the

activity by which organizations decide what must be done and how resources must be used if designated goals are to be achieved with maximum effectiveness. ... In particular, the economic paradigm of rational choice under scarcity, introduced by Margolis, captured Banfield's imagination and led to the successful *packaging* of the rational action model (Sarbib, 1983, p. 80; see Section 2.3 below).

This redefinition was to no avail. The "Chicago School" closed down in 1955 (allowing students to complete their research degrees for somewhat longer). To Perloff this signified lack of acceptance of planning by the Social Science Division. At that time ideological resistance to a progressive faculty may have been a contributory factor. But in times of financial stringency it was perhaps inevitable that the new programme should give way to long-established departments. In fact, several other interdisciplinary programmes were closed down at the same time. With hindsight we can say that this was no reflection on the quality of the "Chicago School". The challenge of having to develop academic programmes has always been an incentive for developing the core of any discipline. Where that discipline integrates the contributions of others, the challenge is twice as great. In response, and for the first time, a planning curriculum was developed which, rather than mimicking architecture, drew on the social sciences. The Chicago answer to the question of how this should be done was a core curriculum based on the assumptions (1) that planning is a *generic* term; (2) that it refers to *decision-making*, as well as *implementation*; and (3) that it relates to *public policy*.

Planning may be applied in various fields. To cover all of them is impossible, so Chicago offered specialisations. Planning in Puerto Rico (where Perloff, Meier and others were consulting) provided the opportunity for specialisation in "Regional and Underdeveloped-Area Planning", and the laboratory, which Chicago itself was, for one in city planning.

Among the Ph.D. degrees conferred were John Friedmann, John Dyckman and Ira Robinson. They represented a group described by Meier as "persons who wanted to do good competently" (Perloff, 1957, p. 150; on the roots of this desire in Dewey's pragmatist philosophy see Hoch, 1984). It is hard to overestimate the impact of the "Chicago School", chiefly through the work of students such as these.

2.2 Education for Planning: City, State & Regional

This section gives a more detailed account of the ideas of the "Chicago School" based on Perloff (1957), Burns and Friedmann (1985) and Robinson (1985). The following section goes into more depth as regards the core of planning knowledge which evolved around the rational planning model.

That *planning core* refers to those elements of the planning curriculum which all students are required to take. It is said to reflect the "generalist" element in planning education. This relates to the view of the planner as a "*generalist-with-a-speciality*": somebody with a grounding in general principles and a detailed knowledge of their application to one area of concern.

Perloff's account starts by identifying a professional and an administrative tradition in planning. Under the former the individual planner learns the skills required for serving his clients in a form of education akin to apprenticeship. It reflects what the previous chapter, criticising it as methodologically unsound, identifies as classic planning thought. The second tradition sees the planner as scheduling public works and recommending the means to encourage private development "in the same way that the budgeting agencies or the central personnel office is concerned with civil service administration influencing all or most of the departments within the local government" (Perloff, 1957, p. 7; the influence of the moderate version of institutionalist economics is evident).

The "Chicago School" embraced the second view of planning as a "staff function". Perloff stresses the difficulties of preparing students for this varied and rapidly changing role:

The history of city planning serves to underline very sharply why planning education cannot rely on the transmission of existing knowledge and methods ... but must be geared to the continuing search for new knowledge and methods and the development of a basic "core" curriculum at the heart of planning education. ... The students being trained today must be prepared for many ... changes during their working lifetime (pp. 21-2).

He sees many professions and disciplines contributing to planning but

the very breadth of the actual and potential intellectual and professional contributions makes it evident that a sound planning education cannot be pieced together by drawing on a little bit here and a little bit there. Only if planning students are required to have a rounded general education as a prerequisite for graduate training, and if the training of city planners centres about a carefully designed core curriculum, can this surrounding richness be a source of strength for city planning education rather than a source of confusion and dilution (p. 22).

Perloff claims that the rationale itself for professional education is related to this core, arguing that the "progress of a profession usually depends upon ... the extent to which the profession comes to base its techniques of operation upon principles rather than rule-of-thumb procedures or simple routine skills" (p. 34).

The major task of professional education thus becomes one of developing and advancing the basic principles to be used in the profession and providing an integrated set of learning experiences which would permit the student, in essence, to rediscover these principles himself and learn to apply them in a problem-solving setting (p. 35).

We see the idea also of the planner as a "generalist-with-a-speciality" taking shape, together with the requisite model of planning education. The core programme:

should center about the basic principles and methods of planning (which, one soon finds, are quite limited in number and scope). It should permit ... the student to rediscover the validity of the basic propositions. ... Similarly, he should learn to use the basic methods by employing them in a problem-solving context. ... The core program should serve other purposes as well. It should make it possible for the student to become acquainted first-hand with ... primary sources. It should enable him to come to understand various kinds of interrelationships. ... It should help to develop in him basic attitudes and approaches to the planning field. ... In other words, the core program should develop a sound basis on which advanced, more specialized, and lifetime planning education can be built (pp. 38-9; see also Perloff, 1974; Faludi, 1978).

Part III, written with the assistance of John Friedmann, raises the issue of whether there could be a generic planning theory-a theme which we have seen above to stem from institutionalist economics. The answers are still valid:

It is natural for educators ... to consider whether the various types of planning activities have common elements and to ask whether the study of these elements makes up a distinguishable field of intellectual endeavor. If the answer is Yes-and there is strong evidence for such a view-then it should be possible to advance knowledge and techniques in planning as a whole through a university education and research program which seeks to develop a systematic body of theory or principles underlying every form of planning (ibid.).

This is what Chicago attempted to do:

From the first, the Chicago group used "planning" as a generic term to refer broadly to the ways in which men and women, acting through organized entities, endeavour to guide developments so as to solve pressing problems around them and approximate the vision of the future which they hold.

Planning ... thus centers on the making of decisions and scheduled effectuations of policies. It takes form in a number of closely integrated steps, from the analysis of problems, the setting of broad objectives and the survey of available resources, to the establishment of specific operating targets; and through various succeeding states until the results can be checked against the targets established and needed adjustments proposed (pp. 141-2).

This shows Chicago as the mainspring of modern planning thought. The essay indicates the sources also on which it draws: theories of budgeting, public choice and decision theory, political science, economics, sociology, anthropology, statistics, and philosophy. Due to Tugwell's influence, interest centred on long-term commitments.

These ideas were pursued in the core-curriculum: planning theory, socio-economic and physical elements of planning, planning methods and studios, or project work. Indeed, schools of design where this tradition is strong apart, the "Chicago School" seems to have been the first to see the potential of studios in teaching the planning process. This remains a strong point of planning education up until the present (see Faludi, 1978).

Perloff also gives his account of why Chicago folded up. As indicated, problems centred on the relationship with the Social Science Division. It had expected a collaborative effort, but Tugwell regarded planning as a separate field of study which, to flourish, should draw together a number of full-time persons. This spelt the end of all interdisciplinary efforts, "but if general financial stringency had not set in, it is likely that the halfway arrangement would have turned out to be a truly effective arrangement" (Perloff, 1957, pp. 153-4).

Apparently the idea had also been mooted of locating planning education in schools of public administration, because the essay points out the advantage of city planning over public administration, at the same time suggesting that the two might fruitfully be joined together:

> To date, the academic study of public administration has largely focused on procedure and process; other social science fields and the applied social sciences have chiefly emphasized content. Planning studies and planning education might well develop ways of bringing these together in the solution of clusters of problems, such as those involved in the physical development of the city ... the study of such subjects-preferably in co-operation with students of public administration-holds high promise of advancing effectiveness of public operations. In fact, there is much to be said in favor of developing a certain number of what might be called "programs of public affairs" which would be concerned with problems of both content (policy) and procedures and which would join the study of public administration and the study of planning (pp. 160-1).

Developments since have shown this to be prophetic. Many schools of planning have indeed joined with public administration.

Planning academics have multiplied since publication of this book. They have organised themselves on both sides of the Atlantic, and in the United States there even exists a *Journal of Planning Education and Research,* published by the *Association of Collegiate Schools of Planning.* But there is still no monograph on planning education that matches Perloff's (see also Robinson, 1985).

2.3   Politics, Planning, and the Public Interest

This book by Meyerson and Banfield (1955) is rightly famous, mainly for having introduced the *"rational planning model"*, as formulated by Simon (1976, 1st edition 1945), into the planning literature. Of course, neither Meyerson and Banfield nor Simon were the first to discuss rationality as such. Rather, it is a longstanding topic of discussion in the social sciences. There is a long footnote in *Politics, Planning and the Public Interest* referring to Parsons (1949), *The Structure of Social Action*. Through him there is a link back to the beginning of the century when Max Weber discussed rationality. The merit of Meyerson and Banfield lies in having made this body of thought accessible to planners. One of the aims of Part One of this work is to demonstrate the lasting importance of their rational planning model.

Meyerson and Banfield's definition follows below, but I should say at the outset what the rational planning model refers to: the quality of decisions. This is not the same as the quality of information on which decisions are based. Rationality is, rather, a matter of drawing the proper conclusions from such information, and values play an important role.

Politics and the *public interest*, too, are explained below. At this stage I merely point out what the treatment of these concepts in this book signifies. It is often said triumphantly, by critics of the rational planning model that "planning is political", and that there can be "no such thing as the public interest". These issues are anything but new. From the very start they formed part of the discourse on rational planning.

Politics, Planning and the Public Interest is the product of a unique form of cooperation. Meyerson had been seconded from the university as planning director to the Chicago Housing Authority. Banfield must have seen it as an opportunity to test out his views, influenced, as they were, by the most recent social science literature. The resulting study ranks amongst the top empirical works on planning-most of them showing the same combination of immediacy of involvement and reflectiveness. In the Preface the authors pose the question of generalisability of their case. Because case studies have been used frequently in planning research ever since, their answers are quoted at length:

the Chicago experience should sensitize the reader to certain influences and relationships which are likely to be found, although not in exactly the same form, in most cities.

Furthermore, ... the case ... should be suggestive for certain classes of issues which do not involve housing. Decisions about site selection are likely to have a certain amount in common whether that facility is a public housing project, a sewage disposal plant, a tuberculosis sanatorium, a super highway, or even a church or school. And since decisions regarding locations, along with decisions regarding budget amounts, are the form in which city planning usually comes into political focus ..., issues and problems like those described in this volume are the familiar concern of planners and politicians.

In addition, ... the logic of the planning process is essentially the same whether the planning be done by an agency like a housing authority which is concerned primarily with a single function and secondarily with other functions or by an agency like a city planning commission which is no more concerned with one function than with others (pp. 12-13).

The "Note on the conceptual scheme" at the end of this work by Banfield is the first discussion in the planning literature of the rational planning model. It will not be found wanting in awareness of the problems involved. The first concept he discusses is *politics*, and relates to conflict.

When there is conflict ... between the ends of different actors (or within the end system of a single actor) and not all conflicting ends can be realized, an *issue* exists and the actors whose ends conflict are parties to the issue. ... The ends which are made the basis of action ending a conflict form the *settlement* of an issue (p. 304).

Politics knows four modes: *cooperation* around shared ends; *contention* (straightforward struggle or bargaining); *accommodation*, out of its own accord, of one party to the wishes of the others; and *dictation* (pp. 305-7). In all this, each contending party uses strategies to influence others. A strategy can aim at compromise, that is "a system of incentives ... by which all parties are brought to agree to the settlement. A compromise is therefore the expression in concrete terms of the equilibrium of power which exists among the parties at the time it is made" (p. 308). It rests on actors being seldom interested in single issues only. Thus, *substitution* (*transfers* or *postponements*) is possible. Arranging compromises is an entrepreneurial function.

The second concept discussed by Banfield is *planning*, starting with a plan:

a course of action which can be carried into effect, which can be expected to lead to the attainment of the ends sought, and which someone ... intends to carry into effect. ... If a housing authority, for example, decides to clear slums and to build low-rent projects, these prospective acts which are related to each other as a "chain" of means ... constitute a plan, providing, of course, that the authority has the necessary legal authority, funds, etc., to build projects. ... As distinct from planned ones, *opportunistic* decisions are made as the event unfolds and they are, therefore, not mutually related as a unit having a single design. The execution of any planned course of action involves the making of opportunistic decisions as well as planned ones (pp. 312-13).

As we shall see in Chapter 6, this is remarkably like the "IOR School's" view of "strategic choice" as choice taken with awareness of the interrelations between decisions. Banfield distinguishes between *comprehensive* and *partial* plans and between *public* and *corporate* planning. *Community planning* is a special case of public planning for a whole community. He then introduces the rational planning model:

Since planning is designing a course of action to achieve ends, "efficient" planning is that which under given conditions leads to the maximization of the attainment of the relevant ends. We will assume that a planned course of action which is selected rationally is most likely to maximize the attainment of the relevant ends and that therefore "rational" planning and "efficient" planning are the same. As a practical matter, of course, this assumption may in many cases be unwarranted: sometimes the most careful deliberation will result in a worse selection than might be made by flipping a coin (p. 314).

Then the model is elaborated:

By a *rational* decision, we mean one made in the following manner: 1. the decision-maker considers all of the alternatives (courses of action) open to him; i.e., he considers what courses of action are possible within the conditions of the situation and in the light of the ends he seeks to attain; 2. he identifies and evaluates all of the consequences which would follow from the adoption of each alternative; i.e. he predicts how the total situation would be changed by each course of action he might adopt; and 3. he selects that alternative the probable consequences of which would be preferable in terms of his most valued ends (*ibid.*).

This is where awareness of the limitations of the rational model comes in:

Obviously no decision can be perfectly rational since no one can ever know all of the alternatives open to him at any moment or all the consequences which would follow from any action. Nevertheless, decisions may be made with more or less knowledge of alternatives, consequences, and relevant ends, and so we may describe some decisions and some decision-making processes as more nearly rational than others (pp. 314-15).

So, if only to various degrees, and depending on circumstances, planning practice can approximate this normative model. This idea has been accepted by many writers since. My *Planning Theory* (on which more in Chapter 4) is but one example. The model gives direction also for research into how plans would have to be made in order to be more effective (see p. 315). It gives direction also to the development of planning method as defined in the previous chapter: a way of rendering explicit the reasons behind decisions in planning. Nowadays, a range of such methods is available for handling each of the steps of the rational planning model which Banfield describes as follows:

1. *Analysis of the situation*: various aspects of the situation in which an actor finds himself must be investigated: the *limiting conditions* restricting the range of actions open to him, and *opportunity areas* as comprising "all those acts or courses of action which the effectuating organisation is not precluded from taking" (p. 316).

2. *End reduction and elaboration*: this refers to the selection of the relevant ends and the weights attached to them. Banfield distinguishes between *active* and *contextual* elements of ends:

> In designing a course of action the planner must find a way to attain the active elements of the end. But although this is a necessary condition ... it is not a sufficient one. For if the end is fully stated, the desired situation is seen to consist ... of several ... elements, and it is, of course, all elements-the desired situation as a whole-which the course of action should attain.
>
> When the content of an end is fully elaborated, it may appear that its active elements cannot be attained without sacrifice of certain contextual elements. In such a case, if the contextual elements are valued more highly, the end may be rejected altogether (p. 317).

So, Friedmann's contention that Banfield's rational planning model treats ends as given (Friedmann, 1973, p. 3) is ill-founded.

3. *The design of courses of action*: here, Banfield identifies decision with commitment, that is "an action which obliges the effectuating organization to take certain other acts or which limits its choice of acts in the future by foreclosing certain action possibilities which would otherwise exist" (p. 318). He distinguishes between *developmental*, *program* and *operational* levels of choice and relates them to functional and substantive rationality. Accordingly, a lower-level course of action may be a highly rational elaboration of a higher-level course of action which is irrational. Such a course of action becomes thereby substantially irrational. This pair of concepts, drawn from Mannheim (1940), will be discussed again in Chapter 4.

4. *The comparative evaluation of consequences*: Banfield defines a consequence as "a change in the situation which is caused by an act ... i.e. which follows the act and would not occur without it. Consequences may be *anticipated* or *unanticipated*, and anticipated consequences may be either *sought* or *unsought*" (p. 319). He adds in a statement, the importance of which will become clear in Chapter 8: "The situation consists only of those objects which have relevance in terms of the end-system of the organization: therefore, consequences ... exist only in relation to ends" (*ibid.*).

Banfield further distinguishes between advantages and disadvantages and calls quantifiable consequences costs and benefits, and others intangibles. He explores the distinction also between private and public organisations in terms of the range of consequences taken into account. This is because, the "greater the number of ends sought, the more difficult it becomes to design a course of action which will attain *all* of them" (p. 320). A private organisation can be selective as regards the ends it wishes to pursue, but a public one "is expected to take into account a very wide range of contextual elements along with the active element of its ends and it is expected to serve many incidental ends and discard old ones" (p. 321).

The significance of this for planning by public agencies is four-fold: a) end reduction is likely to be immensely more complicated in public than in private agencies; b) the ramification of consequences ... which have significance to some end, is likely to be far greater ...; c) the number of courses of action which can be devised that will attain all principal ends decreases as the number and stringency of the contextual elements increases, so that it becomes more probable that there will be no course of action at all which will attain the relevant ends of the public agency, and d) the hazard of unanticipated consequences of radical importance in terms of some of the ends increases; in seeking to attain an incidental end …, a housing authority may unexpectedly provoke the ire of a politician who may destroy the agency altogether (pp. 321-2).

The concept of the *public interest* is closely related: "A decision is said to … be in the *public interest* if it serves the ends of the whole public rather than those of some sector of the public" (p. 322). Banfield distinguishes:

(a) *Unitary conceptions* whereby the public interest is a single set of ends pertaining to all members of the public, either because the public is seen as a corporate entity (the *organismic* conception), or because the ends are almost universally shared (the *communalistic* conception).

(b) *Individualistic conceptions* whereby the relevant ends are those of individuals, whether shared or unshared, which should be aggregated, so that "a decision is in the public interest which is consistent with as large a part of the 'whole' as possible" (p. 324). The subtypes are the *utilitarian* conception, according to which the relevant ends are the ends of individuals and the public interest the sum of gains and losses in utility that are likely to be caused by that decision (pp. 324-5); the *quasi-utilitarian* conception, whereby a greater utility is attached to some men's views than to those of others; and the *qualified individualistic* conception according to which the relevant ends are selected from among certain classes of ends of individuals: community-rather than self-regarding; stable rather than transitory; general rather than particular; pertaining to the role of citizen rather than to some private one; those statistically frequent rather than infrequent; those morally justified rather than neutral.

A different decision-making mechanism is implied by each conception. A unitary one implies a central decision-maker whose role is technical, but endowed with the power at the same time to assert the interest of the "whole" over lesser interests. An individualistic one implies compromise, in the case of the utilitarian and quasi-utilitarian conceptions, by means of bargaining in which representatives act as instructed by their constituents. Under the quasi-individualistic conception, finally, there must be a mechanism for excluding inappropriate ends.

A representative process in which the representative gives more weight to his constituents' "real ultimate interest" … and special weight to "higher motives and more comprehensive and distant views" is implied. This is likely to be a system in which the representative can be called to account only infrequently and then by relatively large constituents" (pp. 328-9).

It is difficult to overestimate the importance of this work. Discussing it helps substantiate one of the arguments of this book: that planning thought can look back on decades of cumulative development, and that the critics of rationality since have said little which the "Chicago School" was not fully aware of.

Conclusions

There is no dearth of criticisms of the rational planning model. They will be discussed in Sections 3.4 and 7.1, where we shall see also that many have been pre-empted by Banfield. Even uncertainty-one of the major points of the "IOR School"-was appreciated at Chicago, based on awareness of work in statistical decision theory.

Two criticisms are possible. First, the "Chicago School" is ambiguous about where to start. Perloff has been quoted as saying that planning starts with the analysis of problems. At one point Meyerson and Banfield seem to be on the same track. But elsewhere they say that the decision-maker starts by considering all the alternatives open to him. Chapter 8 shows why the latter view is to be preferred. Second, the "Chicago School" conceived of the rational planning model as a behavioural prescription. But planning can never be rational, as Meyerson and Banfield fully realise themselves. They have not been able to square this circle. As noted before it is possible, though, to conceive of rationality as a rule for testing decisions *after* they have been proposed, and irrespective of how they have been formulated. Chapters 4 and 8 develop this quite different view.

A further improvement concerns not the rational planning model but its application. Plans, albeit ones based on rational considerations, still occupied the centre stage at that time-and continued to do so for years to come. Presently, it is not plans but the quality of day-by-day decisions which does.

References

Bacon, E. N. (1964) "Comment on 'A task-force approach to replace the planning board' ", *Journal of the American Institute of Planners*, **30**, 25-6.

Beer, S. (1966) *Decision and Control: the Meaning of Operational Research and Management Cybernetics*, John Wiley, London and New York.

Blanco, H. (1985) "Pragmatism, abduction, and wicked problems", *Berkeley Planning Journal*, **1**, 93-119.

Buckley, W. F. (1967) *Sociology and Modern Systems Theory*, Prentice-Hall, Englewood Cliffs, NJ.

Burns, L. S. and Friedmann, J. (eds) (1985) *The Art of Planning: Selected Essays of Harvey S. Perloff*, Plenum Press, New York.

Deutsch, K. W. (1966) *The Nerves of Government: Models of Political Communication and Control*, MacMillan, New York.

Dewey, J. (1929) *The Quest for Certainty: a Study of the Relations of Knowledge and Action*, Minton, Balch & Co., New York.

Etzioni, A. (1968) *The Active Society*, Collier-Macmillan, London.

Faludi, A. (1973) *A Reader in Planning Theory*, Pergamon Press, Oxford.

Faludi, A. (1978) *Essays in Planning Theory and Education*, Pergamon Press, Oxford.

*Foley, D. L. (1960) "British town planning: one ideology or three?ı", *British Journal of Sociology*, **11**, 211-31.

Friedmann, J. (1973) *Retracking America: a Theory of Transactive Planning*, Doubleday Anchor, Garden City, New York.

Friedmann, J. and Weaver, C. (1979) *Territory and Function: the Evolution of Regional Planning*, Edward Arnold, London.

Gelfland, M. I. (1985) "Rexford G. Tugwell and the frustration of planning in New York City", *Journal of the American Planning Association*, **51**, 151-60.

Gellen, M. (1985) "Institutionalist economics and the intellectual origins of national planning in the United States", *Journal of Planning Education and Research*, **4**, 77-85.

*Glass, R. (1959) "The evaluation of planning: some sociological considerations", *International Social Science Journal*, **11**, 393-409.

Hibbersheimer, L. (1944) *The New City: Principles of Planning*, Theobald, Chicago, Ill.

Hoch, C. J. (1984) "Doing good and being right", *Journal of the American Planning Association*, **50**, 335-45.

Howard, J. T. (1951) "In defence of planning commissions", *Journal of the American Institute of Planners*, **17**, 46-9.

Howard, J. T. (1964) "Comment on 'A task-force approach to replace the planning board' ", *Journal of the American Institute of Planners*, **30**, 24-5.

Mannheim, K. (1940) *Man and Society in an Age of Reconstruction*, Kegan Paul, London.

Meyerson, M. M. and Banfield, E.C. (1955) *Politics, Planning and the Public Interest: the Case of Public Housing at Chicago*, Free Press, New York.

Nash, P. H. and Durden, D. (1964) "A task-force approach to replace the planning board", *Journal of the American Institute of Planners*, **30**, 10-12.

Needham, B. (1971) "Planning as problem-solving", *Journal of the Royal Town Planning Institute*, **57**, 317-19.

Parsons, T. (1949) *The Structure of Social Action*, Free Press, Glencoe, Ill.

Perloff, H. S. (1957) *Education for Planning: City, State, & Regional*, Johns Hopkins University Press, Baltimore.

Perloff, H. S. with Klett, F. (1974) "The future of planning education", in: *Planning in America: Learning from Turbulence*, ed. D. R. Godschalk, American Institute of Planners, Washington, DC, pp. 161-80.

Robinson, I. M. (1985) "Appreciation (to Harvey S. Perloff)", *Canadian Journal of Regional Science*, **8**, 299-306.

Sarbib, J. L. (1983) "The University of Chicago program in planning: a retrospective look", *Journal of Planning Education and Research*, **2**, 77-81.

Simon, H. A. (1976; 1st edition 1945) *Administrative Behavior: a Study of Decision-Making Processes in Administrative Organisations*, Free Press, New York.

Walker, R. A. (1950) *The Planning Function in Urban Government*, University of Chicago Press, Chicago.

* Included in Faludi, A. (ed) (1973) *A Reader in Planning Theory*, Pergamon Press, Oxford.

CHAPTER 3

High Points and Diversions

THIS chapter describes high points in the development of the rational planning model and a diversion which is how I regard the "systems approach" which has created the illusion in the minds of planners of a specific area of competence and a role for themselves as "helmsmen" of the city-a metaphor coined by McLoughlin (1969, p. 86).

The chapter starts with an account of "A choice theory of planning" by Davidoff and Reiner (1962). Then I discuss the move *from social science to social engagement. The systems and models craze* concerns the systems approach. *Rational planning?* introduces criticism of the rational planning model claiming that it is an impossible prescription.

3.1 "A choice theory of planning"

Two decades after its publication this article is still the most widely used text in the United States (Klostermann, 1981). Discussing it, I show how ideas generated at Chicago have spread and borne fruit. In the next section I describe their modification in the light of emergent social concerns.

Davidoff and Reiner define planning "as a process for determining appropriate future courses of action through a sequence of choices" (in Faludi, 1973a, p. 11), an early example of a "procedural" notion of planning. They mean determining in the sense of finding out and assuring. Choice relates to goals, alternatives and the guidance of action towards ends. The authors show the need for, and the means of, rendering judgments explicit. This is a recurring theme in the literature on the rational planning model. It means no disregard for intuition, as Dakin (1963) alleges. But, as Davidoff and Reiner (1963, p. 27) retort, intuition is a "weak reed" on which to rest choices.

In Chapter 8 I relate rational planning to legal requirements that reasons be given for each governmental intervention. Davidoff and Reiner endorse such requirements, saying that planners must act in a non-arbitrary manner. Their propositions relate to (a) the *subject matter* of planning and the *environment* in which it takes place; (b) to its *purpose*; and (c) its *characteristics*.

As regards subject matter, they point out that individuals have variable preferences; production is subject to the law of diminishing return; resources are scarce; the entity for which planning is undertaken generally consists of parts which are in flux, thus generating a network effect and a need for coordination; and man operates with imperfect knowledge, making the interesting comment-reminding one of the "IOR School" to be discussed in Chapter 6-that there are severe conflicts "between demands for immediate action and for non-arbitrary decision" (p. 14).

The first of their three purposes of planning is efficiency, this being a re-statement of Meyerson and Banfield's views. Efficiency, of course, is measured in terms of the ends of planning. This provides the springboard for discussing rationality. Davidoff and Reiner make a curious distinction between rationality as "increasing the reasonableness of decision" and involving "full knowledge of the system in question":

In the former sense (a) the task of planning may be to provide information to decision-makers, and, in certain cases, to the clients and the public at large about what presently exists and what may be expected in the future under alternative conditions. With this information the actors can better satisfy their own wants. The latter concept of rationality (b) is far more demanding of planning, for it requires identification of the best of all alternatives evaluated with reference to all ends at stake. The alternative thus selected as optimal implies, and is implied by, an efficient course of action (p. 15).

Optimisation requires full knowledge, therefore. Since such knowledge is unavailable, Davidoff and Reiner think that optimisation makes no sense. But their alternative, rationality as increasing the reasonableness of decisions, implies nothing else than searching for an optimal solution (hopefully knowing that it will not in fact be possible to identify it with certainty).

A second-related-purpose of planning stems from market failures. The conditions of an ideal market seldom exist-about which more in Chapter 10. There are those who want (a) to supplement and (b) to replace the market; the radical and conservative wings amongst institutionalist economists discussed in the previous chapter being cases in point for this division. The expectation of both groups is that choices would become more rational by following their strategy.

The last purpose of planning is the widening of choice. Here a concern becomes apparent which permeates Davidoff's subsequent work discussed below. In modern society, choice is mostly delegated:

Delegation often decreases individual opportunity to choose, but this decrease has limits; the decision-maker can both question and inform the individual client about the issues at hand. The planning process can be specifically employed to widen and to publicize the range of choice of future conditions or goals, as well as of means. This function may be extended to include opportunities where choice can be exercised. Lack of techniques and of willingness often holds back urban planners in this realm (p. 16).

Under planning *characteristics*, Davidoff and Reiner consider the overlap between planning, operational research, decision-making, and problem-solving. They distinguish planning by its orientation towards the achievement of ends, the exercise of choice, the future, to action and by its comprehensiveness. In view of many muddled ideas about the two, it is interesting to note how future-orientation and comprehensiveness are related to the rational planning model:

Estimates of future states are ... important for what they imply for present behavior; thus, points are identified where control is required if ends are to be achieved. Moreover, planning involves assigning costs to deferred goal satisfaction and to losses arising from postponed actions (p. 18).

So, there is nothing mystical about planning's future-orientation. It is implied in the notion of rational choice. The same is true for comprehensiveness. Planning "serves to relate the components of a system. In order to allow decision-makers to choose rationally among alternative programs, the planner must detail fully the ramifications of proposals" (*ibid.*). No notion of "synthesis" is implied.

Davidoff and Reiner identify *value formulation*, *means identification* and *effectuation* as the necessary and sufficient characteristics of planning. Associated with each are distinct methods. Under the first they discuss the responsibility of the planner for widening choice, suggesting that planners must identify their clients, which is another forerunner of Davidoff's "advocacy planning". The authors relate this to the time perspective of plans, drawing a familiar distinction between long-range and short-term plans (see Meyerson, 1956; Friedmann, 1965, 1966, 1967). Long-range plans explore alternative value positions, short-range ones concentrate on what is attainable now. Middle-range plans mesh the two. In all of them value formulation comes first, this being an attack on "survey-before-plan" and the underlying assumptions exposed in Chapter 1:

Even where goal selection is placed first, there is a tendency to underplay this and to return to familiar territory-"survey and analysis". We do not understand the logic that supports ventures in research before the objectives of the research have been defined. Such emphasis on research is premised on an ill-founded belief that knowledge of facts will give rise to appropriate goals or value-judgments. Facts by themselves will not suggest what would be good or what should be preferred (pp. 29-39).

It seems that Davidoff and Reiner's is a sequential view of the planning process, saying that it must *start with* value formulation, proceed to means identification and culminate in effectuation. *Means identification*, then, provides instruments to achieve a stated end. It falls into two parts: the identification of a

universe of means consistent with a value. The alternatives identified would be those which were conditions sufficient for achievement of the goal. This is the deductive element of the model, a task which may take the form of identifying all the feasible alternatives, or a finite number, or possibly only one for comparison with existing conditions (p. 31).

The second task is the evaluation of alternatives in terms of (a) the satisfaction of the ends sought and (b) the probability of achieving them. The composite score gives the optimal alternative. This is superior to their earlier identification of optimality with full knowledge of the system. But before long, by drawing a distinction between optimising studies and comparative impact analyses, they show themselves not to have come to terms with optimality. Surely, what the latter aims for is the best solution from among those available. Indeed, Davidoff and Reiner discuss "means identification" (the generation of alternatives) in these very terms: "We seek to identify a set of means so related to the given purpose as to include the one that is 'best'. Thus, the set of alternatives identified ... must not omit one ... clearly superior to the one selected" (p. 32). It follows that "comparative evaluation of alternatives" is the same as optimisation. The "IOR School" will be shown in Chapter 6 to be similarly inconsistent, rejecting optimality whilst at the same time advocating evaluation of all alternatives.

Under *effectuation*, Davidoff and Reiner refer to the administration of programmes misfiring-thereby anticipating the implementation studies of a later era (see Section 7.3). Their paper is an early example also of the importance given to monitoring, ascribing to the planner "the role of an overseer, one who aids policy makers by observing the direction programs are given and by suggesting means for redirecting these towards the intended goals" (p. 33).

Finally, they say that effectuation begins already at the stage of value formulation, using the publication of a master plan as an example. This passage affirms that theirs is a sequential view of planning. Controls are "derived from" the comprehensive plan. Admittedly they state also that, in suggesting various forms of control, the planner is subject to many constraints, but they do not draw the conclusion-obvious, as we have seen, to Meyerson and Banfield-that these constraints must be assessed at the outset-that, as I shall argue in Chapter 8, planning should start not with end-reduction and elaboration but with an analysis of the "decision-situation".

Davidoff and Reiner are charged with idealism by Cooke (1983, p. 16), that is "an approach in which a conceptual framework of values triggers off the planning process". They are rationalists, also, by virtue of the fact that they "give primacy to correct principles, rather than material processes, in the derivation of knowledge". Cooke signals the presence, lastly, of "a belief that positivistic empirical testing of these principles ... is the only sure way to produce valid knowledge on which to base plans". Whether the first charge amounts to idealism is not relevant to this discussion. The second and the third completely miss the point. Davidoff and Reiner are nowhere concerned with the derivation of knowledge, nor with empirically testing principles. They are writing about values and facts in decision-making. So, these charges do not hold. But two problem have been indicated: (a) the meaning of optimisation which is sometimes wedded to the assumption of certainty; and (b) the idea that planning is a sequential process beginning with the setting of goals. Also, of course, Davidoff and Reiner are concerned with plan-making. Implementation is thought to follow suit.

3.2   From social science to social engagement

How does the rational planning model relate to the quest for relevance of planning which was the reaction in the sixties to the recognition of persistent poverty and discrimination in the midst of a society which Galbraith (1953) had characterised earlier as affluent? In this section I show that this quest does not so much signify the-often heralded-demise, as rather a more radical interpretation of the rational planning model. My witnesses are Webber (1963) and Davidoff (1965), both of whom take the rational planning model as their frame of reference. They address the issue also of whether the planner's professional responsibility should continue to be limited to land-use planning and design.

Comprehensive planning and social responsibility

As with the leading lights of the "Chicago School", Webber has a background in institutionalist economics (see Gellen, 1985, p. 77). He sees three reasons for planning. Taking note of the charge of physical determinism, he argues that the locations of activities do matter, if for nothing else then for *access* to *opportunities*. So, public decisions demand the most deliberate effort to help assure:

> *one*, that the distribution of the benefits and the costs among the city's publics is consciously intended and democratically warranted; *two*, that levels and priorities of investments are so staged as to induce the desired repercussions in the private market; and, *three*, that public resources are used for those projects and programs promising the highest social payoffs (Webber, 1963, in Faludi, 1973a, pp. 97-8).

Integrating programmes is the second reason. "Planning for the locational and physical aspects of our cities must ... be conducted in concert with planning for all other programs that governmental and non-governmental agencies conduct" (p. 102). This is where the rational model (demanding that the likely consequences of programmes should be evaluated) comes in:

> As a minimum condition necessary to this task, each municipal agency should be expected to trace the probable and significant consequences that its programs would have upon the aspects of the city that other agencies focus upon. In this way, each agency would be better informed about likely conditions in the future and hence better able to make rational recommendations of its own (*ibid.*).

Webber continues: "All proposed programs must be subjected to systematic valuation, if intelligent choices are to be made among them." Here, he refers to new techniques "permitting us to simulate what would happen if given policies were adopted, and thus to pretest the relative effectiveness of alternative courses of action in accomplishing stated ends" (p. 103). But he cautions that they must be applied wisely. He refers to uncertainty, conflicting goals, and unwillingness of elected officials to confront the real issues as problems. As will become evident below, Webber has since become an outspoken critic of such approaches. But in the sixties he is still optimistic that information and analysis will improve political, as well as market, choices (which is why Klosterman, 1976, pp. 58-65, characterises this school of thought as "adjunctive planning"). Webber is optimistic, too, about cooperation between professional staffs and the role of city planners: "As men who have specialized in the general, the truly effective city planners have functioned as catalysts for synthesizing the developmental plans prepared by the more specialized groups in government" (p. 106).

Under *expanding choice* as the third reason for planning, Webber points out the growing appreciation of cultural diversity-this being another of his recurrent concerns. Expanding choice requires government action so as to prevent social costs, redistribute income, provide collective goods and public information services. Webber argues, though, that regulatory approaches should be applied with restraint and sensitivity to their redistributive effects. Later these ideas should acquire fame under the name of permissive planning (see Section 7.1). The present article cumulates in a plea for a broader interpretation of the planner's social responsibility:

Although many ... activities do not fall within the city planner's area of special competence, he is nonetheless a key agent in setting municipal-investment priorities; and he is thus in a position to guide municipal policies toward the issues that really matter (p. 111).

This is an indictment of any narrow concern with physical planning. "Comprehensiveness" in the title of his paper means therefore that planning concerns more than physical arrangements. Critics of comprehensiveness sometimes lose sight of the context in which it has been put forward: the struggle for a more inclusive definition of the planner's professional role.

A few years later, similar discussions concerning the role of the planner took place in the United Kingdom (see The Royal Town Planning Institute, 1976). There was hope that "comprehensiveness" in Webber's sense might be approximated. Efforts were made to plan on a broad front, and town planners were in the vanguard of the movement. But such hopes were to be dashed by the crisis that overtook Britain.

Advocacy and pluralism in planning

On the basis of this article, Davidoff (1965) has sometimes been described as being opposed to rational-comprehensive planning (see Healey *et al.*, 1982; Hoch, 1984). This is a misinterpretation. It is not only that, as Stegman (1985, p. 375) says in his obituary, Davidoff's earlier contribution on planning as a generic process (see Section 3.1) is "no less significant to planning education or practice today than are his later and more widely known writings on advocacy and pluralism", the latter are organically related to the former.

Davidoff opens flamboyantly: "The present can become an epoque in which the dreams of the past for an enlightened and just democracy are turned into reality" (in Faludi, 1973a, p. 277). The distinct contribution of planners is based on (a) their command of the planning process as defined in the article with Reiner discussed above, and (b) their substantive skills. But the following statement sets this article apart from the earlier one:

The prospect ... is that of a practice which openly invites political and social values to be examined and debated. Acceptance of this position means rejection of prescriptions ... which would have the planner act solely as a technician (p. 277).

Davidoff rejects the technical role for the planner suggested by Harris (1960) as too timid, admitting at the same time that his joint paper with Reiner is subject to the same criticism. Now he claims that "the planner should do more than explicate the values underlying his prescriptions for courses of action; he should affirm them; he should be an advocate for what he deems proper" (p. 279). Davidoff defends this by saying that determination of what is in the public interest is an adversary process. Planners should openly advocate the interests "both of government and of such other groups, organizations, or individuals who are concerned with proposing policies for the future" (p. 279).

The recommendation that city planners represent and plead the plans of many interest groups is founded upon the need to establish an effective urban democracy, one in which citizens may be able to play an active role in the process of deciding public policy. Appropriate policy in a democracy is determined through a process of political debate. The right course of action is always a matter of choice, never of fact. In a bureaucratic age great care must be taken that choices remain in the area of public view and participation (p. 279).

What a difference, compared with the planning efforts of noble but distant experts of the classic era! Their unconscious positivism has been replaced by awareness of the distinction-already evident in Simon (1976, 1st edition 1945), Meyerson and Banfield (1955) and Davidoff and Reiner (1962); between facts and values, the more modest role of experts which this implies, and a sense of obligation to get involved at the same time. This appealed to the generation of the sixties and seventies, in Europe as much as in the United States. But Davidoff remains firmly committed to pluralism:

The idealized political process in a democracy serves the search for truth in much the same manner as due process in law. Fair notice and hearings, production of supporting evidence, cross examination, reasoned decision are all means employed to arrive at relative truth: a just decision. Due process and ... political content in both rely heavily upon strong advocacy by a professional (pp. 279-80).

This relates to participation. Unitary plans tend to inhibit it, so there should be more than one plan. But, compared with many of his followers, rather than rejecting the rational planning model, Davidoff sees advocacy planning as complementary to it. The reason is that it helps with articulating and evaluating alternatives:

"rational" theories of planning have called for consideration of alternative courses of action by planning agencies. As a matter of rationality it has been argued that all of the alternative choices open as means to ends should be examined. But those, including myself, who have recommended agency consideration of alternatives have placed upon the agency planner the burden of inventing "a few representative alternatives". The agency planner has been given the duty of constructing a model of the political spectrum. ... This duty has placed too great a burden on the agency planner (p. 281).

But advocacy planning does not diminish the role of the public planning agency-again a point which has been lost sight of by latter-day "advocacy planners". That agency

must decide upon appropriate future courses of action for the community. But being isolated as the only plan maker in the community, public agencies as well as the public itself may have suffered from incomplete and shallow analysis. ... Lively political disputes aided by plural plans could do much to improve the level of rationality in the process of preparing the public plan (*ibid.*).

Davidoff expects that (a) the public will obtain better information about alternatives; (b) there will be competition between various plans; (c) those critical of the "establishment" would be forced to come up with suggestions of their own.

Again in contrast to his latter-day followers, in 1965, Davidoff is impressed by methods like cost-benefit analysis, but their weak spot is the determination of values. Advocacy planning helps with making this explicit. "Furthermore, it would become clear ... that there are no neutral grounds for evaluating a plan; there are as many evaluative systems as there are value systems" (p. 283).

Davidoff's second concern-not fully integrated with the first-is a more inclusive definition of planning than that of the *American Institute of Planners*. At that time its Constitution stated that the Institute's "particular sphere of activity shall be the planning of the unified development of urban communities and their environs and of states, regions and the nation as *expressed through the determination of the comprehensive arrangement of land and land occupancy and regulation thereof*" (p. 293). Davidoff had suggested at the 1964 convention that the clause in italics should be deleted. "The planner limited to such concerns is not a city planner, he is a land planner or a physical planner" (*ibid.*). Like the "Chicago School", he conceived of the planner's role as that of a staff adviser in various fields. This

does not imply the termination of physical planning, but it does mean that physical planning be seen as part of city planning. Uninhibited by limitations on his work, the city planner will be able to add his expertise to the task of coordinating the operating and capital budgets and to the job of relating effects of each city planning program upon the others and upon social, political, and economic resources of the community.

An expanded scope reaching all matters of public concern will ... bring planning practice closer to the issues of real concern to citizens (p. 294).

Davidoff discusses planning education also. Starting from the view of city planning as coordination, he reaffirms the Chicago model with its orientation towards the planner as a "generalist-with-a-speciality". Thus, the

practice of plural planning requires educating planners who would be able to engage as professional advocates in the contentious work of forming social policy. The person able to do this would be one deeply committed to both the process of planning and to particular substantive ideas (p. 295).

Davidoff had a great deal of influence. It is not the purpose of this chapter to trace it, nor to discuss the contradictions which advocacy planning allegedly suffers from under capitalism (see Goodman, 1970). The argument here is about the approach to planning which Davidoff puts forward. It is well-attuned to uncertainty, in the sense in which the "IOR School" will be shown to conceive of this concept, including uncertainty concerning values. It is well-attuned also to the need for balancing commitment and criticism in planning.

3.3   The systems and models craze

Davidoff's followers associate the rational planning model with excessively refined methods, seemingly giving the edge of advantage to expert-planners over lay people (Rafter, 1983, p. 367). Systems analysis and model-building did promise a rock-solid base for professional experts in planning. One cannot blame them for jumping on this bandwagon; but in retrospect we know that this has diverted attention away from the recognition of planning as decision-making under uncertainty and conflict. In discussing systems thinking and the development of methods generally, I seek to increase awareness of the dangers of uncritically accepting such promises.

The *systems approach to planning* is difficult to delineate. Like the rational planning model it advocates the generation and evaluation of alternatives prior to making a choice. Thus, Batty (1982) sees the key-work by McLoughlin (1969) as being "not about the city as a system but about planning as a process of designing new city systems", adding that it contains the somewhat different notion also of the "overall planning system being a social control mechanism to manage city systems" (p. 255). Implicitly, Boguslaw (1982), in *Systems Analysis and Social Planning*, equates the systems approach also with rational-comprehensive planning (Hibbard, 1983). Taylor (1984, p. 109), on the other hand, sees the essence of the systems approach in its substantive assumptions. At its heart is a view of the object of planning as forming a system of inter-related parts, thus promising a holistic understanding leading to effective control. This is where *model-building* comes in. Models are representations of the object-system. They help analyse and simulate its behaviour under a variety of conditions. They thus promise to increase system control at the same time.

It is here that the most characteristic features of the systems approach to planning come in. In the British context, McLoughlin (1969) and Chadwick (1978, 1st edition 1970) represent this school. There, planning was already firmly established as a governmental activity but was somewhat insecure as regards its expertise. The achievement of these two authors is to have packaged approaches developed in the United States in such a way as to make their application to the making of statutory plans seem attractive. The symbiosis of governmental and expert authority seemed promising indeed. *Alas*, in due course both sources of legitimacy were to be challenged.

It would be easy to give a mocking review as others have done before. It is said that large models forming the core of the systems approach, "like dinosaurs, collapsed rather than evolved" (Lee, 1973, p. 163). Expectations were exaggerated:

With arrogant confidence, the early systems analysts pronounced themselves ready to take on anyone's perceived problem, diagnostically to discover its hidden character, and then, having exposed its true nature, skillfully excise its root causes. Two decades of experience have worn the self-assurance thin (Rittel and Webber, 1973, p. 159).

No doubt there has been arrogance. The sixties had seen the rapid development of the application of operational research, systems analysis and quantitative model-building to planning problems. The backlash of the seventies resulted from lack of attention to their limitations:

There are plenty of dramatic failures in practice, where the demands were so ambitious that none were met. Yet these failures were rarely the result of the inadequacy of the theory itself in informing practice. ... More usually, failures were the result of inability to perceive the appropriate environment in which such models could be constructed; the management of available resources was totally misconstrued in that the scale of the modelling effort was frequently out of all proportions to resources involved (Batty, 1979, p. 871).

Rather than lashing out against such excesses, I challenge McLoughlin and

Chadwick, who are generally careful to avoid falling into any obvious traps. My purpose is to show that-sheer self-aggrandisement apart-the systems approach is defective as a *planning approach*. In fact, it resembles classic planning thought. At its simplest its message is that "everything is related to everything else". It replaces unidirectional causality with the idea of mutual interdependence between phenomena. At the same time, systems analysts draw boundaries around clusters of high interdependence, referring to them as systems. Man-environmental relations form an example.

This approach shares the notions of feedback with cybernetics, or the study of guidance in material, biological, and social systems. Systems analysis and cybernetics promise practical advantages. Indeed, it was their uses during and after World War II-culminating in the landing on the moon-which made them known.

The attractions to planners are obvious, in particular when seen in the context of the United States of the fifties and early sixties, when massive investments took place in highway construction. Land use and transport seemed to condition each other and thus form systems. To come to grips with their interrelations was necessary, in particular on a regional scale; and it was in land use transportation studies that the approach was tried for the first time. Obviously, such efforts were "continually spurred on by the glamour of the computer age" (Batty, 1982, pp. 252-3). Indeed, the large models which Lee criticises are characterised by the fact that, being spatially disaggregated, "the only practical way to operate them is on a computer" (Lee, 1973, p. 163). Of course, planning was not the only field to experience the impact of these developments. Of great influence for planning was the parallel development of a "new geography" (for instance, Chorley and Haggett, 1967).

Even before the often sobering experiences had been fully assimilated, the systems approach made a great impression on planning theory and education. The second edition of Chapin's classic on *Urban Land Use Planning* (1965; see also Chapin and Weiss, 1962) emulates it (for the first edition see Section 1.3), followed by a lively interest in the systems approach in Britain resulting in the publication of *Urban and Regional Planning: A Systems Approach* (McLoughlin, 1969) and *A Systems View of Planning* (Chadwick, 1978, 1st edition 1971) at a time when scepticism in America was already on the increase (see Hall, 1983). In these works the assumption of the object of planning being a system, and that of planning as a process of rational choice, come into conflict with each other. The authors embrace both, their predominant interest being in providing a basis for professional expertise. They fail thereby to examine critically the choice of adapted spaces and communication channels as the object of planning. In other words, they fail to examine the choice of system boundaries. "As planners", McLoughlin says for example, "we are interested in only a small aspect of the motivations which drive individuals and groups", that is with those "which people feel because of dissatisfaction ... with ... *place related* aspects of their lives (pp. 38-9). He justifies this by pointing out that "a system is *not* the real world, but a way of looking at it. Definitions of systems therefore depend in part on the purpose and objectives for which they are being used" (p. 79; see also Kuhn, 1966, p. 49). But freedom in drawing systems boundaries puts the onus to show that his choice is appropriate on the analyst. As we have seen, neither Webber (1963) nor Davidoff (1965) thinks that traditional physical planning addresses the right problems. But McLoughlin's angle is that of a physical planner delighted with the tools which systems analysis provides, and which offer "an elegant and beautiful means of understanding the man-environmental relationship and a potentially powerful means for its control and guidance" (p. 91).

It is only fair to add that, allowing himself to be influenced by Marxist thinking, McLoughlin is now very critical of his own earlier work: "The system approach, operational research, mathematical models and cybernetics provided at the end of the 1960s a wonderful justification for a bureaucratised profession and its academic counterpart", he says, referring to his own work, mine and Chadwick's as examples (McLoughlin, 1983, p. 18). As far as my work is concerned, the discussion must wait until Chapters 4 and 5.

It is true that Chadwick (1978, 1st edition 1971) is ultimately interested also in rationalising, rather than critically evaluating, physical planning. But demonstrating this point would require discussing his concept of space in more detail than is possible within the scope of this book (but see Faludi, 1973b). Still, generally, the critics of the systems approach have a stronger case where its applications, rather than its conceptual foundations, are concerned. Even McLoughlin-the resounding success of whose book is due to his ability to make the systems approach accessible to planners who lack a grounding in scientific methodology (see Batty, 1982, p. 255)-has been shown to be well aware of the voluntaristic element in drawing systems boundaries. When Rittel and Webber lash out against systems planners (see above), they seem to have something cruder in mind. Bolan (1967, p. 241) puts succinctly what the systems approach meant to land use planning: the discredited "comprehensive" approach to land use planning of survey before plan (see Section 1.2) "dressed up in a fancier garb". (For a critique of the "hyper-comprehensiveness" of land use transportation models see Lee, 1973, pp. 164-5). Hall (1983, p. 42) comments that the systems approach and

comprehensive planning shared a belief that outcomes were predictable and plannable; that particular planning actions would achieve determinable results; that planning objectives could be specified by professional experts ... in sum, that rational decisionmaking was applicable to complex social systems.

In fact, though, the systems approach does little to overcome the tension, evident in planning from the start, between the political system on the one hand and the requirements of such planning on the other. But the theorists of systems analysis can be faulted not so much for committing this error but for failing to prevent practitioners from developing illusions about the systems approach. This is why, to the practitioners, the attractiveness of the idea of scientific planning has been hard to resist, for it held out the promise of right answers, of revealing what we should want, and of saying what we need to do. It seduces with the prospect of certainty, and thus with the prospect of relief from the discomforts of ambiguity and of having to decide things in the face of conflicting evidence and competing wants. But scientific planning is a mirage.

Science and planning are very different sorts of enterprise. ... scientists seek to observe, describe, and explain. ... Planners are quite the opposite; their purposes are to change whatever it is they are confronting, preferably, of course, to improve it (Webber, 1978, p. 152).

Webber adds that "this simple-minded distinction ... has evaded a great many planners. It has also evaded far too many public officials and laymen who have been led to believe that, through science, planners could tell them what is right and hence what they want" (p. 153).

It is not surprising that systems planning did not stand up to the strains of the sixties and early seventies. Physical planning, for which it seemed eminently suited, gave ground to "social planning", and the role of the planner changed from expert-analyst to that of advocate. Far from being the helmsman, the planner was reduced to but one among many participants in a complicated political game which probably defies coordination. Anyway, some argue, integration "does not require a single steersman or a single map. Coordination occurs, perhaps even best, as the resultant of the vectors of all agents' actions" (Webber, 1983, p. 98).

So one can agree with Batty's claim that, far from heralding a new era, McLoughlin's work is "best seen now as the culmination of a previous one in which planning was still a professional, expert-oriented activity rather than some function of social politics and advocacy" (1982, p. 256). It is the rear-guard action of classic planning thought, based on the nineteenth-century concept of science criticised in Chapter 1. It sees the epitome of planning as the making of a plan so thoroughly researched that it must be followed during implementation.

So the reason why the systems approach is treated as a diversion is that, rather than belonging to contemporary planning thought, characterised by recognition of social and political realities, it seems the last convulsion of the classic approach. Rittel and Webber (1973) argue that it should be replaced with approaches of the "second generation", "based on a model of planning as an argumentative process in the course of which the image of the problem and the solutions emerge gradually among the participants, as a product of incessant judgment, subject to critical argument" (pp. 161-2). "Strategic choice" (see Chapter 6) should meet with their approval, as with that of Lee, who ends his "requiem for large models" with the following three guidelines: a better balance between theory, objectivity, and intuition; starting with particular policy problems that need solving; and starting simply (Lee, 1973, pp. 175-6).

It is clear that the systems approach and associated methods have been a mixed blessing. Their acceptance was premature. Important issues had not yet been thought out. Disappointments were inevitable, and the effects are still with us. There is mistrust now of everything "scientific" in planning, which is associated with "number-crunching". As we shall see, this has also affected the perception of procedural planning theory as being "technocratic".

3.4 Rational planning?

What are the criticisms of the rational planning model? From the very beginning, as we shall see, there were doubts about the literal application of rationality in planning which resulted in modifications of the rational model. These relate to the approaches of the "second generation" which the critics of the systems approach were quoted as demanding. The next chapter shows *Planning Theory*, also, to have been greatly concerned with criticisms of the rational model.

In Chapter 2 I noted the influence of Simon on the development of the rational planning model. In his seminal *Administrative Behavior* (1976, 1st edition 1945) he had introduced the notion of "administrative man" making rational choices, as does "economic man". He made a distinction also between objective and subjective rationality (for a slightly different use of the same pair of concepts see Etzioni, 1968, p. 254). Subsequently, Simon put the emphasis more on the limitations of the human mind to formulate and solve complex problems. In the introduction to the third edition he asserts that administrative man does not optimise, he satisfices, that is "looks for a course of action that is 'good enough' " (1976, p. xxix).

This refinement is the result of being involved in research on psychology and artificial intelligence (see Simon, 1968). Works on these subjects had influenced Lindblom in his books on decision-making and the criticisms of the rational model (quoting amongst others the Meyerson and Banfield study; see Braybrooke and Lindblom, 1963, pp. 47, 50, 122). The alternative is described variously as consisting of "limited comparisons" (Lindblom, 1959), an incremental process of dispersed decision-making ("disjointed incrementalism"; Braybrooke and Lindblom, 1963), or "mutual adjustment" (Lindblom, 1965). As Etzioni (1968, pp. 271-2) comments, the formulations have in common their reliance on market-like structures.

In these studies, Popper (1961, first published 1944/45) is sometimes quoted as providing "philosophical support" (Etzioni, 1968, p. 268). Indeed, his "piecemeal engineering" seems close enough to what they propose. But my parallel work on Popper (Faludi, 1986) reveals "piecemeal engineering" to be equally compatible with the rational planning model.

Etzioni himself integrates social theory with cybernetics and systems analysis, and combines rationalism with incrementalism. His "mixed scanning" (Etzioni, 1967, 1968) is an approach by which the decision-maker quickly scans his field of action, identifying the preferred strategy on the basis of incomplete information. He then explores that strategy in more detail, occasionally returning to the general level to re-establish his overall direction. Etzioni illustrates mixed scanning with a variety of examples, including the strategy of infantrymen moving into unknown territory. Chadwick (1978, pp. 341-3) bases his "mixed programming" on Etzioni.

Such adaptations arise out of a concern for the limitations of the human mind in performing the feats which the rational model asks of it. Responses vary. Alexander (1984) distinguishes five reactions to what he describes as the breakdown of the "rational paradigm": the *ritual* response, reaffirming the validity of the rational model in the face of evidence to the contrary; the *avoidance* response, accepting such limitations as there are but refusing to draw consequences-this being a common response amongst social scientists whose "descriptive orientation relieves them of the obligation to repair or replace the normatic model their research has exposed as flawed" (pp. 64-5); the *abandonment* response, relying either on the conventional wisdom of practitioners or on faith in substantive ideology (Alexander refers to Castells, 1977; Clavel *et al.*, 1980; Paris, 1982); the *search* response, looking for alternatives like ecology and transactive planning (see Section 7.2), focusing on problem-definition instead of problem-solving (see Section 7.1), or advocating the transfer of philosophical insights from phenomenology, existentialism, or critical theory into planning. Lastly, Alexander refers to the *contingency model* advocated by Bolan (1969), Hudson (1979) and himself (Alexander, 1972). Maybe, though, there has never been a breakdown in the first instance, but only a few reasonable adaptations.

Conclusions

The last section concerns the rational planning model as a prescription for how to act in planning. Indeed, it cannot be followed in practice. There is also the use of the rational planning model, referred to in the conclusions to Chapter 2, as a critical yardstick for determining whether decisions are correct. It is not affected by such criticisms, and so-called alternatives to the rational planning model, like Lindblom's incrementalism, and Popper's piecemeal engineering are no substitute for it (see Faludi, 1986, p. 74). As their proponents rightly insist, decisions are necessarily incremental, or piecemeal. It follows that neither incrementalism nor piecemeal engineering are capable of discriminating between correct and incorrect decisions. That is where the rational planning model comes into its own. Chapter 8 expands upon this core idea of the decision-centred view of planning.

Also, it is often said that the breakdown of the so-called "consensus-view" of society and the recognition of conflict have spelled out the demise of the rational planning model. But who holds a consensus view? Meyerson and Banfield were shown in Chapter 2 to be free from it. Davidoff, Reiner, or Webber are not afflicted by this malady either. But the application of the systems approach and of model-building to planning-Webber's "engineering style"-comes close to it. As Taylor (1984, p. 109) comments, that is what many critics of procedural planning theory and the rational planning model have in mind. In so doing, they mistake an aberration of the rational planning model for the real thing.

References

Alexander, E. R. (1984) "After rationality, what?: a review of responses to paradigm breakdown", *Journal of the American Planning Association*, **50**, 62-9.

Batty, M. (1979) "Progress, success, and failure in urban modelling", *Environment and Planning A*, **11**, 863-78.

Batty, M. (1982) "Planning systems and systems planning", *Built Environment*, **8**, 252-7.

Boguslaw, R. (1982) *Systems Analysis and Social Planning: Human Problems of Post-industrial Society*, Irvington, New York.

Bolan, R. S. (1967) "Emerging views of planning", *Journal of the American Institute of Planners*, **33**, 233-45.

Bolan, R. S. (1969) "Community decision behavior: the culture of planning", *Journal of the American Institute of Planners*, **35**, 301-10; see also: A. Faludi (ed.) (1973) *A Reader in Planning Theory*, Pergamon Press, Oxford, pp. 371-94.

Braybrooke, D. and Lindblom, C. E. (1963) *A Strategy for Decisions*, Free Press, New York.

Castells, M. (1977) *The Urban Question: a Marxist Approach*, MIT Press, Cambridge, Mass.

Chadwick, G. A. (1978; 1st edition 1970) *A Systems View of Planning*, Pergamon Press, London.

Chapin, F. S. (1965; 1st edition 1957) *Urban Land Use Planning*, Harper, New York.

Chapin, F. S. and Weiss, S. F. (eds) (1962) *Urban Growth Dynamics in a Regional Cluster of Cities*, John Wiley, New York.

Chorley, R. J. and Haggett, P. (1967) *Models in Geography*, Methuen, London.

Clavel, P., Forester, J. and Goldsmith, J. (eds) (1980) *Urban and Regional Planning in an Age of Austerity*, Pergamon Press, New York.

Dakin, J. (1963) "An evaluation of the choice theory of planning", *Journal of the American Institute of Planners*, **29**, 19-27.

*Davidoff, P. (1965) "Advocacy and pluralism in planning", *Journal of the American Institute of Planners*, **31**, 331-8.

*Davidoff, P. and Reiner, T. A. (1962) "A choice theory of planning", *Journal of the American Institute of Planners*, **28**, 108-15.

Davidoff, P. and Reiner, T. A. (1963) "A reply to Dakin", *Journal of the American Institute of Planners*, **29**, 27-8.

Etzioni, A. (1968) *The Active Society*, Collier-Macmillan, London.

Faludi, A. (1973a) *A Reader in Planning Theory*, Pergamon Press, Oxford.

Faludi, A. (1973b) "The systems view and planning theory", *Socio-Economic Planning Sciences*, **7**, 67-77.

Faludi, A. (1986) *Critical Rationalism and Planning Methodology*, Pion Press, London.

*Friedmann, J. (1965) "A response to Altshuler: comprehensive planning as a process", *Journal of the American Institute of Planners*, **31**, 195-7.

Friedmann, J. (1966) "Planning as a vocation (1)", *Plan Canada*, **6**, 99-124.

Friedmann, J. (1967) "Planning as a vocation (2)", *Plan Canada*, **7**, 8-25.

Galbraith, J. K. (1953) *The Affluent Society*, Houghton Mifflin, Boston, Mass.

Gellen, M. (1985) "Institutionalist economics and the intellectual origins of national planning in the United States", *Journal of Planning Education and Research*, **4**, 77-85.

Goodman, R. (1972) *After the Planners*, Penguin, Harmondsworth.

Hall, P. (1983) "The Anglo-American connection; rival rationalities in planning theory and practice, 1955-1980", *Environment and Planning*, **B** (10), 41-6.

Harris, B. (1960) "Plan or projection", *Journal of the American Institute of Planners*, **26**, 265-72.

Healey, P., McDougall, G. and Thomas, M. J. (1982) "Introduction", in: *Planning Theory: Prospects for the 1980s*, eds P. Healey, G. McDougall and M. J. Thomas, Pergamon Press, Oxford, pp. 1-22.

Hibbard, M. (1983) "Review of R. Boguslaw, 'Systems Analysis and Social Planning: Human Problems of Post-Industrial Society' ", *Journal of the American Institute of Planners*, **49**, 111-12.

Hoch, C. J. (1984) "Doing good and being right", *Journal of the American Planning Association*, **50**, 335-45.

Klosterman, R. E. (1976) "*Towards a normative theory of planning*", Cornell University, Ph.D., Urban and Regional Planning.

Klosterman, R. E. (1981) "Contemporary planning theory education: results of a course survey", *Journal of Planning Education and Research*, **1**, 1-11.

Kuhn, A. (1966) *The Study of Society: a Multidisciplinary Approach*, Tavistock, London.

Lee, D. B. Jr (1973) "Requiem for large-scale models", *Journal of the American Institute of Planners*, **39**, 163-78.

*Lindblom, C. E. (1959) "The science of muddling through", *Public Administration Review*, **19**, 79-88.

McLoughlin, J. B. (1969) *Urban and Regional Planning: A System Approach*, Faber & Faber, London.

McLoughlin, J. B. (1983) "Planning research and education in Australia", *Urban Policy and Research*, **1**, 16-21.

*Meyerson, M. M. (1956) "Building the middle-range bridge for comprehensive planning", *Journal of the American Institute of Planners*, **22**, 58-64.

Meyerson, M. M. and Banfield, E. C. (1955) *Politics, Planning and the Public Interest: the Case of Public Housing at Chicago*, Free Press, New York.

Paris, C. (1982) "Introduction by the editor, Part One: A Critique of Pure Planning", in: *Critical Readings in Planning Theory*, ed. C. Paris, Pergamon Press, Oxford, pp. 3-11.

Popper, K. R. (1961; first published 1944/45 *The Poverty of Historicism*, Routledge & Kegan Paul, London.

Rafter, D. O. (1983) "Review of T. N. Clark, 'Urban Policy Analysis: Directions for Future Research' ", *Journal of the American Planning Association*, **50**, 376-68.

Rittel, H. J. W. and Webber, M. M. (1973) "Dilemmas of a general theory of planning", *Policy Sciences*, **4**, 155-9.

Royal Town Planning Institute (1976) *Planning and the Future: a Discussion Document*, London.

Simon, H. A. (1976; 1st edition 1945) *Administrative Behavior: a Study of Decision-Making Processes in Administrative Organizations*, Free Press, New York.

Stegman, M. A. (1985) "Paul Davidoff: symbol and substance", *Journal of the American Planning Association*, **51**, 375-7.

Taylor, N. (1984) "A critique of materialist critiques of procedural planning theory", *Environment and Planning*, **B** (11), 103-26.

*Webber, M. M. (1963) "Comprehensive planning and social responsibility: towards an AIP consensus on the profession's role and purpose", *Journal of the American Institute of Planners*, **29**, 232-41.

Webber, M. M. (1983) "The myth of rationality: development planning reconsidered", *Environment and Planning B: Planning and Design*, **10**, 89-99.

* Included in Faludi, A. (ed.) (1973) *A Reader in Planning Theory*, Pergamon Press, Oxford.

CHAPTER 4

Procedural Planning Theory

WHAT does procedural planning theory stand for? How does it relate to authors discussed so far? Answering these questions should give insight into the background, intentions and propositions of the work in which the decision-centred view of planning is rooted.

Procedural planning theory is an umbrella term for theories about the planning process and organisational forms of planning. Its opposite is substantive theory, concerned with the subject matter of planning-sometimes also referred to as its object. Examples are: theories of land use, theories of urban growth, theories of the housing market.

This chapter discusses procedural theory as represented by my *Planning Theory* (Faludi, 1984, 1st published 1973). Critics insist it represents a high point in the development of this type of theory (see Scott and Roweis, 1977, p. 113; Thomas, 1979, in Paris, 1982, p. 24; Healey *et al.*, 1982, p. 8). It figures also in the "proceduralist" versus "substantivist" controversy discussed in Chapter 5.

Part I of *Planning Theory* outlines the domain of procedural planning theory and explains the distinction between normative and positive theory of planning. Part II gives the rationale of planning theory as promoting human growth, develops a model of planning agencies based on the analogy with the human mind as an information-handling system, and explores strategies for handling the perennial problem of information overload, as well as creativity in planning. Part III concerns three hypotheses about the relationship between the mode of planning on the one hand and the object of planning and its societal context (the "planning environment") on the other. Part IV puts forward principles to be followed in the absence of a fully fledged empirical theory of planning.

"Planning Theory"-concerns and approaches gives details concerning Parts I-III. *Planning principles* relates to Part IV. *Comments and criticisms* gives an account of points by Reade, Taylor, Low and Hooper.

4.1 "Planning Theory"-concerns and approaches

When I was writing *Planning Theory* the distinction between procedural and substantive theory was not a major concern. It seemed uncontroversial-as, indeed, did its implication that, as at Chicago, planning theory and education should concentrate on the former. Procedural theory concerned the very activity of planning, the role, or roles, which planners play, its purpose also: questions important enough to occupy the centre stage. The American planning literature devoted to these issues at that time was impressive, as I had demonstrated in *A Reader in Planning Theory* (Faludi, 1973). It was a surprise that the debate which followed focused on this distinction. Major concerns were rather (a) the research strategy for planning theory; (b) the limitations of the human mind in planning rationally.

The research strategy for formulating planning theory

The reason why this was a major concern should please critics who alleged that *Planning Theory* is concerned with technical rationality (limited to selecting the means to achieve given ends; see Thomas, 1979, in Paris, 1982, p. 14; see also Forester, 1984, p. 125) and/or that it is without context or content (Healey *et al.*, 1982, p. 8). Mannheim (1940), Meyerson and Banfield (1955), Braybrooke and Lindblom (1963), Friedmann (1959, 1966a,b, 1967a) and Etzioni (1968) had led me to conceive of planning as the application of reason to collective decision-making (see Friedmann, 1959, pp. 327-8). That seemed to translate into the rational planning model. (On the contrary view now held by Friedmann see his transactive planning, 1973, p. 9; see also Section 7.2.) But two problems remained. One evolved around *functional* and *substantive rationality* (Mannheim, 1940, pp. 51-7). The former remains on the level of technical rationality. The latter stands for intelligent overall insights. Conceived during the thirties in Germany, this distinction reflects concern for the lack of precisely these insights, making democracies easy prey for Fascism. As we have seen, this debate was revived at Chicago (see Section 2.3); and it figures prominently in Friedmann's works influencing my own.

The second problem stemmed from the *difficulty of rational planning* discussed in Section 3.4. My treatment of this issue has earned me the title of the "last of the rational planners" (Friedmann, 1974, p. 311). But more than a decade later the issue is still alive (see Alexander, 1984; Breheny and Hooper, 1985; Christensen, 1985). Analysts continue to emphasise the political nature of planning, pointing out that, next to their expert role, planners fulfil other roles as well; and that the organisation of planning inhibits rationality. They identify the rational mode also as but one out of a number of modes of decision-making (see Healey, 1983). Fortunately, none of this is very far from what *Planning Theory* says.

The reason is that, in dealing with this problem, I was influenced by Friedmann (1966a, 1967b); Bolan (1967, 1969), Mann (1964) and Rabinovitz (1969) who argued that planning depends on the context in which it takes place-which I refer to as the "planning environment". This "contingency approach" of formulating strategies to match types of problems and organisational settings has become popular since (see Cartwright, 1973; Bryson and Delberq, 1979; Alexander, 1984; Hudson, 1979; Masser, 1983; Christensen, 1985).

The notion of a planning environment offered a way of coping with both problems identified above. Though decision-making in practice was undoubtedly "muddling through" (Lindblom, 1959), differences existed as regards the *degree* to which planning approximated rationality. (That that ideal was worthwhile had been affirmed by Meyerson and Banfield, 1955; See also Banfield, 1959, in Faludi, 1973, p. 149). Whether planning was restricted to considering means to given ends on the level of "functional rationality", or whether it included the evaluation of alternative ends (which was my understanding of substantive rationality at the time; but see Reade, 1985, p. 111 and my reply in Faludi, 1985) might depend equally on the context of planning. The British planning environment, for instance, appeared to hold out hope for a realistic form of "rational-comprehensive planning" as proposed by Meyerson (1956) and Friedmann (1965). (In a sense, therefore, I *was* living in a different world from that of US theorists, as Clavel, 1979, p. 365, surmises.)

I conjectured also that various concepts in the literature could be paired, each forming the extreme end of a continuum, thus bringing order into the conceptual jungle of planning theory. Where along that continuum planning was located depended on a number of factors, the context and the content of planning among them. I identified three such "dimensions": *blueprint planning* and the *process approach*; *rational-comprehensive planning* and *disjointed incrementalism*; *normative* and *functional* planning.

From here it was but a small step to the realisation that my aim was formulating a "positive" theory about how planning takes place in practice. Again I followed Friedmann (1967b), Bolan (1967, 1969), and Dror (1963), arguing for empirical research into forms of planning. With them I held also that the aim was not theory as such but to improve planning-to bring it closer to the ideal represented by the rational planning model. That, then, was why the relationship between normative and positive theory became a prime concern.

Two issues arose. The first related to the normative base of positive theory. All theory-formation rests on normative assumptions. Minimally, the assertion is that the object of theorising is worthy of attention. I proposed that the "rationale of planning theory" be seen as the view of planning as promoting "human growth" in the sense of learning about the environment, but *also* about constraints on self-fulfilment. (Cooke, 1983, p. 106, misconstrues this to mean that the "essense" of planning is the furtherance of human growth. But there is a difference between essence and rationale.) The notion of advocacy planning influenced me in this, as did ideas emerging from the European student movement concerning self-enhancement (see Grauhan and Strudelt, 1971).

So, "positive" planning theory was never thought of as "value free". By clearly outlining my commitments I hoped to escape the charge of "positivism". In this I was singularly unsuccessful (see Hebbert, 1974; Thomas, 1979; Taylor,

1980; Hooper, 1982; Cooke, 1983). Perhaps the very term "positive theory" raised too many eyebrows at a time when the rumbling of the "positivist dispute" in Germany had just about reached the shores of the Anglo-American linguistic empire (see Adorno *et al.*, 1976; Fay, 1975). That dispute concerned whether the social sciences should explain phenomena, like the natural sciences did, or whether their purpose was to examine society critically, with the latter position receiving most of the acclaim. (It is ironic that materialist critics of procedural planning theory like Scott and Roweis, 1977, 1978, can describe theirs as a positive theory of planning with impunity.)

The second issue concerned the *relationship* between positive and normative theory of planning. Regrettably this point has been misunderstood, as we shall see. The works by which I had been impressed did not build on positive theory. Think about Davidoff's argument presented in Section 3.2 for planners acting as advocates, the "middle-range bridge for comprehensive planning" (Meyerson, 1956) and Dyckman's fine pieces in the *Journal of the American Institute of Planners* (Dyckman, 1961, 1962, 1966). Even Friedmann's and Bolan's and Dror's papers, mentioned above, though arguing for positive theory, were not themselves based on such a theory. Were all these works mere expressions of personal predilection?

The normative theory in Part IV of *Planning Theory* was *not* based on positive theory either. My case for making recommendations, the absence of positive theory notwithstanding, rested on Kaplan (1964, pp. 332-46) who distinguished two models of explanation. "Deductive" explanation offered by positive theory shows that an observation can be derived from general propositions, or laws. The "pattern model" is weaker, in that it "explains" what one observes by merely fitting it into a pattern of interlocking concepts so that one can make sense of it. It has the advantage, very often, of being the only explanation available. I thought that procedural planning theory could at least provide explanations following the pattern model, but was aware that these were not recommendations based on causal knowledge.

The limitations of the human mind

In *Planning Theory* I discuss how, limitations notwithstanding, the human mind copes. The work draws on social psychology, the psychology of communication, linguistics, cybernetics, and the literature on artificial intelligence. Of particular influence were Argyle (1967), Miller *et al.* (1960), and, of course, Etzioni (1968).

This throws more light on the charge of "positivism", because I go beyond a "stimulus-response" model and, incidentally, also beyond the thermostat, my use of which Cooke (1983, p. 40) makes some play of, forgetting that I take it as the starting point for exploring the reflective qualities of the human mind. I portray it as working with a "technology-image" which influences what it perceives and how it reacts to problems. The idea of objective facts-being the assumption on which positivism rests-is absent, therefore. On the contrary, the technology-image evolves around goals, and around a self-image (formed on the basis of interaction with others). This gives due attention to the role of values in human knowledge and conduct, and should avoid the danger, which Cooke (1983, p. 165) signals, of a professional sub-culture that "promotes the fallacious belief that given policies can be better than others in some objective sense".

Planning Theory is said not only to be positivistic, but also to represent a "consensus view" of society (in particular: Thomas, 1979, in Paris, 1982, p. 22; Clavel, 1979). Now, the "model of planning agencies" in *Planning Theory* is indeed based on an analogy with the human mind as an "information-handling system", investigating its environment, comparing new information to the existing technology-image and taking decisions on that basis-this being an influence on my work of the systems approach. It may indeed seem to suggest that planning agencies are-or should be-seen as unified entities.

But when using something as a model for something else, one does not thereby claim that the two are identical. My interest in the human mind focused on information-handling in relation to action. It is in that respect only that I looked at planning agencies as being analogous to the human mind. The argument was that planning agencies, too, relate information to action-and get bogged down in the problems involved. Cooke (1983, p. 262) claims that such an analogy "is bad because it requires that we reduce the complex social forces operating in any human organization to the psychologistic level of the individual brain". But, as Banfield has been quoted as saying in Section 2.3, conflicting ends are not specific to organisations. Individuals have difficulties also in integrating their ends. So they, too, face "political" issues. Whether they are less complex than those faced by organisations is not at issue here. Cooke does not indicate where he would draw the line. He merely postulates that there is no comparison between the two, which I deny.

Anyway, as will become evident when discussing the planning principles in *Planning Theory*, I see conflict as a source of strength. It helps with finding creative solutions. Admittedly it aggravates the problem of information-handling. The more divergent views there are, the more information is needed to define, let alone resolve, planning issues, and the more our limited capacity for handling information is taxed. But that is not at issue here. What is, is whether I hold a consensus view, which I do not.

How, then, can one reconcile the emphasis on rationality with the constrained position of planners working on the coal face of planning, "unable and certainly disinclined to move human destinies and to make the really 'big' decisions" (Friedmann, 1966b, pp. 122-3)? *Planning Theory* gives two answers. The more conventional one embraces mixed scanning (Etzioni, 1968; see Section 3.4). Structure and local plans-then being developed in Britain-seemed to fit this approach. We may extend mixed scanning to include the cultural context of action as well. Language embodies technologies and concepts. They are based on world views in turn which influence what we deem to be acceptable and effective in terms of action. Figuratively speaking, such views represent the result of a first "scan". So rational planning never works with a clean slate, literally evaluating all alternatives in the light of all their consequences. As Lindblom rightly points out, we consider only those alternatives encompassed by the dominant technology-image. Most planners work within these confines- and they should not be made to feel the worse for that. (See also the stance taken by Harris, 1978a,b, in his debate with Scott and Roweis, 1977, 1978, discussed in Section 5.4 below, and the discussion of planning doctrine in Section 8.5).

Rational planning does not attempt the impossible, therefore. Rather, it takes account of limitations. Its requirements must be relaxed. But this must be done consciously. Mixed scanning and other "planning strategies" show how. Uncertainty management forming part of "strategic choice"-to be discussed in Chapter 6-provides more examples. These approaches free energies for really important decisions. We might call this "rationality of the second order". It takes account of our strengths and weaknesses. (As Chapter 8 below has it: the definition of the decision situation includes awareness of the limitations of the planning subject.) This is more sensible than pursuing rationality in any literal sense of the word-which only means abandoning it sooner rather than later.

This is fairly conventional. The more radical answer to the problem of reconciling rationality with our limitations is to reformulate the issue around the distinction between the rational planning model as a prescription for how to act in planning, and for testing decisions once they have been made. Looking back, this seems one of the more satisfactory ideas in *Planning Theory*. Decision-making, planning, indeed, human thought processes generally, cannot be straight-jacketed by rules. The mind works differently, as critics of rationality are quick to point out. Nor does it matter whether thought processes are systematic, methodical, "rational". In a passage that has received little attention I explain that the point is rather:

to present one's choices in a form which could have resulted from a rational planning process, even if this has not actually been the case. Much as in science ... the effort of presenting a course of action in this way has the advantage of facilitating criticism and of establishing an unambiguous basis for agreement or conflict (Faludi, 1984, p. 38).

This foreshadows my current interest in critical rationalism (see Faludi, 1983, 1985, 1986) which leads me to describe rationality as a methodological rule for identifying which decisions are correct in a given situation. Section 8.5 discusses this further.

4.2 Planning principles

Ordinarily, the term principle is used in planning to describe desirable end-states, like the separation of conflicting uses, or the clustering of housing, together with a strategy for achieving it: controlling land uses, or building housing in larger, planned unit developments (PUD; see Chapter 13), as the current American term goes. *Planning Theory*, too, asserts certain aims, and gives guidelines for how to move towards them. In retrospect, it seems that what I was concerned with were *planning principles* in the sense of reasoned proposals of what we should strive for in terms of the organisation and procedures of planning, and a strategy for approximately that state.

The hypotheses in *Planning Theory* refer to contextual variables, amongst others, as having a firm influence on the conduct of planning. But should planners merely adapt to the prevailing planning environment (as the literature tends to suggest, with Friedmann's "innovative planning"-a form of institution building-being the exception confirming the rule; see Friedmann, 1967b)? The alternative is to make that environment more conducive to the preferred planning style. *Planning Theory* points out that, collectively, planners can-and do-have policies on these matters. This is my starting point.

If we had our way, then, planning would be evaluating all alternatives. It would include considerations of alternative goals, and respond flexibly to new situations. But this ideal planning style cannot be practised, and all we can do is try. The planning principles in *Planning Theory* for meeting this challenge are: (1) division of labour in "multi-planning agencies"; (2) planners engaging in public controversy; (3) teamwork within planning offices; (4) participation in planning.

Multi-planning agencies

Multi-planning agencies are clusters of related planning agencies. They allow for specialisation and hold out the promise of coordinated attacks on problems such as Webber (1963) and Davidoff (1965) were shown in Section 3.2 to demand. The minimum one can ask for is that decisions of public agencies should not be at cross-purposes-that there should be "negative coordination" ("positive coordination" being reserved for really joint planning). One must be sceptical, at the same time, about all-out efforts at coordination. The necessary negotiations are time-consuming and frustrating.

How should multi-planning agencies be given overall direction? The main concern of such "strategic planning", according to *Planning Theory*, must be to balance problems of coordination against the desire for comprehensiveness. Strategic planning must beware of getting bogged down in details, leaving them to others with a more direct involvement in the issues at hand. But this begs the question as to what the strategic elements are-an issue which has concerned Mannheim describing them as *principia media* (see also Friedmann, 1973). The question can only be answered from case to case. Beyond this, strategic planning must keep an eye on overall performance of the multi-planning agency, thus generating self-awareness which increases rationality. These proposals are similar to those by Webber (1983, p. 97; see Section 7.1) for the organisation of development planning.

The next two principles should foster criticism, exempting neither facts nor values from scrutiny.

Planners as political actors

The exploration of real alternatives requires committed planners, as Davidoff has been shown to argue (see Section 3.2). They must not merely be the loyal servants of their political masters, as the bureaucratic role model of the planner has it (see Beckman, 1964). In fact, as leftist critics of the British Civil service complain (see Hill, 1981, p. 209), under the cover of neutrality, bureaucrats often manipulate politicians. They should be encouraged to engage in public controversy instead.

But their role is not the same as that of politicians. *Planning Theory* draws on Friend and Jessop (1977; 1st edition 1969; see Section 6.1) who distinguish between decision-making and decision-taking. Decision-making should allow for free discussions between all those concerned, including planners of course (Lichfield *et al.*, 1975, p. 6, drawing also on Friend and Jessop, forget this last point). Decision-taking, on the other hand, involves the shouldering of political responsibility, and planners have no part in it. For better or for worse, representative democracy relies on elected politicians. Clearly the hope is that, in assuming their role, they benefit from free discussions.

This distinction relates to the one above between rationality as a prescription for action and as a guideline for testing decisions. Decision-taking takes place on the basis of arguments previously formulated. How, by whom, and with which ulterior motives, should be of no consequence for their acceptance. In particular it should be of no concern to the decision-takers whether the process of formulating proposals has been "rational"-whatever that may mean. Their concern should be with whether the recommendations follow from the premises, and whether those premises are acceptable in themselves.

Planning as teamwork

Discussions should not be limited to chief planners and politicians, but should extend to all echelons. Party factions should form coalitions with groups of planners, thus ensuring that real alternatives are explored. This should obviate the problem of planners having "the duty to construct a model of the political spectrum" (Davidoff, 1965, in Faludi, 1973, p. 281, see also Section 3.2). Also, it should prevent planning agencies from developing policies which bear the stamp mainly of their chiefs-which is what bureaucratic policy mainly amounts to. What it all comes down to is that planning must be teamwork. (In this I was influenced by Grauhan, 1969, in Faludi, 1973.)

Participation

This is another means of furthering criticism, thereby expanding the range of options considered. As Popper (1981, p. 190) observes, hearings and the like do make situations more transparent. This should recommend it as improving planning.

The democratic aim is, of course, that those affected come to feel the subjects rather than the objects of planning. So, control in planning should be by persuasion and the setting of a framework within which actors can do their own planning, this being an application of a distinction by Etzioni (1968, pp. 357-9) between sources of power. His preference is for persuasive rather than coercive or utilitarian power. Like the "humanistic planners" (see Section 7.2), he is concerned at the same time that even persuasion might become oppressive lest it is "authentic".

Undoubtedly this all has a naïve ring about it. More often than not, participation results in awareness of conflicts, thus raising the issue of whether the preconditions for democratic decision-making exist. But whether democracy is able to resolve conflicts which, thanks to participation, become apparent, is not an issue of planning theory. That striving for rationality ultimately poses the question of whether ours is a rational society should not, however, surprise us. "Human growth" was described as confronting us with such issues from the start.

This touches upon a persistent criticism levelled against *Planning Theory*: its alleged idealism. The concern in it is for fostering criticism whilst simultaneously maintaining the drive towards rationality. In my parallel work on *Critical Rationalism and Planning Methodology* (Faludi, 1986, p. 109), I quote *The Poverty of Historicism* as giving an "institutional theory of progress". It underlines the importance of maintaining the preconditions of criticism. Objectivity, Popper argues, rests upon the public character of science "which imposes a mental discipline upon the individual scientist" (Popper, 1961, first published 1944-5, p. 155). This applies as well to politics and planning. This is because holistic control, "which must lead to the equalization not of human rights but of human minds, would mean the end of progress" (p. 159). The Epilogue in *Planning Theory* on "The Planning Society" shows-as Friedmann (1974) readily grants-that *Planning Theory* seeks to avoid this danger.

4.3 Comments and criticism

This section starts by relating comments by Reade and Taylor that *Planning Theory* confounds normative and empirical inquiry. Low adds "personal construct theory" to the arsenal of approaches on which planning thought can draw. Hooper forges a link with the "positivist dispute" mentioned above.

An unhappy mixture?

Reade persistently rejects my normative planning theory summarised in the previous section, saying that "those who provide such normative theories, due to their understandable desire to influence events, 'jump the gun'. While some of their prescriptions arise from accepted causal connections, others rest on supposition" (Reade, 1974, p. 444; see also Reade, 1973, 1976, 1982). Taylor (1980) also thinks that theories of planning have generally been an "unhappy mixture of philosophical judgement and sociological theory-'unhappy' because the philosophy has typically been unclear and questionable, and the sociology has often been superficial and naïve" (p. 159). To him, my work too, overlays the "plea for an improvement of our empirical understanding of planning with the philosophical judgement that it should be the aim of planning to foster 'human growth' " (p. 160; see also Hooper, 1982, discussed below). Which leads Taylor to distinguish between philosophy and sociology of planning, a distinction running parallel to the one between normative and positive theory of planning. He examines the role of philosophy and identifies two areas relevant to planning: ethics and methodology of science. Criticising logical positivism as one of the schools in the methodology of science, he suggests that, where I speak "of developing 'positive' theory of planning by means of empirical research into the process of planning" (p. 159), I, too, can be suspected of positivism. Taylor fairly admits, though, that he is not sure about this. My proposed hypotheses for subsequent testing should have put his mind to rest: this is not in conflict with the Popperian method which Taylor recommends.

I have already given my reasons for combining normative and positive theory in one work. But in *Planning Theory* I am apologetic about not being able to base recommendations on a fully fledged empirical theory. Since then I have come to regard the formulation of normative theory as a pursuit more in its own right. Also I readily admit that, as regards the relation between normative and empirical inquiry, my earlier work is liable to be misunderstood.

New horizons?

Low (1979) rightly characterises mine as a learning model of planning and affirms that the planner's job is "essentially that of facilitator, or catalyst. Planners have resources available, they can show people alternatives, help people to understand what they want, but should not take decisions for them". Indeed, he says that my claim that the "planning society leaves maximum reign to individuals and groups" represents the essence of my model of planning (p. 97, see also Sorensen and Day, 1981, p. 397).

But Low puts some emphases differently. First, he agrees the input of planning to be information obtained by means of surveys, but "the independent stirring of an angry citizens' action group is just as much real information for the relevant agency as, say, 'scientific' investigation of road capacities and traffic flows" (p. 97). Second, he specifies how the "technology-image" determines what information is received:

Faludi describes the impact of the value system as that of a filter but a more active image might be more appropriate since . . . the positive attempt to constrain the information flow is a normal part of the agency's response to uncertainty (p. 98).

Third, planning indeed involves interaction between an investigative body (the planners) and a selector (the decision-takers). But it

is important to note that the form of interaction need not be a linear one proceeding from general goals to particular programmes. On the contrary, goals can only be specified and made real with reference to programmes; the process is as much one of learning about goals in terms of programmes as of devising programmes in terms of goals. The function of the "selector" is to choose, to narrow down, to converge upon a single course of action in contrast to the function of the "memory" ("technology-image" in Faludi's model) which is to open up options, to diverge (p. 99).

Lastly, Low comments that I give rather a small box to automatic programmes, whereas in planning the largest amount of time is spent on set routines. He feels also that the model of planning agencies places the environment in a subordinate position. But public participation "has the effect of returning the community to the dominant position of 'selector' " (p. 105):

Urban managers have to deal with a complex of community learning processes in which the community appears as both "environment" and "selector". Policy essentially arises from interaction between the community and its specialist advisers, usually but not necessarily through the mediation of the community's representatives. The speciality of the urban manager lies in understanding this interaction (ibid.).

Low (1982) criticises general systems theory, on which *Planning Theory* draws, starting with process linearity. Mine is an "input-transformation-output" model. But when the cycles get shorter, "the concepts portrayed in sequence are actually held simultaneously" (p. 224), as when tennis players enter into each other's planning. Low claims that this invalidates my model. However, when considering the self-image-see Section 4.1-I come to similar formulation.

As regards conflict, Low does not go into any detail over and above claiming that general systems theory cannot cope with it. He says also that I treat inter-organisational conflict by resorting to hierarchies in multi-planning agencies:

It is obviously wise not to abandon the idea of hierarchy altogether but it is necessary to supplement it with an understanding of what happens in negotiation, compromise and collaboration, and with an appreciation of the significance of these concepts in policy making and implementation. The realm of conflict requires appropriate strategies as much as the realm of consensus (p. 225).

Concerning boundaries-a key-concept in systems theory-the criticism is that social-as against biological-systems do not have clearly defined boundaries:

Organisations ... are composed of ... "individual-systems" who belong to many groups and take on many roles most of which fall into the "environment" of the organisation in question. Planners are also voters, consumers, members of political parties and of community lobby groups (p. 226).

Planning Theory says much the same (see p. 119). Low goes on to argue that the problem is to relate the goals of planners to each other, something which general systems theory cannot grasp:

If "negative co-ordination" in Faludi's terms means that planning agencies come to appreciate that they are in one another's environment ... positive co-ordination means that they interpenetrate one another through the interactions of their members.

In inter-corporate planning individuals are not only in one another's environment but in one another's "system". What we are looking at can perhaps better be described as a scheme of linkages among individuals, a network. What were formerly seen as discrete systems can also be seen as clusters of relationships and knots of interactions among individual-systems (p. 226).

Low concludes that "Faludi's theory contains a fundamental contradiction between his repeated emphasis on the human mind and his use of general systems theory" (*ibid.*). Such criticisms provide a stepping stone for introducing "personal construct theory". He describes it as being based on the fact that we "live not so much in the world, as in a model of the world made of words and word-like things". The role of the planner should be that of helping people to make sense out of this world by providing interpretative schemes.

The idea needs to be applauded. I would like to think that it is already implied in *Planning Theory*. Centring on goals, the technology-image is a subjective construct. This is also true of the outcome of "strategic choice" to be discussed in Chapter 6, the definition of the decision situation. Chapter 8 shows that this concept takes the place of the technology-image in my current decision-centred view of planning. Meanwhile, personal construct theory has been put to practical uses by Eden *et al.* (1983), just as Low demanded. It is encouraging to note that the outcomes are similar to the approaches in this book.

A new positivist dispute?

In his retrospective assessment Hooper (1982) points out that most critics of *Planning Theory* seize upon the distinction between procedural and substantive theory. He relays the frequent comment that this reifies an analytic distinction,

condemning planning theorists either to reflect endlessly upon procedural practices of planning, or to advocate some unattainable but ethically-desirable ideal of rational planning. ... The qualified relationship ... to rational-comprehensive planning ... has usually been neglected with the startling consequence that attempts to identify rational-comprehensive planning with a particular philosophy of scientific method-logical positivism (p. 224).

Hooper might have quoted Gillingwater (1975) and Camhis (1979). Against this he points out my opposition to positivism. Some of the blame for the confusion must be laid at my doorstep though, for my research strategy is ambiguous. It (a) implies a fixed path for the development of scientific disciplines; (b) starting with "raw data", as I suggest, indicates "an empiricist, not to say inductivist, stance" (p. 245); and (c) the identification of laws with hypotheses which have passed experimental tests is a tenet of logical positivism. But my use of a pattern, alongside with a deductive, model of explanation is at variance with this. Hooper associates it with a "reflexive critical stance in relation to the values embodied in theory construction (and apparently defined-out in the context of 'deductive models')." He sees this as betraying "dissatisfaction with the artificial constraints of logical positivism as a basis for the development of a science concerned with human action and practice" (p. 245), and claims that this led me to "critical rationalism as a potential resolution of the self-imposed dualism in the 'scientific method' characteristic of *Planning Theory*. But the absence of critical rationalism in that text provided the occasion for ... some theoretical confusion" (*ibid.*), especially where normative theory is concerned. Hooper complains about the "fundamentally non-sociological, cybernetic treatment (of human growth), its evolutionary perspective and teleological ethic of progress" (*ibid.*). He is amongst those who object to the homology between the human mind and planning, and joins Reade and Taylor in saying that the normative theory is based on a poorly articulated mix of values and empirical observations. In particular I conflate two uses of normative theory: as a basis for formulating hypotheses and as an ethically based theory of planning-which is true, although Hooper does not show that the two are necessarily different.

Furthermore, to him, my attitude towards scientific method signifies methodological monism: "the idea of the unity of scientific method amidst the-diversity of subject matter of scientific investigation" (p. 245; quoting Frisby, 1976). What characterises my work is the tension, therefore, between science as "nothing other than methodology, namely a procedure" (Frisby, 1976) and a meta-methodological concern with the relevance of planning theory to practice which Hooper translates, again in terms drawn from Frisby's introduction to the English translation of *The Positivist Dispute in German Sociology* into "the problem whether reason is practical, whether norms can be grounded in reason" (*ibid.*).

He sees a further complication in relation to the planning subject. He starts by pointing out my concern (see Section 4.1) to link the procedural and substantive realms of planning.

This is attempted less at the levels of epistemology or ontology, but rather through a theory of action involving a planning "subject". The limitations on rationality which Faludi explores in terms of information, resources, organization and politics are among the more neglected aspects of Planning Theory, and this neglect accounts for the perpetuation of the myth of "rational comprehensiveness" mistakenly associated with his procedural theory (pp. 246-7).

This is gratifying to hear, but for Hooper it is the starting point for exposing an alleged methodological individualism which he thinks becomes evident in my work on critical rationalism (quoting Faludi, 1983). He detects a shift. In *Planning Theory*, the limitations on rational-comprehensive planning are introduced "externally", through the medium of the planning environment. In 1983 they are said to be approached "internally" by invoking Simon's administrative man (see Section 3.4.). Following Lukes (1977, p. 183), Hooper argues that it is one of the tenets of methodological individualism that "the relevant features of the social context are, so to speak, built into the individual". An important question then is the extent to which the rationality principle "embodies rationality rules deriving from, and constrained by, the structure of a capitalist social formation" (p. 247 quoting Godelier, 1972, p. 46). Without elaborating, Hooper claims that the implications for the rationality of any planning theory are profound.

He is right: I internalise external constraints. That is particularly so in my notion of the definition of the decision situation (see Chapter 8) which reflects the power structure, amongst other things. Whether this amounts to "methodological individualism" I am not sure. The "Epilogue" in *Planning Theory* professes to a "qualified holistic" view of society, and this still makes sense to me. Anyway, as we have seen, other critics are more inclined to attack my "consensus view". In debates with Needham (see Faludi, 1971; Needham and Faludi, 1973) and my analysis of Popper (see Faludi, 1986, pp. 30-1), I criticise rather than endorse methodological individualism, pointing out that it is an ethical stance rather than a methodological precept. Perhaps Hooper wrongly identifies decision situations with individual choices. Institutions face choices also. They define their decision situations from their points of view (taking account of such constraints as there are). So, "subjective" is not the same as "individual".

Hooper appreciates the methodological issues in *Planning Theory*. Whether "methodological monism" is acceptable or not is a matter of legitimate debate. My current understanding is that the "unity of science" idea holds. It need not conflict with "personal construct theory" advocated by Low, nor with the concerns of critical theory, on which Hooper obviously draws.

Conclusions

Positive theory of planning-"sociology of planning" in the terms of Taylor (1980)-gets less of my attention now. Paradoxically, this is the result of involvement in empirical research. Like Meyerson and Banfield (see Section 2.3) and Friend and Jessop (see Chapter 6), that research has proved more fruitful for the occasions which it provided for reflecting on planning than for formulating a positive theory. My parallel work (Faludi, 1986, p. 6) describes the process by which it is formulated as "methodological reflection" (see also Faludi and Mastop, 1982).

Friedmann (1974, p. 311) is the only critic who has drawn attention to my treatment of implementation. Having just completed his *Retracking America* (Friedmann, 1973, see Section 7.2) where he takes the radical position of fusing plan-making with implementation into one overall notion of societal action (see also Friedmann, 1969), he feels that a mere chapter at the end on implementation was not enough. Now, whilst one whole chapter on this subject is more than books on planning theory used to devote to it, I quite agree that my thinking at the time focused on plan-making. It did not yet surpass Davidoff and Reiner, nor indeed Meyerson and Banfield, where they argue the case for taking good account of constraints on implementation early on during plan-making. Before discussing the further development of planning theory-a development which concerns this very issue, amongst others-a major controversy surrounding it needs to be discussed.

References

Alexander, E. R. (1984) "After rationality, what?: a review of responses to paradigm breakdown", *Journal of the American Planning Association*, **50**, 62-9.

Argyle, M. (1967) *The Psychology of Interpersonal Behaviour*, Penguin, Harmondsworth.

Banfield, E. C. (1959) "Ends and means in planning", *International Social Science Journal*, **11**, 361-8; see also A. Faludi (ed.) (1973) *A Reader in Planning Theory*, Pergamon Press, Oxford, pp. 139-49.

*Beckman, N. (1964) "The planner as a bureaucrat", *Journal of the American Institute of Planners*, **30**, 325-7.

Bolan, R. S. (1967) "Emerging views of planning", *Journal of the American Institute of Planners*, **33**, 233-45.

Bolan, R. S. (1969) "Community decision behavior: the culture of planning", *Journal of the American Institute of Planners*, **35**, 310-10; see also A. Faludi (ed.) (1973) *A Reader in Planning Theory*, Pergamon Press, Oxford, pp. 371-94.

Braybrooke, D. and Lindblom, C. E. (1963) *A Strategy for Decisions*, Free Press, New York.

Breheny, M. J. and Hooper, A. (eds) (1985) *Rationality in Planning: Critical Essays on the Role of Rationality in Urban & Regional Planning*, Pion Press, London.

Bryson, J. M. and Delbercq, A. L. (1979) "A contingent approach to strategy and tactics in project planning", *Journal of the American Planning Association*, **45**, 167-79.

Camhis, M. (1979) *Planning Theory and Philosophy*, Tavistock, London.

Cartwright, T. J. (1973) "Problems, solutions, and strategies: a contribution to the theory and practice of planning", *Journal of the American Institute of Planners*, **39**, 179-87.

Christensen, K. S. (1985) "Coping with uncertainty in planning", *Journal of the American Planning Association*, **51**, 63-73.

Clavel, P. (1979) "Review of Essays in Planning Theory and Education, by: A. Faludi", *Journal of the American Planning Association*, **54**, 364-5.

Clavel, P., Forester, J. and Goldsmith, J. (eds) (1980) *Urban and Regional Planning in an Age of Austerity*, Pergamon Press, New York.

Cooke, P. N. (1983) *Theories of Planning and Spatial Development*, Hutchinson, London.

*Davidoff, P. (1965) "Advocacy and pluralism in planning", *Journal of the American Institute of Planners*, **31**, 331-8.

*Dror, Y. (1963) "The planning process: a facet design", *International Review of Administrative Sciences*, **29**, 93-116.

*Dyckman, J. W. (1961) "What makes planners plan?", *Journal of the American Institute of Planners*, **27**, 164-7.

Dyckman, J. W. (1962) "New ideas in planning", *Journal of the American Institute of Planners*, **28**, 63-5.

Dyckman, J. W. (1966) "Social planning, social planners, and planned society", *Journal of the American Institute of Planners*, **32**, 66-76.

Eden, C., Jones, H. and Sims, D. (1983) *Messing About in Problems*, Pergamon Press, Oxford.

Etzioni, A. (1968) *The Active Society*, Collier-Macmillan, London.

Faludi, A. (1971) "Problems with problem-solving", *Journal of the Royal Town Planning Institute*, **57**, 415.

Faludi, A. (1973) *A Reader in Planning Theory*, Pergamon Press, Oxford.

Faludi, A. (1983) "Critical rationalism and planning methodology", *Urban Studies*, **20**, 265-78.

Faludi, A. (1984; 1st published 1973) *Planning Theory*, Pergamon Press, Oxford.

Faludi, A. (1985) "The return of rationality", in: *Rationality in Planning: Critical Essays on the Role of Rationality in Urban and Regional Planning*, eds M. J. Breheny and A. J. Hooper, Pion Press, London, pp. 27-47.

Faludi, A. (1986) *Critical Rationalism and Planning Methodology*, Pion Press, London.

Faludi, A. and Mastop, J. M. (1982) "The I. O. R. School: the development of a planning methodology", *Environment and Planning B*, **9**, 241-56.

Fay, B. (1975) *Social Theory and Political Practice*, Allen & Unwin, London.

Friedmann, J. (1959) "The study and practice of planning: Introduction", *International Social Science Journal*, **11**, 327-39.

Forester, J. (1984) "Lest planning be seen as a tool ...", *Built Environment*, **10**, 124-31.

*Friedmann, J. (1965) "A response to Altshuler: comprehensive planning as a process", *Journal of the American Institute of Planners*, **31**, 195-7.

Friedmann, J. (1966a) "The institutional context", in: *Action under Planning*, ed. B. Gross, McGraw-Hill, New York, pp. 31-67.

Friedmann, J. (1966b) "Planning as a vocation (1)", *Plan Canada*, **6**, 99-124.

Friedmann, J. (1967a) "Planning as a vocation (2)", *Plan Canada*, **7**, 8-25.

*Friedmann, J. (1967b) "A conceptual model for the analysis of planning behavior", *Administrative Science Quarterly*, **12**, 225-52; see also A. Faludi (ed.) (1973) *A Reader in Planning Theory*, Pergamon Press, Oxford, pp. 345-69.

Friedmann, J. (1969) "Planning and societal action", *Journal of the American Institute of Planners*, **35**, 311-18.

Friedmann, J. (1973) *Retracking America: a Theory of Transactive Planning*, Doubleday Anchor, Garden City, New York.

Friedmann, J. (1974) "Review of A. Faludi, 'Planning Theory' ", *Regional Studies*, **8**, 311.

Friend, J. K. and Jessop, W. N. (1977; 1st edition 1969) *Local Government and Strategic Choice*, Pergamon Press, Oxford.

Frisby, D. (1976) "Introduction to the English translation", in: *The Positivist Dispute in German Sociology*, T. W. Adorno, H. Albert, A. Dahrendorf, J. Habermas, H. Pilot and K. R. Popper, Heinemann Educational Books, London, pp. ix-xliv.

Gillingwater, D. (1975) *Regional Planning and Social Change*, Saxon House, Westmead, Farnborough, Hants.

Godlier, M. (1972) *Rationality and Irrationality in Economics*, New Left Books, London.

Grauhan, R. R. (1969) "Zur Struktur der planenden Verwaltung", *Stadtbauwelt*, **60**, 132-7; see also "Notes on the structure of planning administration", in A. Faludi (ed.) (1973) *A Reader in Planning Theory*, Pergamon Press, Oxford, pp. 297-316.

Grauhan, R. R. and Strudelt, W. (1971) "Political rationality reconsidered", *Policy Sciences*, **2**, 249-70.

Harris, B. (1978a) "A note on planning theory", *Environment and Planning A*, **10**, 221-4.

Harris, B. (1978b) "Planning theory: a reponse to Scott and Roweis", *Environment and Planning A*, **10**, 349-50.

Healey, P. (1983) "Rational method as a mode of policy formation and implementation in land-use policy", *Environment and Planning B*, **10**, 19-39.

Healey, P., McDougall, G., and Thomas, M. J. (1982) "Introduction", in: *Planning Theory: Prospects for the 1980s*, eds P. Healey, G. McDougall and M. J. Thomas, Pergamon Press, Oxford, pp. 1-22.

Hebbert, M. (1974) "Review of A. Faludi, 'Planning Theory' ", *Planning Outlook*, **14**, 43-7.

Hill, M. (1981) "The policy-implementation distinction: a quest for rational control?", in: *Policy and Action: Essays on the Implementation of Public Policy*, eds S. Barrett and C. Fudge, Methuen, London and New York, pp. 207-23.

Hooper, A. (1982) "Methodological monism or critical dualism? Reflections on Andreas Faludi's Planning Theory", *Built Environment*, **8**, 247-8.

Hudson, B. M. (1979) "Comparison of current planning theories: Counterparts and contradictions", *Journal of the American Planning Association*, **45**, 387-98.

Kaplan, A. (1964) *The Conduct of Inquiry: Methodology for Behavioral Science*, Harper & Row, New York, Hagerstown, Philadelphia, San Francisco and London.

Lichfield, N., Kettle, P. and Whitbread, M. (1975) *Evaluation in the Planning Process*, Pergamon Press, Oxford.

Lindblom, C. E. (1959) "The science of muddling through", *Public Administration Review*, **19**, 79-88; see also A. Faludi (ed.) (1973) *A Reader in Planning Theory*, Pergamon Press, Oxford, pp. 151-69.

Low, N. (1979) "Urban management: some models for policy making", *Long Range Planning*, **12**, 91-109.

Low, N. (1982) "Beyond general systems theory: a constructivist perspective", *Urban Studies*, **19**, 221-33.

Lukes, S. (1977) *Essays in Social Theory*, Macmillan, London.

Mann, L. D. (1964) "Studies in community decision-making", *Journal of the American Institute of Planners*, **30**, 58-65.

Mannheim, K. (1940) *Man and Society in an Age of Reconstruction*, Kegan Paul, London.

Masser, I. (1983) "The representation of urban planning processes: an exploratory review", *Environment and Planning B: Planning and Design*, **10**, 47-62.

*Meyerson, M. M. (1956) "Building the middle-range bridge for comprehensive planning", *Journal of the American Institute of Planners*, **22**, 58-64.

Meyerson, M. M. and Banfield, E. C. (1955) *Politics, Planning and the Public Interest: The Case of Public Housing at Chicago*, Free Press, New York.

Miller, G. A., Galanter, E. and Pribhan, K. H. (1960) *Plans and the Structure of Behavior*, Holt, Rinehart & Winston, New York.

Needham, B. and Faludi, A. (1973) "Planning and the public interest", *Journal of the Royal Town Planning Institute*, **59**, 164-6.

Paris, C. (1982) "Introduction by the editor, Part One: a Critique of Pure Planning", in: *Critical Readings in Planning Theory*, ed. C. Paris, Pergamon Press, Oxford, pp. 3-11.

Popper, F. J. (1981) *The Politics of Land-Use Reform*, University of Wisconsin Press, Madison, Wisc. and London.

Popper, K. R. (1961; first published 1944/45) *The Poverty of Historicism*, Routledge & Kegan Paul, London.

Rabinovitz, F. F. (1969) *City Politics and Planning*, Atherton Press, New York.

Reade, E. J. (1973) "Review of A. Faludi, 'A Reader in Planning Theory' ", *Town Planning Review*, **44**, 407-9.

Reade, E. J. (1974) "Review of A. Faludi, 'Planning Theory' ", *Town Planning Review*, **45**, 444-6.

Reade, E. J. (1976) "The context of theory courses in town planning education", Working Paper, No. 25, Department of Town Planning, Oxford Polytechnic, Oxford, pp. 94-136.

Reade, E. J. (1982) "The theory of town and country planning", in: *Planning Theory: Prospects for the 1980s*, eds P. Healey, G. McDougall and M. J. Thomas, Pergamon Press, Oxford, pp. 43-58.

Reade, E. J. (1985) "An analysis of the use of the concept of rationality in the literature of planning", in: *Rationality in Planning: Critical Essays on the Role of Rationality in Urban and Regional Planning*, eds M. J. Breheny and A. J. Hooper, Pion Press, London.

Scott, A. J. and Roweis, S. T. (1977) "Urban planning theory and practice: a reappraisal", *Environment and Planning A*, **9**, 1097-19.

Scott, A. J. and Roweis, S. T. (1978) "A note on planning theory: a response to Britton Harris", *Environment and Planning A*, **10**, 229-31.

Sorensen, A. D. and Day, R. A. (1981) "Libertarian planning", *Town Planning Review*, **52**, 390-402.

Taylor, N. (1980) "Planning theory and the philosophy of planning", *Urban Studies*, **17**, 159-72.

Thomas, M. J. (1979) "The procedural planning theory of A. Faludi", *Planning Outlook*, **22**, 72-6; see also C. Paris (ed.) (1982) *Critical Readings in Planning Theory*, Pergamon Press, Oxford, pp. 13-25.

*Webber, M. M. (1963) "Comprehensive planning and social responsibility: towards an AIP consensus on the profession's role and purpose", *Journal of the American Institute of Planners*, **29**, 232-41.

Webber, M. M. (1983) "The myth of rationality: development planning reconsidered", *Environment and Planning B: Planning and Design*, **10**, 89-99.

* Included in Faludi, A. (ed.) (1973) *A Reader in Planning Theory*, Pergamon Press, Oxford.

CHAPTER 5

The "Proceduralist" versus "Substantivist" Controversy

WRITING about Britain, Breheny (1983, p. 110), finds that "there is virtually no work on planning theory in the last decade that does not begin with a swingeing critique of procedural planning theory". Hague (1986), who dismisses it on the first page as "repressive and partial", is a case in point. This chapter deals with this debate.

Where reference is made to a *proceduralist* position, it should be clear from Chapter 4 that this entails the following: (a) organisations and procedures are worthy of separate attention; (b) they are within limits similar, whatever is being planned; (c) planning theory and education should give prominence to generic theory and skills. The *substantivist* position will be shown to comprise two camps, united only in their critique of procedural theory for its alleged neglect of the substance of planning. Under *The context of the debate* we learn that this critique reflected, amongst others, misgivings in the seventies about planning and the planning profession. The following sections review the two substantivist schools under *The conventional substantivist position* and *The new substantivist challenge*. Under *An abstract theory*, it is affirmed that, as some critics claim, planning theory is abstract, or formal.

5.1 The context of the debate

The seventies were suspicious of everything "scientific". By espousing rational decision-making, planning theory was found guilty by association.

Of course, this was a reaction to what had gone before, when planning had been seen neither as the object of conflict, nor as a matter for designers any more, but as applied social science and essentially a "problem of procedure and method" (Friedmann, 1959, p. 328; see also Section 3.1 for Davidoff and Reiner's saying that planning is a "set of procedures"). Influenced as it was by operational research and systems analysis (see Section 3.3), the planning method was thought to be "largely independent of the planned" (Webber, 1963, p. 320). So planning theory was regarded as "generic".

Reaction is threefold: against the rational planning model; against the alleged support by planning theory of professionalism; and one view claiming that it is counter-revolutionary. There is another, more diffuse, criticism that a procedural planning theory neglects substantive knowledge. The main motive seems a defence against claims by proceduralists for a pre-eminent role in planning theory and education.

The first reaction is evident in the review of planning theory by Healey *et al.* (1982) claiming that disjointed incrementalism and advocacy planning (see Chapter 3), as well as the "IOR School" (to be discussed in Chapter 6) are opposed to procedural planning theory. It seems to have escaped these authors that, as Galloway and Mahayni (1977, p. 67) put it so well, these approaches are chained to the rational planning model in that "deficiencies of the precursor generate further conceptualizations which shape the new model". Healey *et al.* signal the demise of procedural planning theory, nevertheless, claiming that its "ambitions were stalled in the mid-seventies by the academic criticism of the concept of synoptic co-ordinated planning (particularly the incrementalists' attack) and the practical problems of operationalizing the approach" (p. 13). But procedural planning theory advances a form of planning that takes account of limitations of the human mind. Hooper (1982) has been shown to understand this well. Also, recognising its practical problems of planning rationally is not an achievement that academic critics of the mid-seventies should take credit for. We have seen that they formed the object of planning-theoretical discourse from the start.

Concerning alleged support for professionalism, in Britain this amounts to the charge of assisting The Royal Town Planning Institute to retain its hold on planning practice and education. More generally, it is tantamount to advocating "technocracy", or a strong role for experts in planning. In this vein, Healey *et al.* (1982) give an account of procedural planning theory as the view gaining acceptance by the profession in the early seventies. Apparently, it "offered both a new position to replace the naïve deterministic assumptions of the design tradition and a basis of enlarging professional status" (p. 13). As evidence they refer to the discussion document by the Royal Town Planning Institute, *Planning and the Future* (1976). They do not elaborate on what they have in mind. McLoughlin (1983, p. 18) similarly relates the acceptance of procedural planning theory to the "territoriality of planners and their desperate need to solve a chronic identity crisis". Reade (1982) perpetuates the charge of support for professionalism:

Town and country planning is a profession in which pretentious verbal obscurity is cultivated: ... Such an occupational group ... was a sitting duck ... for the blandishments of the peddlers of procedural theory. The latter, by showing that the whole world could be reduced to a series of boxes, with purposeful arrows pointing from one to the next, restored to planners their sense both of omniscience and of omnipotence (pp. 49-50).

Reade resents the invocation of principles of "good planning" in justifying their proposals. But Breheny (1983, p. 110) counters that he fails to demonstrate that the profession has ever adopted the procedural position, and this criticism also applies to other authors. By making planners give reasons for either rejecting or recommending alternatives, the rational planning model

counteracts professional wisdom being substituted for analysis. Sorensen and
Day (1981, p. 397) describe the advocacy of this model even as "antithetical
to the notion of professional planning judgement as it is generally understood".
Also, I, for one, am known to resent the Royal Town Planning Institute's hold
on planning education to the point where Cockburn (1970, p. 105) describes
me as "inimical" to the profession. So what is the substance of the charge of
supporting professionalism? Also, it is not clear why substantive theory of
planning-whatever that may be-should not be similarly charged.

The alleged counter-revolutionary character of procedural planning theory
requires more elaborate discussion. Publication of *A Reader in Planning
Theory* and *Planning Theory* coincided with that of *Social Justice and the City*
(Harvey, 1973) which gave a Marxist analysis of urban inequality. The
distinction in it between revolutionary and counter-revolutionary science was
invoked by Thornley (1974) in her review of *A Reader in Planning Theory*.
To her, without question, that book represented counter-revolutionary science.
Cooke and Rees (1977), Frost (1977), Thomas (1979), Scott and Roweis (1977)
in their critique of "mainstream planning theory", and Healey *et al.* (1982),
quoted above, echo the same theme. There is a presupposition that underlies
it, present also in a review by Friedmann (1974), pointing out the degree to
which economic power is concentrated. It is that the only credible position is
to address issues such as, in Frost's words, "features of the historical
development of mankind as the uneven pattern of economic growth, and the
underdevelopment of vast areas of the world; persistent poverty and
homelessness in metropolitan countries; unemployment; racism, etc." (Frost
1977, p. 221). Argyris (1982) has been challenged on a similar point by Baum
(1983, p. 239). Discussing the pragmatist roots of American planning theory,
Hoch (1984) claims that its founder, the philosopher John Dewey, is
responsible for the absence in planning theory of the issue of power.

Planning is not alone in being plagued by such disputes. In my parallel work
on Popper (Faludi, 1986, pp. 23-5) I refer to a discussion in operational
research and systems analysis. As it does there, it transpires that the
"proceduralist" versus "substantivist" controversy comprises two debates, and
the "substantivists" two camps. "Conventional" substantivists stress the role
of substantive knowledge as a guide to action. "New substantivists" regard
planning as the object of social-science research aiming to explain its
functioning-or rather malfunctioning-under present, capitalist, conditions. It
is not surprising, then, that they find that "mainstream (procedural) planning
theory, as a set of analytical propositions about the domain of planning, seems
to be remarkably uninteresting from a scientific point of view" (Scott and
Roweis, 1977, p. 1114; for their failure even to perceive such "analytical
propositions about the domain of planning" as are contained in *Planning
Theory* see below). In view of the vast differences between them, how
conventional and new substantivists could be united in their critique of
procedural planning theory remains a source of wonder. Many of their points

apply to the other substantivist position with equal or greater force. At the same time, both have something in common with proceduralists: the conventional substantivists their willingness to consider planning a worthwhile task here and now; the new substantivists their rejection of the crude positivism which is implied in the position taken by most conventional substantivist. Be this as it may, both positions are discussed in turn.

5.2   The conventional substantivist position

Conventional substantivists take three stances. One wrongly assumes that knowledge of its object is a sufficient basis for planning-the "object-centred view of planning". The second rightly insists that causal knowledge provides technologies for intervention, but fails to acknowledge the methodological and organisational problems of applying such knowledge as an area worthy of separate attention. The third rejects that procedures are generic and argues for theories specifically of environmental planning.

The object-centred view of planning

Describing the first substantivist position as "object-centred" (see Faludi, 1982) emphasises what I am against: not the use of substantive knowledge-which would be ridiculous-but the idea that planning is *nothing but* the assembly of such knowledge until the right course of action "emerges".

Geddes's "survey before plan", supplemented, as it was, by the ideology of the creative leap (see Chapter 1), typifies this view. But Harvey (1969) has shown already that there are assumptions involved even in deciding "what questions to assume away and what questions to investigate" (p. 482). With respect to the study of unique situations (as is invariably the case in planning; see de Neufville, 1983; Rittel and Webber, 1973; Faludi, 1985), Popper says that we must make explicit the point of view from which we approach them. Talking about the systems approach, Chadwick (1978) argues that "like beauty, a system lies in the eye of the beholder, for we can define a system in an infinite number of ways in accordance with our interests and our purposes, for the world is composed of very many sets of relationships" (p. 42; for the opposite view that "systemness" must be proven see McDougall, 1973, 1983). The notion of a definition of the decision situation, to be presented in Chapter 8, expresses the same. Neglect of the all-pervasive element of choice, not only in planning, but *also* in research, is what makes the object-centred view untenable. Theoretical conclusions, let alone decisions, never flow from a look at the "facts". So planning requires something beyond research, and it is here that procedural planning theory comes into its own.

Of course, this does not mean that substantive theories do not come into play. Although, as Bristow and Cross (1983, p. 304), have found with respect to their study of British structure planning, "there is no sign ... of a substantive theory of urbanisation, or of environmental change, or location, being used as one of the main tools", such theories do enter on the level of what Friedmann and Weaver (1979, p. 2) call planning doctrine: definite concepts of development underlying planning practice which feed on substantive theories and on ideology. The point is that such doctrines cannot-indeed should not-provide the only intellectual backbone of planning as an activity.

Technologies for intervention

The second stance is not so much untenable as incomplete. Its proponents do not advocate surveys. But they still claim that planning theory should aim at substantive analysis. Their position is epitomised by a parable by Reade (1976) about two books by a certain Galufi found after the Great Obliteration in 1990: *Keeping Theory* and *A Reader in Keeping Theory*. Research by archaeologists had shown, so the tale goes, that these books had formed part of the drive to develop a theory of park-keeping in order to bolster the professional status of park-keepers (the charge of professionalism discussed in the previous section). Eventually, though, park-keepers had become weary of fruitless debates and turned their attention instead to the quality of grass seeds, so that their parks could withstand being trampled upon. Thus, to Reade "the theory of an activity is simply the causal knowledge to carry out that activity" (Reade, 1976, p. 112; see also his views about monitoring in Reade, 1983). Cooke (1983, p. 160) describes this more correctly as substantive theory. It "concerns the probable consequences of alternative spatial patterns and physical forms, and comes from such disciplines as urban and regional economics". This definition is unexceptional. The issue is whether the main object of planning theory and research should be this.

Reade's view that it should do so gets acclaim nowadays from Jacobs, who argues that generic skills are less likely to improve the poor public image of planners than research into substantive matters, for instance concerning "impacts of buildings upon sun and wind. ... That kind of planning is supported. Professional, substantive work, once known, once out there in the public domain is unavoidable" (Jacobs, 1983, p. 60). Now, substantive theory forms part of what *Planning Theory* calls the *technology-image* on which planning draws. We must have more of it in order to better be able to generate and evaluate alternatives. But it does not tell us what to do. Rather, it must be applied with some purpose in mind. This must be done in systematic fashion, stating assumptions, limitations, consequences, and so forth. In other words, some recognised procedure must be followed. All that procedural planning theory does is make this into its special area of concern.

Generic planning theory

The idea that planning theory is generic stems from institutionalist economics discussed in Section 2.1. It is clearly evident in Friedmann's writing. Also, as a matter of historical fact, planning theory does have its roots in the application of concepts and ideas evolving around the rational planning model which the Chicago School has culled from the social sciences-in particular economics and sociology. The subsequent influence of the systems approach, cybernetics and operational research is proof also of its origin and application being broader than just environmental, or land use planning. So there are many others claiming that procedural planning theory is generic (see for instance Webber, 1963b, p. 320; McLoughlin, 1973, p. 111; Hall, 1974, pp. 1-2).

Healey (1982), Reade (1982, 1983), Cooke (1983) and Roweis (1983) are amongst those dissenting. They argue for a theory specifically of environmental planning. I would welcome such a theory, so much so that Part Two of this book is devoted to it. Hopefully, that Part surpasses the controversy described here. At the same time it shows that such a theory is what proceduralists claim it to be: an application of generic planning theory.

Why, then, does the debate persist? The reason lies in its import for the struggle for the centre stage in planning education. Davidoff and Reiner (1962) claimed already that planning education "has been excessively directed to substantive areas and has failed to focus on any unique skills and responsibilities of the planner" (in Faludi, 1973, p. 36). Likewise, Robinson (1972) pointed out that

if planners are to claim a special capability for planning a city's future, then this claim is justified, not because they are experts on the city, but because they are experts on determining what is the most desirable and feasible future to seek and what needs to be done to achieve it. The planner should be an expert on the methodology by which planning is done (p. 27).

The view-already present in the "Chicago School"-of the planner as a "generalist-with-a-speciality" supports this argument. Of course, substantive knowledge is also important, and Davidoff and Reiner, for instance, "do not suggest ... that a planning education should ignore study in subject areas. Rather ... such areas become the testing ground for the application of planning" (in Faludi, 1973, p. 37). But those teaching procedural skills lay claim to the core curriculum, with the prestige that goes with this position, and so those teaching substantive knowledge might find themselves on the periphery. This threat must have contributed in no small way to the lack of consensus concerning planning theory (Hightower, 1970), even before the new substantivist challenge reared its head.

Radical theorists reject generic theory for more respectable reasons. It is said to be a-historic, "an idealized and rationalistic conceptual logic being elaborated whereby, irrespective of location, time or organizational context, only limited variants on a basically rationalistic model of decision-making are derived" (Cooke, 1983, p. 261). Below I argue that procedural planning theory is indeed a conceptual theory at heart. At the same time, as we have seen, *Planning Theory* discussed variations as to the way in which the rational planning model is applied. Cooke recognises this, but finds the variants limited.

Still, in terms of his own analysis this means that the logic does *not* apply irrespective of time, location, and so forth. His statement is contradictory, therefore. Of course, if Cooke's claim is merely that there is insufficient variance, then it is incumbent upon him to be more specific as to what an acceptable degree of variability would be.

5.3   The new substantivist challenge

What is this challenge? What weight does it carry? Answering these questions, this section forms the counterpart to the previous one on the "conventional" substantivist position.

The radical theorists concerned argue that planning theory should deal with the function of planning under capitalism where "the means for dealing with environmental problems are influenced by the ruling class" (Sandbach, 1980, p. 34). Some think "the best the planning system can expect to do is function according to capital's need and help to hold the system together for a while longer" (Cooke, 1983, p. 10; for Cooke's own more subtle position see further below). Clearly, these critics see the central issue as: How does the power-structure explain planning as we experience it? The reasons for poor performance in planning are said to lie "not in the inherent intellectual limitations of the idea of planning, but in the structure of the society in which planning is asked to operate" (Dyckman, 1983, p. 6). Therefore, in the words of Scott and Roweis (1977), "a viable theory of urban planning must be based upon conceptual foundations that permit an analytical derivation of the nature, content and trajectory of urban planning out of those relatively *durable* social phenomena in which urban planning is embedded" (p. 1100).

Thomas (1979) echoes their point when he criticises me for not starting from "the view that planning is a public activity carried out by the State, and, therefore, legitimated politically within a structural situation dominated by particular socio-economic formations to which planning responds" (in Paris, 1982, p. 15). But these authors are dealing with different problems than proceduralists do. Thus, my planning theory has what Frost (1977; see Section 5.1) calls "absences" simply because it is not concerned with the issues he raises. Procedural planning theory does not even pretend to provide a substantive basis for a critical position, as Thomas (*op cit.*, p. 22) says it should, nor are Scott and Roweis's "trajectories of urban development" its concern. It does not even share the more modest aim of Cooke (1983, p. 10), that is "to present a theoretical description of what the urban and regional planning system does for the spatial development process". Its object is-with excuses for the triviality of saying so-the procedure of planning, and its intention normative. "Theoretical description" of the planning system only comes in as a basis for prescription.

Of course it is possible to take exception to this by showing that organisations and procedures have no significance for the outcomes of planning. Indeed, as Hall (1983, p. 44) points out, "the implicit assumption of Marxist analysts ... is that the contradictions of the existing system will themselves produce change so that specific planning-actions are at best irrelevant and at worse pernicious". (See also Hill, 1981, pp. 215-16.)

Now, surely, "the physical planning system itself can clearly not be the main determinant of the pattern of post-war urban development" (Pickvance, 1982, p. 72), but market forces are. At the same time, the importance of organisations and procedures is also evident. In a rare effort to measure the impact of environmental conditions, departmental organisation and individuals on innovation in local planning authorities in England and Wales, Jefferson (1973, p. 294) found that "approximately half of the variance is to be left to be explained with reference to the internal structural features of the planning organisation, to the personalities of the individual planners, or to error of measurement". Pickvance (1976) concedes also that design issues, in particular, are not quite as "structurally determined" as others, and that "there is no reason why analyses of institutions ... should not focus on organizational structure as a feature having distinctive effects irrespective of the functions of the institution concerned" (p. 32). Likewise, Cooke (1983, p. 10) is trying to overcome the "debilitating reductionism" of a position claiming to explain every outcome of planning as but a reflection of forces of production. He conceives of both planning and spatial development as "objects of struggle, the outcomes of which are partly indeterminate" (p. 11). This leaves room for intervention and restores planning action as an area worthy of our attention, even from the materialist position which Pickvance and Cooke represent.

Of course it is arguable that contextual variables in general, and the prevailing power structure in particular, have more influence than procedural and organisational ones. Would that mean that procedural planning theory was irrelevant and "materialist analysis" the only viable alternative, as Scott and Roweis (1977) and Paris (1982) claim? No, because, its explanatory power apart, the distribution of power also happens to be outside the planner's direct sphere of influence. Account should be taken of it, but awareness of the importance of power should not be allowed to stifle planners. As long as there are some prospects of improvements, they should simply try to do a good job *within* their areas of discretion. (Of course, when that prospect disappears, the ethical question arises of whether to quit. It is important for students that such issues should be discussed in planning education.)

In my reply to Thomas (Faludi, 1979), I couched this discussion in terms of two paradigms of planning theory. The concept culled from Kuhn (1962) will inspire me also to introduce the concept of "planning doctrine" in Chapter 8. It refers to an outlook on the world pre-structuring problems and solutions. It also connotes closedness to other schools of thought seeing things differently. But I argued that Thomas's approach and mine were complementary, that there are nets of various types catching fish of various sizes. Thomas and his like seem to aim for the big catches, i.e. the structural conditions in society which set the parameters of planning.

I am quite content with the small fry of decision-making theories, knowing that they will be of more immediate application to the practice of planning. But there seems little reason why we should not sit side by side (Faludi, 1979, in Paris, 1982, p. 38).

The irony of the imagery of fishing side by side, like Marx's worker of the future working in the morning and going fishing in the afternoon, has escaped the editor of the volume containing the exchange with Thomas. He complains:

To view planning theory as a separate, internally coherent set of procedural logics, operating in "given situations" is thus to ignore what is crucial for any real understanding of particular forms of planning, i.e. the inter-relationships over time between the *development* of such forms, the practice of "planning" as a job or profession, and the significance of those forms and practices within particular societies" (Paris, 1982, p. 7).

The problem of planning theory, again, is seen as that of *explaining* the existence, success and failure of planning. Such a position raises suspicion in the mind of Harris. Concerning Scott and Roweis' (1977) adoption of it, he complains that, in the hands of the inexperienced, their theory "provides an easy way out of the difficulties of learning, practicing and accommodating to planning" (Harris, 1978, p. 222; see also the next section). Healey *et al.* (1982, p. 6) confirm this suspicion, saying that they are "not interested in a discipline to which practitioners can relate". For the same reason Paris dismisses procedural planning theory as "a cookbook of instructions for doing planning-as-a-job but at worst it could be a deliberate attempt to focus on the uncontroversial and the mundane at the expense of a critical understanding of the nature and significance of specific institutional forms" (Paris, 1982, p. 7).

Procedural planning theory sets out to be instructive to planners-on-the-job, so this is hardly disturbing. Whether their job is mundane and uncontroversial I hesitate to say. I respect their problems and their struggles. Like Bolan (1981) I believe that planning theory must help planners to improve their performance. Rather than with such mundane things, new substantivists profess to be concerned "uniquely with what planning *is*" (Scott and Roweis, 1977, p. 1097). Interestingly, in searching for explanatory theories they are taking a Popperian stance as regards empirical, or positive, theory of planning, demanding that it should result in falsifiable propositions (see Scott and Roweis, 1977, p. 1113; Roweis, 1983, p. 147). Also, of course, they insist that substantive variables are necessary for explaining planning, because "positive procedural theory cannot make any meaningful statements about observed planning behavior without reference to the specific substantive claims embodied in the various generalizations planners use" (Roweis, 1983, p. 145; see also Cross and Bristow, 1983, p. 292).

But substantive variables do enter into various conceptual schemes of "proceduralists" as a matter of course under the "subject matter" and "general environment of planning" (Dror, 1963); the "decision environment" (Friedmann, 1966); the "decision field characteristics" and "issue attributes" (Bolan, 1969; Bolan and Nuttall, 1975). Rabinovitz (1969) matches effective styles of planning with various types of communities characterised by the prevailing pattern of influence. Howe and Kaufmann (1979), Vasu (1979),

Hudson (1979), Baum (1980a,b), Mayo (1982) and, in the British context, Healey (1983) equally deal with the relationship between planning styles and context, and point to frustrations caused by mismatch between the two. The three hypotheses in *Planning Theory* (see Chapter 4, where this "contingency approach" is also discussed) likewise relate the mode of planning to substantive variables. Most recently, Alexander (1984) has recommended this approach "as capable at once of reflecting the complexity of ... behavior and contexts, and of presenting prescriptive models that are abstract enough to generalize over a set of cases but concrete enough to offer useful guidance for action" (p. 67). Christensen (1985; see Section 7.1) similarly relates strategies to the nature of the problem faced in planning. So, Roweis has been pre-empted by many others, "proceduralists" amongst them.

There is recognition also amongst radical theorists that, "the planner is equipped with powers *vis-à-vis* the production, maintenance and management of the built environment which permit him to intervene" (Harvey, 1978, p. 9). Furthermore, Fainstein and Fainstein (1979) conclude that Marxism "cannot provide a completely satisfactory guide for what planners should do and still remain planners" (in Paris, 1982, p. 166). As an aside, a strategy debate has resulted which aims to identify ways of achieving progressive change. Assessments of alternatives and their evaluation in a way reminiscent of rational planning play their part. So, if even radical strategies can be planned, then, rather than always and necessarily being a tool in the hands of those in power (Grabow and Heskin, 1973; Beauregard, 1978), perhaps planning *is* the generic approach which many of these authors reject? Be this as it may, it is gratifying to read Fainstein and Fainstein defining urban planning theory "as comprising two analytically separable but mutually dependent parts: a theory of planning process or activity and a theory of urban structure and development" (in Paris, 1982, p. 147).

Other authors demand integration. McDougall is amongst those who readily acknowledge that "structuralism is ... a one-sided limited view of social life which overemphasises the de-personalised structure of institutions and practices and which de-historicises social life by analysing it in terms of fixed, universal categories" (1983, p. 50). Based on her critique of the "interactional approach to organisations and planning" represented by Argyris, Schön and Bolan (see Section 7.2) which she identifies as phenomenological, she adds:

If ... structuralism suffers from misplaced abstractness then phenomenology suffers from misplaced concreteness. I would argue that in planning theory and sociology we need social models that are less exclusive and less restrictive and which can combine objectified social structure with the actor's subjective structuring of social reality.

One of the problems with one-sided explanations of social life is that they unnecessarily restrict the possibility of social change. The structuralist explanation, seeing people as incidental to the grand play of social forces, severely restricts the practice alternatives of individuals. Individuals can attempt to widen the cracks in the system exposed by the contradictions and by great efforts of collective action marginally increase the speed at which capitalism meets its downfall (*ibid.*).

Likewise, Hoch (1984), analysing the origin of American planning theory in

Dewey's pragmatism (see Chapter 2), and challenging him for his instrumentalism, imagines

a reconstructed pragmatic theory of planning. ... Such a theory would not separate process from substance; it would focus instead on defining problems in relation to the particular histories and attachments of people in specific locales ... It would explore how uncertainties generated by the control of corporate and governmental bureaucracies became recognized as problems by people subjected to such insecurity, as well as how those people learn to collaborate in overcoming this uncertainty by drawing up a plan of action based on the strength of diverse emotional bonds, the security of common purpose, and the legitimacy of democratic participation (p. 343).

We can conclude that the issue of how "people learn to collaborate in overcoming uncertainty" is an area worthy of attention. Thanks to the "IOR School" (to be discussed in Chapter 6), the recognition of uncertainty, and of uncertainty management, are indeed now central issues in planning theory. The only bone of contention that remains is whether separate attention should be given to procedures. New substantivists aiming to understand society reject this. The trend is to view social structure and action as conditioning each other (see Giddens, 1984). But in planning we are justified in focusing on what can be done within such structural constraints as do exist.

McDougall would counter that widening the cracks in the system, rather than planning within it, is the main issue. But surely the subtle position which she and others take means that "structural constraints" are never precisely known in advance. Rather, they must be established from case to case. Constraints are that which, it turns out, one cannot influence.

Now, assessments of what can and cannot be done form part of the ordinary course of rational planning demanding that all effects of all alternatives be considered. So "structural change"-whatever that may mean-can and should be considered as a matter of course around concrete issues. So, to say that planners should aim for structural change is no more than an exhortation to them to do their job of rational planning well.

5.4   An abstract theory

Central to the position of Scott and Roweis (1977) is that procedural planning theory is abstract. Debates in the wake of their paper involve Harris and Taylor.

We have seen above that new substantivists aim to explain urban planning as a phenomenon. Scott and Roweis contrast this with the literature which treats it "as an *abstract analytical concept*" (p. 1098). What they mean is that "conventional planning theory tends to proceed by initially positing formal and linguistic definitions of planning that have a purely *a priori* or nominalistic character". Apparently forgetting that definitions are not subject to empirical testing anyway, they point out that "it is difficult to think of any empirical test that in principle might refute any of them" (*ibid.*). They put this down to "a definite viewpoint in the literature that suggests that planning theory is, by its nature, a *normative* theory. ... It abstracts away from real, historically determinate parameters of human activity, and gratuitously assumes the existence of transcendent operational norms" (p. 1099). They claim that the "attempt only raises the inevitable question: Under what specific social circumstances will any given imperative be relevant and applicable in practice? And again: What concrete circumstances *give rise* to this imperative rather than that imperative?" (*ibid.*). Theory answering to these criteria would not only tell them what planning is, but also what "progressive planners" can, and must, do.

The demand for a materialist analysis of urban planning as embedded in a particular mode of production makes clear why Scott and Roweis are angry with planning theorists. The charge is that of idealism. They claim that "it is not an independent and autonomous planning *theory* that produces the various facts of actual planning; it is rather the realities of contemporary urbanization" (p. 1101). Further down, they reiterate this point: "in contradistinction to the abstract-idealist formulations of current planning theory, urban planning is not 'invented' in a vacuum, but is structurally produced out of the basic contradiction between capitalist social and property relations (and their specifically urban manifestations) and the concomitant necessity for collective action" (p. 1105). So, mainstream theory seems singularly uninteresting, because it is "not so much ... incorrect as it is simply trivially true. For example, assertions that the planning process involves various forms of goal formulation, evaluation, implementation and control, learning, and all the rest, are no doubt true, but they are also plainly vacuous" (p. 1113). This theory cannot cope with the mismatch between what it says on the one hand and the real world of practical urban intervention on the other hand. So, instead of explaining reality, it sets out to be normative. Here comes a fuller exposition of the criticism of abstract, normative theory as reflecting idealism:

Planning theory then sets itself the task of rationalizing irrationalities, and seeks to materialize itself in social and historical reality (like Hegel's World Spirit) by bringing to bear upon the world a set of abstract, independent, and transcendent norms. Herein lie the idealist-utopian roots of contemporary planning theory. They are idealist in the specific sense that conventional theory takes consciousness (ideas, will, psychic states, etc) as the autonomous and unilateral determinants of social existence. They are utopian in the sense that conventional theory sees human society as being endlessly renegotiable by means of simple, if heroic, acts of will (p. 116).

The counterpart to mainstream theory is also explained more fully. First, Scott and Roweis agree that

the world as it is certainly presents innumerable *opportunities* for intentional collective action and choice. But these opportunities are objectively given; they are neither invented in the minds of planners nor created by astute theoretical analysis; *they may simply be revealed for what they are, or are not* (ibid.; note the difference as against McDougall's imagery above of exploiting the "cracks in the system").

Second, planning ideas are "born within and are reflections of a given historical situation" (*ibid.*). Thus urban transport planning appears subsequent to the emergence of circulation problems in large cities; hence its "essentially materialist origin". Scott and Roweis conclude that the imperatives of urban planning are intertwined with the central conflict in capitalist society over income distribution.

Harris (1978a) begins his comments by distinguishing between social and planning theory, and normative and positive theory. Scott and Roweis provide examples of positive social theory of large-scale urban phenomena. Besides, "a great deal of disaggregated positive social theory is necessary ..., and at this level political conditions play an auxiliary but not a dominant role" (p. 221).

Normative social theory is political in nature. Harris is surprised that Scott and Roweis turn away from it. He states that there is " a need for utopian planning, but it is hardly the role of the planners themselves and not one to which questions of planning theory can be directed. Constructing the future society is a major political and social task which far transcends planning, but which would draw upon the essence of normative social theory" (p. 222). Positive theory of planning, on the other hand

cannot avoid talking about what planners do. If the article of Scott and Roweis is examined in detail, it turns out that such an examination is almost entirely missing from their discussion. The illustrations ... do not present the details of the planning response to social problems, but only the context in which whatever planning there may have been proceeded, and the broad response of society. ... To design a new town or a system or routes and schedules for public transportation is nontrivial in any social context. (*ibid.*)

This has earned Harris the comment by Cooke (1983, p. 29) that, like myself, he conflates planning and planners, and neglects the institutional dimension of planning.

Harris continues that there is no good positive theory "which tells us in a formal way what planners do and how they do it. Such a positive theory would facilitate comparisons across cultures and put an end to a certain amount of empty vaporing. At the same time it would provide an intellectual rather than an artistic basis for the teaching of planning method" (*ibid.*). This is a re-statement of the motive behind the development of procedural planning theory.

Lastly, normative theory of planning concerns "the purposes of planning itself, just as normative theory of society must be normative with respect to the purposes of society" (pp. 222-3). Here, Harris affirms that this theory is abstract, and *necessarily so*:

I conceive normative theory of planning to be one which describes how planning should be conducted in order effectively to fulfill the social objectives which are laid upon it. In any given context, planning has to solve certain problems. The concept of efficiently and effectively solving these problems suggests that an abstract analysis of planning is possible, one which is not limited to historically observed planning activity nor to the behavior of planners and designers and their organizations; such an analysis could follow a much more deductive approach. This is not to imply that the experience of various branches of society planning their activities can or should be disregarded, but this experience is not necessarily the best or the only starting point for a normative theory. The possible behaviors of individuals and social groups in a social and a planning situation may be constraints on a normative theory, but they do not provide its motive power (p. 223).

Harris summarises his critique by saying that to

confound social theory with planning theory as Scott and Roweis have done diverts attention from a significant sphere of human activity which requires additional research and understanding. It may very well be that the problems which they address are much more important than the problems which they overlook, but the implication that their approach will solve the problems of planning is not legitimate. No more is the normative implication that a change in the social order will also automatically solve the problems of planning (p. 223).

Like I do in the debate with Thomas, Harris wants to bridge the gap between Scott and Roweis's approach and his. In a statement which is interesting because of the hints which it gives of his approach in a forthcoming book-still eagerly awaited-he explains how this might be achieved by starting from mathematical programming as the paradigm for planning organisation and procedures.

It is then possible to predict and diagnose situations in which planning fails because it deals improperly with one or more of the elements of this paradigm. For example, the objectives may have been improperly conceived; the outcome of planning decisions may have been inadequately predicted; the search for alternatives may have been unnecessarily truncated; and so on. Scott and Roweis' social theory would come into play in explaining why political and institutional factors prevented one of the desiderata from having been met; such an analysis is in the realm of positive social theory (p. 223).

Scott and Roweis (1978) retort that Harris is wrong on four counts. Here, the most central issue is his claim that they confound social with planning theory. Harris's paradigm suggests that planning theory is a set of problem-solving algorithms and procedures. But to

reduce planning theory to something akin to mathematical programming is to reduce planning itself to an arbitrary autonomous "conception" that appears, literally, out of nowhere; and this forever puts barriers in the way of discovering what planning *is* as a definite phenomenon with definite social content and a definite historical trajectory to be explained and accounted for in terms of observable material manifestations (building regulations, land-use zoning, public housing, etc.) (p. 230).

In his somewhat exasperated reply, Harris (1978b) exclaims that "it is logically self-evident that social theory and planning theory are intrinsically different if society and planning are different" (p. 350). Even more important is the fact that, in insisting that planning theory should be subject to empirical testing, Scott and Roweis misapprehend the conceptual nature of Harris's proposal. This is the core issue of the subsequent debate between Taylor and Scott, which is no less frustrating for the lack of any mutually acceptable outcome. In his "A critique of the materialistic critiques of procedural planning theory", Taylor (1984) describes Scott and Roweis's approach as "sociology of planning". He claims that procedural planning theory is different in that it is

arrived at by conceptual or logical analysis of what would be required for a decision to be rational in a purely formal or logical sense. ... First there is the analysis of what is being done in making decisions. ... Thus the making of any decision implies that *some* objective is being sought, that *some* course of action is needed to achieve this objective, that a course of action is evaluated in relation to the objectives and chosen in preference to other courses of action, and so on. ... a second condition must be satisfied. ... For the final decision to be demonstrably rational, the various steps ... must be logically related one to another so that the whole process leading to a decision is logically rational (p. 106).

Procedural planning theory does not say anything about *which* problems should be tackled, nor about *whose* interests should be satisfied. Rather, it "confines itself to demonstrating that any exercise in decisionmaking ... necessarily or logically presupposes *some* problem to be solved ... *some* course of action or plan for action, *some* choice between alternative courses of action or plans, and so on" (p. 107).

Taylor clarifies also what is meant by "normative" planning theory. Rather than being normative in itself, procedural planning theory, evolving as it does around the rational planning model, has normative implications, in the sense that, "*if* planning does seek to be ... rational, *then* it ought to be approached in a manner that conforms to the basic theory or model of rational planning" (*ibid*).

Taylor concludes that procedural planning theory cannot be criticised for not being what it does not want to be: empirical, making its materialist critique seem misconceived. He demonstrates also that Scott and Roweis themselves commit sins which they criticise mainstream theorists for; for instance, starting from a conceptual framework that is not based-indeed cannot be based-on facts. Now, the familiar pattern of the previous debate repeats itself. Scott (1984) replies that Taylor's critique has no empirical foundation and dwells on the fact that procedural planning theory does not arise out of practice, concluding that it is self-validating-immune to external critique, as it were. He challenges Taylor to show "the grounds for his belief that theoretical questions about the activity of planners can indeed be usefully raised and resolved *in advance* of any enquiry as to what planning really is" (p. 129). He seemingly forgets that, prior to investigating something "as it is" one must always formulate concepts of that which one is looking at.

In his rejoinder, Taylor (1985) affirms the conceptual nature of the theory of rational planning, but shows that it does suggest empirical inquiries and practical improvements. Taylor thus replies to Scott, demanding a demon-stration of the usefulness of procedural theory to practice, using the identification of goals as his example. This necessary element of the basic theory of rational planning points at research into how actual planning agencies come to identify goals. Such research might expose biases of the kind such as Scott and Roweis claim exist. It might also raise the normative issue of whose goals should prevail. So, Taylor claims, empirical research is useful (a) in a purely descriptive sense; (b) in revealing practices which ought to be changed; (c) as a theoretical base for improving planning. The latter two applications involve the use of precisely the kind of conceptual theory which procedural planning theory is.

Thus, if we have a conceptual theory of rational planning ... which specifies that, in order to be rational a process of planning must make explicit the identification and definition of problems and interests and any evaluation in relation to these problems and interests, then it is in relation to this concept of rationality that we can criticize (the planning agency) for failing to make these matters explicit and thus failing to act in a truly rational way. ... What this shows is that concepts and conceptual analysis are crucial not only in clarifying but also in criticizing social practices (p. 238).

Taylor responds also to Scott's challenge that he makes procedural theory immune to criticism, pointing out the many criticisms that have in fact been made against the rational planning model. He ends by affirming that social-scientific theory "which seeks to explain state intervention in urban planning in terms of the political economy of advanced industrial capitalism is extremely valuable in extending our understanding of the origin and role of urban planning in capitalist societies". He continues that procedural planning theory "is also theoretically and practically useful, and in ways which are complementary rather than antagonistic to such social scientific theory" (p. 239), this being the view held also by Harris and myself. I concur also with Taylor that Scott nowhere confronts his arguments. His latest reply (Scott, 1985) suggests that he is still caught up in the illusion that theory is necessarily explanatory, and thus empirical. It is only then that his insistence that theory must not be made immune against meaningful confrontations with reality makes sense. But Los (1981, p. 81) had pointed out to Scott and Roweis some time ago that falsifiability is a meaningful criterion *only* with respect to empirical, and not to conceptual, inquiry. As one of the editors of the volume in which that paper appeared, Scott might have taken account of this.

All this throws light on my changing perspective on planning theory. In 1973, as we have seen, I did set out to construct a positive theory of planning. Scott and Roweis are adamant always that their critics must specifically address the points they make, but fail to recognise this crucial fact. Had they done so, they might have taken *Planning Theory* up on the hypotheses it offers, showing perhaps (since they profess to a Popperian methodology recommending conjectures and refutations) how they could be refuted. As far as my present position is concerned, I agree now with Taylor and Harris. Procedural planning theory is at heart conceptual, or formal, theory. My attempt to develop positive or empirical procedural planning theory (and, as far as the methodology is concerned, nobody has yet been able to fault it) has been somewhat of a digression. I shall return to the nature of the type of enquiry which my work has involved since as being methodological (conceptual, in Taylor's and Harris's words) in Section 8.5.

Conclusions

The cause of the new substantivists is credible, but their critique of procedural planning theory unwarranted. The materialist analysis which they advocate cannot explain planning "as is". Organisational and procedural variables are needed also. And even if new substantivists were to explain planning under capitalism at 100 per cent, it would still be a worthwhile task to explore the logic and the conditions of planning, once the shackles of capitalism were broken, and planning could begin. This does involve abstract analysis, but that is hardly a valid criticism of something that sets out to be an abstract, or conceptual, theory.

Nor-and this has been shown to frustrate Harris and Taylor as much as myself-is the critique of procedural planning theory a necessary part of the new substantivist position. Understandable though the attack on "mainstream theory" may have been a decade or so ago, whilst the struggle was on for the hearts and minds of planning students, the new substantivists can easily do without it. And, in between the serious analyses of planning which they are surely engaged in, they might spare a glance for their brethren in arms, in their struggle against proceduralists. They might find ideological distortion and lack of methodological awareness in the conventional substantivist position: more so than is the case with proceduralists whom they are so well-practised in dismissing.

The "decision-centred view of planning", to be presented in Chapter 8, is also abstract, or formal, at heart. Its abstractness notwithstanding, this view relates to the work-situation of planners in the business of preparing policy. This practical orientation is what parts "new substantivists" and myself.

Much concern is expressed about the academician-practitioner gap (see Susskind, 1974; Perloff, 1974; Galloway and Mahayni, 1977; Bolan, 1981; Breheny, 1983; Breheny and Hall, 1985). It relates to this discussion. Planning education owes society effective, as well as educated, practitioners. So planning academics should debate the challenges of practical decision-making, even more so than the functions of planning in capitalism. The latter are important, to be sure. The ability to reflect on such issues is the mark of an *educated* practitioner. But it is not the *only* distinguishing characteristic of an *effective* one.

The intellectually credible challenge to procedural planning theory comes from the "new substantivists". But they turn out not to be interested in procedural theory. Far be it from me to criticise them for that. Only, it would help if the recognition that our concerns *are* different were mutual, because then the two perspectives could coexist.

Such tolerance is impossible as regards the conventional substantivist position, especially as far as the object-centred view of planning is concerned (the other variants within that view having been shown to be based on misunderstanding). Compromise with a view that is clearly untenable is a non-starter.

References

Alexander, E. R. (1984) "After rationality, what?; a review of responses to paradigm breakdown", *Journal of the American Planning Association*, **50**, 62-9.

Argyris, C. (1982) *Reasoning, Learning and Action: Individual and Organizational*, Jossey-Bass, San Francisco.

Baum, H. S. (1980a) "Analysts and planners must think organizationally", *Policy Analysis*, **6**, 479-94.

Baum, H. S. (1980b) "The uncertain consciousness of planners and the professional enterprise", *Plan Canada*, **20**, 39-53.

Baum, H. S. (1983) "Review of C. Argyris, 'Reasoning, Learning and Action: Individual and Organizational' ", *Journal of the American Planning Association*, **49**, 238-9.

Beauregard, R. A. (1978) "Planning in an advanced capitalist state", in: *Planning Theory in the 1980s: A Search for Future Directions*, eds R. W. Burchell and G. Sternlieb, Centre for Urban Policy and Research, New Brunswick, NJ.

*Bolan, R. S. (1969) "Community decision behavior: the culture of planning", *Journal of the American Institute of Planners*, **35**, 301-10.

Bolan, R. S. (1982) "Do planning theory courses teach planning?", *Journal of Planning Education and Research*, **1**, 12-14.

Bolan, R. S. and Nuttall, R. L. (1975) *Urban Planning and Politics*, Lexington Books, Lexington, Mass.

Breheny, M. J. (1983) "A practical review of planning theory", *Environment and Planning B*, **10**, 101-15.

Breheny, M. J. and Hall, P. (1985) "The strange death of strategic planning and the victory of the know-nothing school", *Built Environment*, **10**, 95-9.

Chadwick, G. A. (1978; 1st edition 1970) *A Systems View of Planning*, Pergamon Press, London.

Christensen, K. S. (1985) "Coping with uncertainty in planning", *Journal of the American Planning Association*, **51**, 63-73.

Cockburn, C. (1970) "Opinion and planning education", Information Paper No. 21, Centre for Environmental Studies, London.

Cooke, P. N. (1983) *Theories of Planning and Spatial Development*, Hutchinson, London.

Cooke, P. N. and Rees, G. (1977) "Faludi's sociology in planning education: a critical comment", *Urban Studies*, **14**, 219-22.

Cross, D. T. and Bristow, M. R. (1983) *English Structure Planning: A Commentary on Procedure and Practice in the Seventies*, Pion Press, London.

*Davidoff, P. and Reiner, T. A. (1962) "A choice theory of planning", *Journal of the American Institute of Planners*, **28**, 108-15.

*Dror, Y. (1963) "The planning process: a facet design", *International Review of Administrative Sciences*, **29**, 93-116.

Dyckman, J. W. (1983) "Reflections on planning practice in an age of reaction", *Journal of Planning Education and Research*, **3**, 5-12.

Fainstein, N. I. and Fainstein, S. S. (1979) "New debates in urban planning: the impact of marxist theory within the United States", *International Journal of Urban and Regional Research*, **3**, 381-403; see also C. Paris (ed.) (1982) *Critical Readings in Planning Theory*, Pergamon Press, Oxford, pp. 147-73.

Faludi, A. (1973) *A Reader in Planning Theory*, Pergamon Press, Oxford.

Faludi, A. (1979) "Towards a combined paradigm of planning theory: a rejoinder by Andreas Faludi", *Planning Outlook*, **22**, 77-80; see also: C. Paris (ed.) (1982) *Critical Essays in Planning Theory and Education*, Pergamon Press, Oxford, pp. 27-38.

Faludi, A. (1982) "Three paradigms of planning theory", in: *Planning Theory: Prospects for the 1980s*, eds P.Healey, G. McDougall and M. J. Thomas, Pergamon Press, Oxford, pp. 81-101.

Faludi, A. (1985) "The return of rationality", in: *Rationality in Planning: Critical Essays on the Role of Rationality in Urban and Regional Planning*, eds M. J. Breheny and A. J. Hooper, Pion Press, London, pp. 27-47.

Faludi, A. (1986) *Critical Rationalism and Planning Methodology*, Pion Press, London.

Friedmann, J. (1959) "The study and practice of planning: introduction", *International Social Science Journal*, **11**, 327-39.

Friedmann, J. (1966) "The institutional context", in: *Action under Planning*, ed. B. Gross, McGraw-Hill, New York, pp. 31-67.

*Friedmann, J. (1967) "A conceptual model for the analysis of planning behavior", *Administrative Science Quarterly*, **12**, 225-52.

Friedmann, J. (1974) "Review of A. Faludi, 'Planning Theory' ", *Regional Studies*, **8**, 311.

Friedmann, J. and Weaver, C. (1979) *Territory and Function: the Evolution of Regional Planning*, Edward Arnold, London.

Frost, D. (1977) "Sociology in planning education: A comment", *Urban Studies*, **14**, 221-2.

Galloway, T. D. and Mahayni, R. G. (1977) "Planning theory in retrospect: the process of paradigm change", *Journal of the American Institute of Planners*, **43**, 62-71.

Giddens, A. (1984) *The Construction of Society: Outline of a Theory of Structuration*, Polity Press, Cambridge.

Grabow, S. and Heskin, A. (1973) "Foundations for a radical concept of planning", *Journal of the American Institute of Planners*, **39**, 106-16.

86 A Decision-centred View of Environmental Planning

Hague, C. (1984) *The Development of Planning Thought: A Critical Perspective*, Huchinson, London.

Hall, P. (1974) *Urban and Regional Planning*, Penguin, Harmondsworth.

Hall, P. (1983) "The Anglo-American connection: rival rationalities in planning theory and practice, 1955-1980", *Environment and Planning B*, **10**, 41-6.

Harris, B. (1978a) "A note on planning theory", *Environment and Planning A*, **10**, 221-4.

Harris, B. (1978b) "Planning theory: a response to Scott and Roweis", *Environment and Planning A*, **10**, 349-50.

Harvey, D. (1969) *Explanation in Geography*, Edward Arnold, London.

Harvey, D. (1973) *Social Justice and the City*, Edward Arnold, London.

Harvey, D. (1978) "On planning the ideology of planning", in: *Planning Theory in the 1980s*, eds R. W. Burchell and G. Sternlieb, Centre for Urban Policy Research, New Brunswick.

Healey, P. (1982) "Understanding land use planning: the contribution of recent developments in political economy and policy studies", in: *Planning Theory: Prospects for the 1980s*, eds P. Healey, G. McDougall and M. J. Thomas, Pergamon Press, Oxford, pp. 81-101.

Healey, P. (1983) "Rational method as a mode of policy formation and implementation in land-use policy", *Environment and Planning B*, **10**, 19-39.

Healey, P., McDougall, G. and Thomas, M. J. (1982) "Introduction", in: *Planning Theory: Prospects for the 1980s*, eds P. Healey, G. McDougall and M. J. Thomas, Pergamon Press, Oxford, pp. 1-22.

Hightower, H. C. (1970) "Planning theory in contemporary professional education", *Journal of the American Institute of Planners*, **35**, 326-9.

Hill, M. (1981) "The policy-implementation distinction: a quest for rational control?", in: *Policy and Action: Essays on the Implementation of Public Policy*, eds S. Barrett and C. Fudge, Methuen, London and New York, pp. 207-23.

Hoch, C. J. (1984) "Doing good and being right", *Journal of the American Planning Association*, **50**, 335-45.

Hooper, A. (1982) "Methodological monism or critical dualism? Reflections on Andreas Faludi's planning theory", *Built Environment*, **8**, 247-8.

Howe, E. and Kaufman, J. (1979) "The ethics of contemporary American planners", *Journal of the American Planning Association*, **45**, 243-55.

Hudson, B. M. (1979) "Comparison of current planning theories: counterparts and contradictions", *Journal of the American Planning Association*, **45**, 387-98.

Jefferson, R. (1973) "Planning and the innovation process", in: *Progress in Planning*, eds D. Diamond and B. McLoughlin, Pergamon Press, Oxford, pp. 233-312.

Kuhn, T. S. (1962) *The Structure of Scientific Revolutions*, University of Chicago Press, Chicago.

Los, M. (1981) "Some reflexions on epistemology, design and planning", in: *Urbanization and Urban Planning in Capitalist Society*, eds M. Dear, and A. J. Scott, Methuen, New York.

Mayo, J. M. (1982) "Sources of job dissatisfaction: ideals versus realities in planning", *Journal of the American Planning Association*, **48**, 481-95.

McDougall, G. (1973) "The systems approach to planning: a critique", *Socio-Economic Planning Sciences*, **7**, 79-90.

McDougall, G. (1983) "The interactional approach to organisations and planning: a critique", in: *Evaluating Urban Planning Efforts*, ed. I. Masser, Gower, Aldershot, Hants, pp. 36-53.

McLoughlin, J. B. (1969) *Urban and Regional Planning: a System Approach*, Faber & Faber, London.

McLoughlin, J. B. (1973) *Control and Urban Planning*, Faber & Faber, London.

McLoughlin, J. B. (1983) "Planning research and education in Australia", *Urban Policy and Research*, **1**, 16-21.

Neufville, J. I. de (1983) "The doldrums of planning theory", *Journal of Planning Education and Research*, **3**, 35-45.

Paris, C. (1982) "Introduction by the editor, Part One: A Critique of Pure Planning", in: *Critical Readings in Planning Theory*, ed. C. Paris, Pergamon Press, Oxford, pp. 3-11.

Perloff, H. S. (with Klett, F.) (1974) "The future of planning education", in: *Planning in America: Learning from Turbulence*, ed. D. R. Godschalk, American Institute of Planners, Washington, DC, pp. 161-80.

Pickvance, C. G. (1976) "Introduction: historical materialist approaches to urban sociology", in: *Urban Sociology*, ed. C. G. Pickvance, Tavistock, London, pp. 10-36.

Pickvance, C. (1982) "Physical planning and market forces in urban development", in: *Critical Readings in Planning Theory*, ed. C. Paris, Pergamon Press, Oxford, pp. 69-82.

Rabinovitz, F. F. (1969) *City Politics and Planning*, Atherton Press, New York.

Reade, E. J. (1976) "The context of theory courses in town planning education", Working Paper, No. 25, Department of Town Planning, Oxford Polytechnic, Oxford, pp. 94-136.

Reade, E. J. (1982) "The theory of town and country planning", in: *Planning Theory: Prospects for the 1980s*, eds P. Healey, G. McDougall and M. J. Thomas, Pergamon Press, Oxford, pp. 43-58.

Reade, E. J. (1983) "Monitoring in planning", in: *Evaluating Urban Planning Efforts*, ed. I. Masser, Gower, Aldershot, Hants, pp. 224-42.

Rittel, H. J. W. and Webber, M. M. (1973) "Dilemmas of a general theory of planning", *Policy Sciences*, 4, 155-69.

Robinson, I. M.(1972) *Decision Making in Urban Planning*, Sage, Beverly Hills, CA.

Roweis, S. T. (1983) "Urban planning as professional mediation of territorial politics", *Environment and Planning D: Society and Space*, 1, 139-62.

Royal Town Planning Institute (1976) *Planning and the Future: a Discussion Document*, London.

Sandbach, F. (1980) *Environment, Ideology and Policy*, Basil Blackwell, Oxford.

Scott, A. J. (1984) "A comment on Taylor's procedural theory of planning", *Environment and Planning B*, 11, 127-9.

Scott, A. J. (1985) "A further comment on Taylor's procedural theory", *Environment and Planning B: Planning and Design*, 12, 240.

Scott, A. J. and Roweis, S. T. (1977) "Urban planning theory and practice: a reappraisal", *Environment and Planning A*, 9, 1097-19.

Scott, A. J. and Roweis, S. T. (1978) "A note on planning theory: a response to Britton Harris", *Environment and Planning A*, 10, 229-31.

Sorensen, A. D. and Day, R. A. (1981) "Libertarian planning", *Town Planning Review*, 52, 390-402.

Susskind, L. E. (1974) "The future of the planning profession", in: *Planning in America: Learning from Turbulence*, ed. D. R. Godschalk, American Institute of Planners, Washington, DC, pp. 138-60.

Taylor, N. (1984) "A critique of materialist critiques of procedural planning theory", *Environment and Planning B*, 11, 103-26.

Taylor, N. (1985) "The usefulness of a conceptual theory of rational planning: a reply to Scott's comment", *Environment and Planning B: Planning and Design*, 12, 235-40.

Thomas, M. J. (1979) "The procedural planning theory of A. Faludi", *Planning Outlook*, 22, 72-6; see also C. Paris (ed.) (1982) *Critical Readings in Planning Theory*, Pergamon Press, Oxford, pp. 13-25.

Thornley, J. (1974) "Review of A. Faludi, 'A Reader in Planning Theory' ", *Urban Studies*, 11, 111-12.

Vasu, M. L. (1979) *Politics and Planning: a National Study of American Planners*, University of North Carolina Press, Chapel Hill, NC.

Webber, M. M. (1963) "The prospects of policies planning", in: *The Urban Condition: People and Politics in the Metropolis*, (ed.) L. S. Duhl, Basic Books, Yew York, pp. 319-30.

CHAPTER 6

The Radical Gentlemen from Coventry

THIS chapter prepares the ground for the decision-centred view of planning, based as that view is on the work of the "IOR" (*Institute for Operational Research*). Established as a unit of the *Tavistock Institute of Human Relations*, IOR became a household name after publication of *Local Government and Strategic Choice* (Friend and Jessop, 1977, 1st edition 1969). For many years the base of its planning processes work was Coventry, the site of that study. At present, due to savage cuts in research funding, the IOR is smaller, bearing the name of *Centre for Operational and Organisational Research*. The person who more than anybody else has provided continuity throughout is John K. Friend.

The "IOR School"-a term introduced by Faludi and Mastop (1982)-is second in importance only to the Chicago School, but presents its message in the kind of understatement in which English gentlemen excel. Perhaps this is why it has not received the acclaim which it deserves.

What is its message? How does it relate to mainstream planning thought? In answering these questions, I shall show that the "IOR School" has laid the groundwork for a practicable approach to planning free from pretensions-the hallmark of much academic planning thought-of replacing existing decision-making practices. It has helped also to shift attention away from plan-making.

The chapter begins with the *Origin and orientation* of the "IOR School". *Technology of choice and networks* discusses technical, organisational and procedural aspects of its message. *The missing link with academia* shows that there is a gulf between the "IOR School" and academic theorising.

6.1 Origin and orientation

What are the roots of the "IOR School"? What is its message? Answering these questions helps to appreciate its role.

The founding of the *Institute for Operational Research* in 1963 reflected the desire of British operational researchers to apply themselves to public policy, and to integrate formal approaches with the social sciences (see Lawrence, 1966). The *Tavistock Institute of Human Relations*, with its tradition of qualitative research, provided the ideal context for attention to the human dimensions of organisational decision-making. One of its first projects was concerned with communication in the building industry. Its significance lies in the development of the so-called *Analysis of Interconnected Decision Areas (AIDA)* (see Luckmann, 1967) using graphic representations of the *interrelations* between various *options* per *decision area* to generate alternatives systematically. In simple manner, it lays open the decision-making process so that every assumption can be changed at will. AIDA is the best known part of what later became to be known as the *strategic choice approach*, so much so that many believe that is all there is to it.

The most important project was one on policy research for local government based on field work at Coventry in 1963-67 and resulted in the publication of *Local Government and Strategic Choice: an Operational Research Approach to the Process of Public Planning* (Friend and Jessop, 1977, 1st edition 1969). Its conduct reflects the dual concern for the *formal* as well as the *social* aspects of decision-making. Availing themselves of the advice of a social psychologist and of anthropologists, the team studied decision-makers in their "natural habitat"-offices and council chambers. They did this by seeking to experience at first hand what makes decision-makers tick, their aim being to interpret practice correctly.

Until then, the impetus for innovation in planning had come from systems analysis and cybernetics, as discussed in Section 3.3. Practical examples of the new planning had been the work of exceptional teams drawn from a small group of skilled people. It was worlds apart from the routine of petty squabbles, the tactics of evasion, the dashed hopes and desperate searches for solutions which are just about good enough to survive the next day, which seem to characterise practice. Lee (1973, p. 173) counts lack of organisational learning resulting from this gap amongst reasons for the failure of large-scale models. There is no such gap in the approach of the "IOR School".

The introductory note to the book (Friend and Jessop, 1977, p. xi) conveys a sense of the unique opportunity which virtually unlimited access at Coventry offered. It gives an idea also of the commitment of the team to improving planning. This led them to abandon their initial aim of building a model of the total system, "coupled with the idea then coming into the ascendant in the Tavistock Institute of designing a 'sociotechnical system' in which organisational arrangements would be explicitly matched to the behavioural as well as the operational dimension of the task" (Friend, 1983, p. 64). Rather, attention focused on the development of "intermediate technology", of which AIDA is a prime example.

The reason is that the research showed decision-makers to be frequently in need of help of an immediate and practical kind. They demanded more research, more policy guidance, more coordination. The now classic distinction of types of uncertainty concerning the *environment*, *values*, and *related areas of choice* is based on this. The following quote demonstrates the centrality of the latter concept in particular (foreshadowed by Davidoff and Reiner's reference to the "networking effect" of decisions; for similar views on the need for comprehensiveness see Webber, 1963, and Davidoff, 1965, in Section 3.2) to the view of planning as *strategic choice*. They say that

any process of choice will become a process of planning (or: strategic choice) if the selection of current actions is made only after a formulation and comparison of possible solutions over a wider field of decision relating to certain anticipated as well as current situations (Friend and Jessop, 1977, p. 110).

In view of the opposition, reported below, of the "IOR School" to rationality in the sense of optimisation, it is worth noting that strategic choice is similar in intent to what Etzioni (1968, pp. 260-3) describes as "comprehensive rationality", whereby the effects of instrumental action on other than the immediate goals are taken into account. This may include goals such as the maintenance of legitimacy. (See also Meyerson and Banfield's "contextual ends" discussed in Section 2.3.) What is underlying is the distinction between ordinary decision-making on the one hand and planning on the other. It is based on whether the wider field of choice is explored or not. Many authors neglect it, equating planning with any kind of problem-solving.

For conveying these ideas, *Local Government and Strategic Choice* uses a "dialogue model" of the "governmental system" interacting with the "community system". It reminds one of the systems approach and of *Planning Theory*, but without the dwelling on problems which such a conceptualisation entails (see Low, 1982, in Section 4.3). But this model is only a device for expounding the "agency-centred" view of planning of the "IOR School". Due emphasis is given to the limitations-analysed in other literature as well-which planning agencies confront. These are looked at, not from the point of view of a disinterested observer, but from that of the decision-maker considering his options. This empathy for the situations of practitioners-professionals and politicians alike-sets the "IOR School" apart from others.

The work identifies five operational and six organisational planning problems. The operational problems are: to find solutions, express preferences, expose latent uncertainties, select exploratory actions to help in reducing them, and to select immediate commitments in the face of such uncertainties as remain unresolved (Friend and Jessop, 1977, p. 118). It is here that the technology of choice comes in: a kit-bag with tools that help to explore the "wider field of choice". In some instances conventional methods-like cost-benefit analysis-fit the bill. In others, innovation is called for. Next to Analysis of Interrelated Decision Areas (AIDA), methods for determining the robustness of various courses of action are proposed.

The organisational problems are: to find mechanisms for strategic control, to assemble the authority necessary for the same purpose, to obtain sufficient information, provide democratic guidance, find a common language and induce sufficient motivation (Friend and Jessop, 1977, p. 135). If the formulation of the first set of problems is a call for a technology of choice, the second is a brief for developing an appropriate setting for planning (similar in intention to the planning principles discussed in Section 4.2). Full appreciation of its importance came during the follow-up project to be discussed below.

Neither operational nor organisational problem are defined in unusual terms. Indeed, I shall argue below that they show the essential relationship between the message of the "IOR School" and the rational planning model.

The underlying view of planning is simple, almost to the point of triviality, but has radical implications. Its simplicity lies in the view of planning as a choice between alternative courses of action, a point appreciated ever since the "Chicago School". The "IOR School" added their view of planning as strategic choice under uncertainty and concerned with matters which are interrelated: spatially, or in time, because of budgetary constraints, or whatever reason there might be for linking decisions. Meyerson and Banfield, too, identify planning with coordinated decision-making, but this idea subsequently receded into the background. The distinction in Chapter 8 between *operational decisions* and *planning decisions* is based on this view of planning.

Recognition of uncertainty is not entirely new either. Risk analysis can be found in the operational research literature (see Ackoff, 1962; Bross, 1953), an awareness of which influenced the "IOR School". But the notion came more to life in their analyses of planning documents and decision-making practices than in the technical literature.

The most radical aspect concerns the implications of the proposals of the "IOR School". They counteract the view-present not only in architecture and urban design but also in the systems approach-of planning that is aimed primarily at the production of plans representing a better future to which present action should be subordinated. The "IOR School" thinks of planning as not so much concerned with the description of the future-a future over which there is only limited control-but with providing a firmer case for action which there is power to take now. Planning is not so much concerned with producing a plan as with gaining a better understanding of the problems with which we are faced now and in the future, in order that we can make better decisions now (Centre for Environmental Studies, 1970, p. 16).

This is where there is a real difference, compared with the classic rational planning model. We have seen that Davidoff and Reiner (1962) claim that estimates of future states are "important for what they imply for present behavior". But they fail to take this to its conclusion, which is that planning should never set itself up as an alternative-and allegedly superior-way of decision-making, but should help in improving ongoing choice, and that planning itself never comes to any definite resolution, least of all by adopting a document called "the plan". Or, as Lee (1973, p. 1976) comments: "Long-range planning means evaluating immediate decisions with regard to long-run consequencs, rather than constructing grand plans or big models."

Old hands have always appreciated this, but their adaptations to real life have tended to conflict with cherished planning ideals. The "IOR School" gives a rationale for a viable form of planning which does not reject existing practice, but expands upon it.

The "IOR School' takes us also beyond previous views which assume that what is being planned is *outside* the planning agency: development on the ground, settlements, the environment, human activities, their shells, and the channels between them, or whichever formulation one prefers. Works by sociologists like Gans (1968) in the United States and Broady (1968) in Britain have sharpened our understanding of the human dimensions of development, but never has the assumption been questioned that planning has some part of the real world as its object. The emphasis on day-to-day decision-making undermines it.

Local Government and Strategic Choice describes the object of planning as "the powers for dealing with ... situations" (Friend and Jessop, 1977, p. 120). Ultimately, this means that planning is seen as the arranging of ongoing decisions into packages that make sense from some overall point of view. Appropriately, Friend and Hickling (1987) in a long-awaited work summarising more than 20 years experience, *Planning under Pressure-The Strategic Choice Approach*, talk about "scheming". In Chapter 8 I shall argue that it is decisions which form the object of scheming.

Half a decade after the publication of *Local Government and Strategic Choice*, Drake (1975) reported that the practice of structure planning reflected its influence (see also Hayton, 1981, p. 426). But its impact on theory was not immediately visible. Whilst the gestation period lasted, the work of the "IOR School" continued.

6.2 Technology of choice and networks

Two elements of *Local Government and Strategic Choice* were the idea of a technology of choice and the attention to organisational problems. The line ahead in the case of the technology of choice was to test it in practice. In so doing, the "IOR School" took an approach that reflected the Tavistock influence yet again: action research. Researchers joined practitioners; the emphasis was on mutual learning based on a relationship of trust. This turned earlier suggestions into the more definite-yet still flexible-approach to the multitude of problems in planning which now goes under the term *strategic choice*. It owes its appeal to the manifold links with planners which are forged during action research and also to the type of "hands-on" post-experience training which became another of the hallmarks of the "IOR School". It must be admitted, though, that in a book like this it is difficult to convey a sense of what is involved, because strategic choice relates to the experience of real-life situations. The works of the "IOR School" make valiant efforts to describe cases, but a real appreciation of the value of their approach can only come from doing strategic choice.

The "LOGIMP Experiment"

If there is one single project that epitomises the philosophy of the "IOR

School", then it is the one known as the "LOGIMP experiment" (LOcal Government IMPlementation). One of the rare examples of cooperation with academics-the *Institute for Local Government Studies* of the University of Birmingham-it tested the technology of choice proposed above.

It is difficult to overestimate the importance of this shoestring operation, funded by the *Centre for Environmental Studies* (then the major promoter of planning research in Britain). Through it, confidence in the technology of choice increased, and the message of the "IOR School" spread. There were frequent discussions, including a debriefing conference. Two papers arising out of it, by Wedgewood-Oppenheim (1972a,b) relate the message of the "IOR School" to mainstream planning thought. Bunker (1973, 1974) analyses the long-term effects in the participating authorities.

The final report (Centre for Environmental Studies, 1970) gives a stream-lined presentation of the process of strategic choice. Centring on the generation and evaluation of alternatives, it shows its roots to be in the rational planning model. The report recognises the discretional and creative elements involved. Every step, from formulating a first "strategic focus" to devising solutions acceptable in the face of uncertainties, in turn entails a decision. "Uncertainty management" represents a new element in the process.

LOGIMP is responsible for the identification of strategic choice with AIDA, and in a way, this is understandable. AIDA is easily adaptable to the conditions of practice and is exemplary for strategic choice. Ideas are not being presented in as "technically sophisticated and glossy packaged a manner as possible", as (Cooke, 1983, p. 9) is claimed to be the case in planning. Its main benefit lies not so much in the actual method as such, to which there are alternatives, for instance morphological analysis developed by Zwicky (see Chadwick, 1978, p. 168; for a comparison see Faludi, 1978, p. 77). Its beauty lies in what it induces. The debriefing in the LOGIMP experiment concluded: "Of particular interest ... was the general view that emerged that the approach was of more value as an attitude of mind and as a communication aid than as a mere technical aid to problem-solving" (Friend and Jessop, 1977, p. 292; for Webber viewing planning as an attitude of mind see Section 3.2). Also AIDA forces the decision-maker to come clean on assumptions, and directs attention to gaps in understanding and new solutions.

But the benefits derive mainly to the initiated. Already during that de-briefing, doubts were voiced as to how far AIDA could be used with lay people. Subsequently, IOR researchers did get involved in applications involving residents and elected representatives (Friend and Jessop, 1977, p. 294). But such examples are rare. On the whole the apparent complexity of AIDA puts people off, but to blame AIDA for this is like blaming the messenger for the content of the message. The complexity is not of its making, but stems from the issues themselves and merely becomes evident thanks to using AIDA.

Other elements of the technology of choice, in particular uncertainty management, are not half as well-developed. Perhaps this is because uncertainty management is even more demanding on decision-makers and violates established views of planning, even more so than AIDA does. Also, as Friend (1983, p. 64) readily admits, uncertainty is less rigorously defined than other concepts in strategic choice.

Wedgewood-Oppenheim (1972a) compares strategic choice with the rational planning model and various of its alternatives. Like Etzioni's "mixed scanning" (see Section 3.4), it is intentionally rational and comprehensive, but imbued with awareness of the fragmentation of real-life decision-making at the same time. Strategic choice accepts that the outcomes of planning are often tentative, leading to small rather than large amounts of change. Even then, it aims to let incremental steps be the outcome of broad analysis, and takes account also of the limitations of the decision-maker, thus reminding us of Simon's "satisficing" (see Section 3.4). In other words, the planning *process* should be comprehensive, taking account not only of the facts of the situation, but also of the limitations of the decision-maker. The *outcome* of such a process may very well be small commitments. Besides, planning often results in exploratory actions aimed at diminishing uncertainty.

The technology of choice was the object of many training sessions for which Hickling (1974, 1975) wrote supporting material. It is attractive, didactically speaking, presenting the process step by step, illustrating every one with diagrams of a distinctive style, and with practical examples drawn from various projects. One of the diagrams expresses the cyclical nature of strategic choice so well that it has become the trademark of strategic choice. Advances concerned (a) recognition of the *invisible products* of planning: learning, better communication within the planning agency and between it and the outside world, and (b) a way of presenting its "visible products" (which Hickling sometimes seems to rate less than the "invisible" ones) in a *commitment package*, bringing together all that flows from a round of strategic choice in one position statement. The outcomes include direct interventions, the commitments to do more research and/or enter into negotiations, deferred actions and contingency plans. So, the commitment package catches the variety of responses to uncertainty. It represents an adaptation to our inability to resolve all issues at once, and complements decision-making in a context often characterised by conflict.

For all intents and purposes the commitment package may be said to replace the plan-drawn-up-in-advance-of-action of the classic rational planning model. That, at least, would seem the implication. But when applying themselves to plan-making, as in the structure-planning project quoted below, the "IOR School" failed to take this to its ultimate conclusion. Approaches to plan-making will concern us again in Chapter 12.

The very success of these booklets raises doubts as to whether strategic choice has not become too smooth a package. Its application is unlikely to be successful in the long run if it is not accompanied by awareness of the underlying view of planning. The research on structure planning (Sutton *et al.*, 1977) increases the suspicion of an element of *l'art-pour-l'art*. It followed the model of the LOGIMP experiment and led to differentiation between scenarios, policy areas and action sets, each representing a level of choice. As indicated, all this smacks more of conventional plan-making than of the commitment-package idea. Some diagrams in the report are startling for their complexity-thus running foul of the philosophy of the "IOR School" of keeping everything simple. Maybe, though, what has been said earlier about AIDA applies, and these diagrams merely demonstrate the real complexity of planning itself.

Perhaps the members of the "IOR School" were plagued by similar doubts. The latest statement on the state-of-the-art in strategic choice by Friend and Hickling (1987) nowhere refers to scenarios or policy areas as separate levels of choice, and the diagrams are of the appealingly simple nature of those in early publications.

Public planning-the inter-corporate dimension

Some loose ends around connective planning demanded more research leading to the recognition of networks in situations where coordination is needed between several organisations. The nodal points of networks are people with negotiating skills. This was the result of yet another participatory-observer study. Against the background of the emphasis at the time on corporate planning (see Eddison, 1973; Stewart, 1971), attention is drawn to the inter-organisational dimension of planning, hence the title *Public Planning-The Inter-corporate Dimension* (Friend *et al.*, 1974). This work clarifies an ambiguity in the earlier one: Which agency does "agency-centred" refer to? The dialogue model above suggests that it is the whole "governmental system". But organisations are far from coherent. Friend and Jessop's statement on organisational problems makes clear that negotiations bear little relationship to formal structure and extend beyond the bounds of any one agency.

The follow-up study takes this as its starting point. It identifies *decision networks* and so-called *reticulists* (persons with a special aptitude for linking decision processes together in negotiations). In so doing, the "IOR School" expands the meaning of one of the three forms of uncertainty: that relating to intentions in related fields of choice. Many such uncertainties come from *other organisations* operating in the planning agency's area of concern.

The planning of an expanded town, Droitwich in the West Midlands, catering for overspill from Birmingham, provides the case in point. The donor authority has to come to terms with the wishes of the recipient county and borough-and vice-versa. From the outset the study emphasises *connective planning*:

Opportunities for *connective planning* arise when people acting in *policy systems* which operate in particular *action spaces* are stimulated by their perceptions of *decision problems* to activate and shape *networks of decision-makers* in order to *explore alternatives* and from among them select *commitments to action* (Friend *et al.*, 1974, p. 56, emphases in the original).

As before, the emphasis is on selectivity. Connective planning is only recommended where there is a need for it. The presence of the "reticulists" described above is of key importance. The book culminates in the plea to treat their placement in strategic positions as key steps in inter-organisational planning. After all, "the practical influence of public planning activities on decision-making depends on the dispositions among public accountable agencies of skills and resources relevant to the selective activation of inter-agency networks" (pp. 372-3).

6.3 The missing link with academia

Public Planning puts awareness of the political and institutional dimensions of planning to practical use. This has not earned the "IOR School" the applause of planning writers, and it has never been fully accepted as a contributor to- and revolutioniser of-planning thought. Discussing this question, I give a critique of works presented in the previous two sections.

The mainspring of planning thought, as we have seen, is in the United States. Works on the purpose and conduct of planning were rare in the Britain of the sixties, which perhaps explains why the "IOR School" relates so uneasily to the planning literature. That the growing literature since largely ignores it reflects the predominant concern of academics with issues other than planning practice.

Initial reviews of *Local Government and Strategic Choice* were favourable, even in the United States (see Krueckeberg, 1970). Parts of it are included in *Decision-making in Urban Planning* (Robinson, 1972). Michael (1973), in *On Learning to Plan-and Planning to-Learn*, refers to it. (Chapter 3 of Chapin and Kaiser's internationally known textbook, *Urban Land Use Planning*, 1979, advances similar ideas, but without making reference to the "IOR School".) But there is no trace of any lasting impact on American planning. Krueckeberg hints why:

One leaves the study with a wholesome and hopeful attitude towards the problems of planning for the future. American case-studies tend to be destructive of their subjects and often breed cynicism in the believing reader (p. 69).

It seems that the, to use a concept from *Planning Theory* (see Section 4.1), "planning environment" of the United States is responsible. The Britain of the early seventies was characterised by enthusiasm for putting planning into practice. Structure plans generated particular excitement-and, as we have seen, Drake (1975) credits the "IOR School" with some influence on the emerging practice of their preparation, even before their work on structure planning got under way. It is its positive yet at the same time realistic attitude to planning which characterises the "IOR School" and which it is difficult to transplant into a different context. Take this away, and what remains are interesting case studies and techniques, neither of which were in short supply in the American literature of the early seventies.

Even in Britain, however, academics pay little attention. A recent review of the development of planning theory refers to the "IOR School" in passing as part of the mainstream of procedural planning theory (Healey *et al.*, 1982, pp. 8-9; see also Darke, 1983, p. 20). Batey and Breheny (1982), in their review of the history of British planning methodology, fail to give due credit to it. The 1982 issue on *Classics revisited* of *The Built Environment* does not review *Local Government and Strategic Choice*. In her critique of the "interactional approach to organisations and planning" represented by Bolan, Schön and Argyris (see Section 7.2), McDougall (1983) fails even to mention the very similar approach of the "IOR School".

With the exception of Bunker, Carter, Power and Wedgwood-Oppenheim, academics have not contributed to the "IOR School" either. (The work of Openshaw, 1975, and Openshaw and Whitehead, 1977, 1978, 1980, is a special case. Based on AIDA, their computerised *decision optimising technique* has never been acknowledged as useful by the "IOR School". Maybe the problem lies in the use of the very term optimisation, about which more below.)

There is a dearth of critical reviews, even from those normally opposed to anything that smacks of procedural matters. Healey (1979) is one of the few that come to mind. She criticises *Public Planning-the Inter-corporate Dimension* for considering the placement of so-called "reticulists" as a solution to inter-organisational problems. This neglect reflects the predominant concern of academics with matters other than the improvement of planning. It leads them to dismiss the "IOR School" on the strength of the argument that it does not give a "detailed analysis of power relations, conflict generation and resolution, and the nature of dominant coalitions" (Cooke, 1983, pp. 32-3). The previous two chapters have commented on the current quest for a "sociology of planning" explaining its very existence and function in the present (capitalist) system.

The "IOR School" is also responsible for its isolation. Although making major contributions to it, it relates uneasily to the general literature. Neither of the main works is thoroughly referenced. Passages in Friend *et al.* (1974) invoking Lindblom (1965) and Etzioni (1968) uncritically embrace their arguments. There is lack of awareness of American research which similarly emphasises the importance of "reticulist skills" (see Daland and Parker, 1962; Bellush and Hausknecht, 1966; Friedmann, 1969; Rabinovitz, 1969; Stanford, 1970). Many links could indeed have been forged. An obvious example is the emphasis on planning as learning, an idea of good currency at the beginning of the seventies (see Friedmann, 1969; Dunn, 1971; Michael, 1973; Eddison, 1973; Chadwick, 1978, 1st edition 1970, and also my own work discussed in Chapter 4). Most important is the link with the rational planning model.

Now, the reader might be excused for thinking that rationality could not be squared with the message of the "IOR School". *Local Government and Strategic Choice* does not refer to it, and *Public Planning-the Inter-corporate Dimension* goes overboard with praising Lindblom's view of planning as mutual adjustment, something which does not seem to go well with rationality. Also, Hickling never gets tired of portraying strategic choice as a way of expanding our understanding, of learning, but nothing like one of finding "optimal" solutions. Since Meyerson and Banfield (see Section 2.3), this search for optimal solutions has been what the rational model stands for. But the "IOR School" sees rationality as being opposed to its pragmatic approach which "sets out to do no more than to articulate, as clearly as possible, the kinds of day to day dilemma that experienced decision-makers repeatedly face in the course of their work" (Friend and Hickling, 1987), adding that the judgements which they make "often seem to be accompanied by a sense of discomfort and even guilt, because those involved feel that they may be departing from certain principles of rational behavior which they have been taught to respect" (ibid.). So, rather than being an exponent of it, the "IOR School" has been characterised by Rosenhead (1980a,b) as offering an alternative to the rational model.

But that model is implied in the formulation of the various "operational problems" and the "technology of choice", particularly so in the case of AIDA, as performing systematic analyses of what the "IOR School" describes as the "policy space". (In Chapter 8 I shall introduce the term "decision situation".) The point of such an analysis is evidently to ensure that the alternatives include the one that best suits the situation. To this end, in AIDA decision areas are defined as exhaustive sets of options. Strategies include all feasible sets of decisions, one from each decision area. Like it or not, the strategy emerging from a comparative evaluation of these sets must be regarded as optimal. Davidoff and Reiner were shown to recognise this as the purpose of systematically generating alternatives as early as 1962. They, too, were criticised for drawing inappropriate distinctions, nevertheless, around optimisation.

But the "IOR School" is reluctant to talk in terms of optimisation or rationality. (See the reply by Friend, 1983, to an earlier demonstration of the roots of the "IOR School" in the rational model by Faludi and Mastop, 1982.) Optimisation is implied nevertheless. It is useless to protest that we cannot be sure whether a strategy is in fact optimal. The "IOR School" itself shows how one can either reduce, or live with, uncertainties. Refined notions of optimality-coming from decision theory-comprise both goals achievement *and* probability scores (see Davidoff and Reiner, discussed in Section 3.1). It is well understood, therefore, that optimality includes an appreciation of uncertainties, as well as recognising that one's idea of what is optimal may change as new information becomes available.

Nor is it an argument against the rational model that "one man's meat is the other man's poison", so that no generally accepted optimum can even be said to exist. The issue is adequately covered by the notion of uncertainty concerning values. This, too, has been recognised by Meyerson and Banfield. The point is that the "agency-centred view" is so defined that strategies are always seen from subjective points of view, and it is only from such a point of view that optimality makes any sense at all. This will be taken further in Chapter 8 where I show that rationality implies a-subjective-definition of the decision situation.

No, in thinking that the rational model becomes defunct in the face of uncertainty, the "IOR School" has gone astray. The reason is that it wrongly identifies it with the fallacious assumption that certain knowledge can be found on which to base recommendations. The model does not entail it, and the recognition of manifold uncertainties in planning does not justify our abandoning it. It entails exactly what Friend (1983), in his reply quoted above, claims for strategic choice by describing it as "rationality-seeking", rather than rational:

a concern to keep moving towards greater rationality and rigor, against whatever obstacles, is the only way of developing a fuller understanding of the scope and limitations of rational methods in a process which must always rest on foundations of an inherently political nature (p. 69).

This is perfectly compatible with the rational planning model as here defined.

The onus of bridging the gap between them and the "IOR School" is, however, on academics. The coming chapters have as their purpose to help assimilating that school into the mainstream of planning thought.

Conclusions

The importance of the "IOR School" can hardly be overestimated. It helps us to appreciate the problems of practitioners. Also, it insists that planning is concerned with improving day-to-day decision-making. For those who assimilate its message planning theory will never be the same again.

But the "IOR School" is party also to the widespread misrepresentation of the rational planning model, wrongly identifying it with the quest for certainty. Protestations to the contrary, an essential relationship exists between their message and the rational model. Neither does that model stand or fall with the availability of certain knowledge; nor is it necessarily wedded to plan-making as a distinct activity, involving expertise of a rarefied kind, as the. systems approach is.

The rejection of model-building of this kind we can follow. But the "IOR School" does engage in some model-building of its own, except that what is being modelled is different. Like Low (1982), who has been quoted as recommending personal construct theory, this school makes models of what is in the decision-makers' minds, like the "cognitive maps" constructed as of late by Eden et al. (1983). AIDA, in particular, makes maps of our thoughts so that we can better use what we know already, and know what we still need to know at the same time.

References

Ackoff, R. L. (1962) *Scientific Method*, John Wiley, New York.

Batey, P. W. J. and Breheney, M. J. (1982) "The history of planning methodology: a framework for the assessment of Anglo-American theory and practice", *Reading Geographical Papers*, No. 79, University of Reading.

Bellush, J. and Hausknecht, M. (1966) "Entrepeneurs and urban renewal", *Journal of the American Institute of Planners*, **32**, 289-97.

Broady, M. (1968) *Planning for People*, Bedford Square Press, London.

Bross, I. D. (1953) *Design for Decision*, Macmillan, London.

Bunker, R. (1973) "Making choices and taking decisions in local government", *Proceedings of the International Congress, Copenhagen*, Volume 2, International Federation for Housing and Planning, The Hague, pp. 325-36.

Bunker, R. (1974) "Making decisions in St Albans", *Built Environment*, **3**, 316-18.

Centre for Environmental Studies (1970) "The LOGIMP experiment", Information Paper 25, London.

Chadwick, G. A. (1978; 1st edition 1970) *A Systems View of Planning*, Pergamon Press, Oxford.

Chapin, F. S. and Kaiser, E. J. (1979) *Urban Land Use Planning*, University of Illinois Press, Champaign, Ill.

Cooke, P. N. (1983) *Theories of Planning and Spatial Development*, Hutchinson, London.

Daland, R. T. and Parker, J. A. (1962) "Roles of planners in urban development", in: *Urban Growth Dynamics*, eds F. S. Chapin and S. F. Weiss, John Wiley, New York, pp. 188-225.

Darke, R. (1983) "Procedural planning theory: explanation or control?", in : *Evaluating Urban Planning Efforts*, ed. I. Masser, Gower, Aldershot, Hants, pp. 16-35.

*Davidoff, P. (1965) "Advocacy and pluralism in planning", *Journal of the American Institute of Planners*, **31**, 331-8.

*Davidoff, P. and Reiner, T. A. (1962) "A choice theory of planning", *Journal of the American Institute of Planners*, **28**, 108-15.

Drake, M. (1975) "Aims, objectives and problems in structure planning methodology", in: *Research Paper 20: Aspects of Structure Planning in Britain*, eds M. Drake, B. McLoughlin, R. Thompson and J. Thornley, Centre for Environmental Studies, London, pp. 131-55.

Dunn, E. S. (1971) *Economic and Social Development*, Johns Hopkins University Press, Baltimore and London.

Eddison, T. (1973) *Local Government: Management and Corporate Planning*, Leonard Hill Books, London.

Eden, C., Jones, H. and Sims, D. (1983) *Messing About in Problems*, Pergamon Press, Oxford.

Etzioni, A. (1968) *The Activity Society*, Collier-Macmillan, London.

Faludi, A. (1978) *Essays in Planning Theory and Education*, Pergamon Press, Oxford.

Faludi, A. and Mastop, J. M. (1982) "The I. O. R.-School: the development of a planning methodology", *Environment and Planning B*, **9**, 241-56.

Friedmann, J. (1969) "Planning and societal action", *Journal of the American Institute of Planners*, **35**, 311-18.

Friend, J. K. (1983) "Reflections on rationality in strategic choice", *Environment and Planning B: Planning and Design*, **10**, 63-69.

Friend, J. and Hickling, A. (1987) *Planning under Pressure: the Strategic Choice Approach*, Pergamon Press, Oxford.

Friend, J. K. and Jessop, W. N. (1977; 1st edition 1969) *Local Government and Strategic Choice*, Pergamon Press, Oxford.

Friend, J. K., Power, J. M. and Yewlett, C. J. L. (1974) *Public Planning: the Inter-corporate Dimension*, Tavistock, London, New York.

Gans, H. J. (1968) *People and Plans: Essays on Urban Problems and Solutions*, Basic Books, New York.

Hayton, K. (1981) "A linear-programming land selection model for structure planning", *Regional Studies*, **15**, 425-37.

Healey, P. (1979) "Networking as a normative principle with particular reference to local government and land use planning", *Local Government Studies*, 5, 55-68.

Healey, P., McDougall, G. and Thomas, M. J. (1982) "Introduction", in: *Planning Theory: Prospects for the 1980s*, eds P. Healey, G. McDougall and M. J. Thomas, Pergamon Press, Oxford, pp. 1-22.

Hickling, A. (1974) *Managing Decisions*, Mantec, Rugby.

Hickling, A. (1975) *Aids to Strategic Choice*, Centre for Continuing Education, University of British Columbia, Vancouver.

Krueckeberg, D. A. (1970) "Review of J. K. Friend and W. N. Jessop, 'Local Government and Strategic Choice' ", *Journal of the American Institute of Planners*, 36, 69.

Lawrence, J. R. (1966) *Operational Research and the Social Sciences*, Tavistock, London, New York.

Lee, D. B. jr. (1973) "Requiem for large-scale models", *Journal of the American Institute of Planners*, 39, 163-78.

Lindblom, C. E. (1965) *The Intelligence of Democracy: Decision Making Through Mutual Adjustment*, Free Press, New York.

Low, N. (1982) "Beyond general systems theory: a constructivist perspective", *Urban Studies*, 19, 221-33.

Luckmann, J. (1967) "An approach to the management of design", *Operational Research Quarterly*, 18, 345-58.

McDougall, G. (1983) "The interactional approach to organisations and planning: a critique", in: *Evaluating Urban Planning Efforts*, ed. I. Masser, Gower, Aldershot, Hants, pp. 36-53.

Michael, D. N. (1973) *On Learning to Plan: and Planning to Learn*, Jossey-Bass, San Francisco.

Openshaw, S. (1975) "An alternative approach to structure planning: the structure plan decision making model (SPDM)", *Planning Outlook*, 17, 10-26.

Openshaw, S. and Whitehead, P. T. (1977) "Decision-making in local plans: the DOT-methodology and a case-study", *Town Planning Review*, 48, 29-41.

Openshaw, S. and Whitehead, P. T. (1978) "Structure planning using a decision optimizing technique", *Town Planning Review*, 49, 486-501.

Openshaw, S. and Whitehead, P. T. (1980) "A rejoinder to Willis and Thompson", *Town Planning Review*, 51, 71-5.

Rabinovitz, F. F. (1969) *City Politics and Planning*, Atherton Press, New York.

Robinson, I. M. (1972) *Decision-making in Urban Planning*, Sage, Beverly Hills, CA.

Rosenhead, J. (1980a) "Planning under uncertainty. 1: The inflexibility of methodologies", *Journal of the Operational Research Society*, 31, 209-16.

Rosenhead, J. (1980b) "Planning under uncertainty. 2: A methodology for robustness analysis", *Journal of the Operational Research Society*, 31, 331-41.

Stanford, J. H. (1970) "Why planners fail", in: *A Geography of Urban Places*, eds R. G. Putnam, F. J. Taylor and Ph. G. Kettle, McHuren, Toronto, pp. 348-52.

Stewart, J. D. (1971) *Management in Local Government: a Viewpoint*, Charles Knight, London.

Sutton, A., Hickling, A. and Friend, J. K. (1977) "The analysis of policy options in structure plan preparation", Internal Paper IOR/932, Institute for Operational Research, Coventry.

Webber, M. M. (1963) "Comprehensive planning and social responsibility: towards an AIP consensus on the profession's role and purpose", *Journal of the American Institute of Planners*, 29, 232-41; see also A. Faludi (ed.) (1973) *A Reader in Planning Theory*, Pergamon Press, Oxford, pp. 95-112.

Wedgewood-Oppenheim, F. (1972a) "Planning under uncertainty", *Local Government Studies*, 2, 53-65.

Wedgewood-Oppenheim, F. (1972b) "The strategic choice approach to planning", *Proceedings of the PTRC Seminar, 17-19 May, 1972*, Planning and Transport Research and Computation Company Ltd., London, pp. 1-5.

* Included in Faludi, A. (ed.) (1973) *A Reader in Planning Theory*, Pergamon Press, Oxford.

CHAPTER 7

Parallel Developments

WITH hindsight, the IOR message seems obvious and could not have escaped others. Which parallel developments exist?

There are *The sceptics*, who labour uncertainty and complexity in planning. The *Humanistic planners* emphasise communicative aspects, which are a development of the planning-as-learning model, paying special attention to the personal qualities of planners. *Implementation studies* address the apparent ineffectiveness of planning as indicated by widespread departures from plans.

7.1 The sceptics

The works discussed have in common the rejection of optimisation which, since Meyerson and Banfield, is at the core of the rational planning model. The aim here is (a) to show parallels with the "IOR School", and (b) to demonstrate that, much as with that school, the sceptics are over-reacting.

"If planning is everything, maybe it's nothing?"

Wildavsky (1973) argues: (a) if it is judged by its results in terms of control over the future, planning has little or no effect; (b) modifications to the concept of planning taking account of such problems make it indistinguishable from ordinary decision-making. He might have referred to the strategic choice approach, which is why I discuss his article.

With its provocative title, it is referred to frequently (for instance: Reade, 1983); but Alexander (1981) complains that it has never received the critical attention which it deserves. He shows that Wildavsky argues from the particular (national planning) to the general (all planning). Also, in order to prove that planning has little effect, one would have to compare it with situations where no planning takes place at all, which Wildavsky does not do. Lastly he wrongly assumes that we can opt for or against planning, but it is "as universal and natural as breathing" (p. 134).

My own comments are complementary. I discuss planning's poor record in terms of control over the future more fully in Section 7.3. Suffice it to say that my criterion of success in planning is whether it can inform day-to-day decision-making. A plan can inform-and improve!-decision-making without being followed during implementation.

Concerning Wildavsky's second point, he argues convincingly against long-term comprehensive planning and hints at what a realistic form of planning would be. Obviously, he knows as much as the "IOR School", that real-life planning is adaptive:

Life is full of small corrections. Rarely is it possible to pursue objectives on a once-and-for-all basis. Relative success in meeting goals depends on new actions in response to changing circumstances. Learning, adjustments, adaptation are the keys to accomplishment (p. 134).

But he alleges that adjusting strategies is the opposite of planning. Though a "virtue", it "smacks of *ad hoc* decisionmaking" (p. 135). The recurring point, alluded to in the title of his article, is that such reasonable adaptations are indistinguishable from ordinary decision-making.

Wildavsky makes some play also of conflict-recognised already by Meyerson and Banfield to affect planning. Owing to conflict,

intention evaporates as a useful criterion for judging the success of planning. The planners lose their hold over intention; it is no longer immutable but problematic, a subject for bargaining, a counter in the flux of events. The stage shifts from the intentions specified in the plan to a multitude of actors whose intentions are alleged to be the real ones. The success of planning depends entirely on whose plan one has in mind (p. 140).

Why does Wildavsky juxtapose this, no doubt realistic, view to an impossible ideal? His answer is that, by "making planning manageable it appears we have made it indistinguishable from ordinary processes of decision. Planning has been rescued by diminishing, if not entirely obliterating, the difference between it and everyday decisionmaking" (p. 141). But why not settle for "diminishing" rather than "obliterating"? That would allow for planning adding an extra dimension to ordinary decision-making (as the "IOR School" would have it), without making the claim of replacing it altogether. In his critique, Alexander, too, pleads for precisely the adaptive ("tentative") style which Wildavsky regards as no different from ordinary action.

This will not substitute inaction for action … but will attempt when possible to articulate implementation in "small doses", to reduce the risks of unanticipated impacts and enable the evaluation of effects, rather than as one "big bang". This approach is constrained, of course, by the inherent indivisibilities of programme economies, infrastructure and physical facility characteristics (Alexander, 1981, pp. 139-40).

It is Wildavsky's privilege to define planning his way. We can console ourselves with the knowledge that adaptations to practice like Alexander's and Friend and Jessop's are reasonable in his eyes. Also, in passing, he gives away what he really thinks ought to happen: attending to the consequences of acting in one way rather than another. This occurs where he discusses the rational planning model. He claims that it puts too much emphasis on "adherence to universal norms rather than on the consequences of acting in one way instead of another. Attention is directed to the internal qualities of the decisions and not to their external effects" (p. 130). But which universal norms does he mean? He mentions efficiency. But that implies precisely what he says it does not: attending to the consequences of actions, so as to be able to compare them and choose the one with the most favourable ratio between costs and benefits-which is what efficiency means. Be this as it may, this "consequentialism" will be shown in Chapter 8 to be the basic on which we can reconstruct the "IOR School" message around the notion of rational planning.

"Permissive planning" and the rational planning model

The term "permissive planning" comes from Webber (1968, 1969). Written whilst he was in Britain to advise on the development of Milton Keynes, the main thrust of these articles is directed against the "engineering style of planning" and the imposition of (elitist) standards. It advocates the market as an, in many instances superior, alternative, prompting Heywood (1969), in an article-length reply, to emphasise the disastrous consequences which permissive planning would have, in the British context anyway. As regards rational planning, though, these articles do not yet show the scepticism of their successors (Rittel and Webber, 1973; Webber, 1978, 1983; see also Webber's criticisms of systems analysis in Section 3.3).

Rittel and Webber claim that the test of efficiency (which since Meyerson and Banfield, has been regarded as synonymous to rationality) is being challenged by equity considerations, and that consensus is being eroded by a growing differentiation of publics. They point also at "waves of repercussions generated by a problem-solving action directed to any node in the network, and we are no longer surprised to find it inducing problems of greater severity at some other node" (p. 159). So planning problems are "wicked". What is clear is that Rittel and Webber would applaud strategic choice as one of the argumentative approaches of the "second generation" (see Section 3.3) they allude to. The same affinity with the "IOR School" is evident in Webber (1978), where he argues for abandoning the search for right solutions. Planning is rather a "cognitive style". In effect, Webber suggests the adaptations to the concept of planning which Wildavsky has been shown to reject as making nonsense of the very idea:

The growing involvement of lay groups bodes well for the prospect of a politically responsive mode of planning. It suggests that an effective style of planning does not call for plans that represent the right answers, rather it calls for procedures which might help plural politics reach decisions in acceptable ways. In that idiom, planning would become an integral aspect of governing, rather than a separate function of government. Its special task would be to help assure that all parties' voices are heard; that all available evidence, theory, and arguments are weighed; that potentially useful options are considered and evaluated; that latent consequences and their distribution among the many publics are identified and assessed (p. 158).

None of this means that planning is value-neutral. Rather, all manner of value positions-especially those of minorities-should be explored, hence Webber's term "difference paradigm of planning". "In this image, permissive planning seeks to formulate those minimal procedural rules that then permit to foster difference, being somewhat indifferent to the substance of those differences" (p. 159). It fosters open argument, "creating the means for inducing debate and the media through which contending parties might effectively engage each other" (*ibid*.). As with constitutionally guaranteed due process, "so too would planners promoting the permissive style seek to frame the few warrantees assuring that all groups' interests are heard" (*ibid*).

Webber (1983) focuses on developing countries and central planning in ways reminiscent of Meyerson (1956), who emphasised the information role of planning. (See also the notion of "strategic planning" discussed in Chapter 4.) He argues that developing nations are being misled by the rational planning model. It

involves preparing portraits of desired future conditions within and among the numerous sectors of the society and economy. Those end-state portraits are usually accompanied by time-sequenced programs-prescribed actions of various kinds needed to bring about the desired future conditions, within and among sectors (p. 91).

His views are similar to those of van Gunsteren (1976), who has clearly been influenced by the Berkeley intellectual climate where Rittel, Webber and Wildavsky teach:

I think that the classical-rational planning model is fundamentally flawed, primarily because it assumes rationality and certainty where neither is possible. ... Neither planners nor anybody else knows enough to be able to do what the development-planning doctrine claims they can do. ... Further, the model assumes unitary collective purposes ... It then relies upon unitary plans ... thereby denying the fact that plural publics seek plural purposes, many of them mutually incompatible.

That error is doubly serious, for to obstruct the separate pursuits of competing objectives is ... to reject the prospect that a better collective outcome might be realized through the simultaneous pursuit of multiple ends/means (Webber, 1983, p. 96).

Rather, all agencies, public and private, should conduct "rigorous technical analyses and, within the constraints of available resources, ... formulate their own plans favoring their own purposes, each virtually independently of the others" (*ibid*.), which is a re-statement of the philosophy of "permissive planning". Planning's role is then that of a central information agency-a "cognitive style"-striving "to promote planning in all agencies of government and in all private organizations, for it champions belief in the instrumental power of ideas, knowledge, analysis, design, and planning" (p. 97).

Webber reiterates the analogy between the constitution and planning, paying attention also to mechanisms for taking decisions, like majority votes, jury decisions, the market place. They rely on procedural rules to approximate correct decisions. In all this, the parallel with the "IOR message" is striking. So is that with Popper's classical argument against "holistic planning" advanced several decades before (see Popper, 1966; first published 1944/45; Popper, 1962, 1st edition 1945; see also Faludi, 1986):

However workable planning may be within a given organization or sector ..., it is nevertheless impossible to integrate program plans for all sectors. I will also argue that, even if it were possible to do so, that it would be a mistake. All plans are inherently susceptible to error, and integrated plans are susceptible to large and compounded error (Webber, 1978, p. 98).

He claims the classic model suffers also from lack of flexibility, and pleads for adaptive planning by a multiplicity of actors. "And, where large collective decisions must be taken, far better that they be made against contingency plans, rather than fixed and unitary ones" (*ibid.*). Then comes the opposite of McLoughlin's heroic view of the planner as a "helmsman" (see Section 3.3): "Integration does not require a single steersman or a single map. Coordination occurs, perhaps even best, as the resultant of the vectors of all agents' actions" (*ibid.*).

Summing up, Webber characterises the preferred style of planning as one that is

essentially procedural at the center but substantive in the thousands of relatively autonomous public and private organizations at the periphery, that is permissive rather than regulatory, that promotes argumentation and innovation in its search for betterment, and that is tolerant of the deviancy and differences that are the generators of development (p. 99).

These views-closely meshed with substantive ideas concerning settlement patterns as forming a "non-place urban realm" (see Webber, 1963, 1968, 1969)- put Webber apart from planning theorists committed to a strong role for planning-their rhetoric about involving people notwithstanding. But his polemic against rationality seems a reaction against exaggerated claims by systems analysts.

Uncertainty rediscovered

Christensen (1985) discusses four possible situations: well-understood technology and agreed-upon goals (which is when optimisation is called for); unknown technology, but still agreed-upon goals; well-understood technology but no consensus; problematic knowledge and no consensus.

Under planning for unknown technology and agreed goals Christensen envisages a "trial-and-error" and a "planning-as-learning" approach. The former is the opposite of the classic rational response to uncertainty:

Instead of trying to predict as many consequences of a potential action as possible, the planner acts first and then waits to see what consequences actually occur. If they are acceptable, then the action is deemed workable and may be repeated. If the consequences are unacceptable, the planner tries a new variation. ... Over time, this process tends to generate knowledge of workable means and thus reduces uncertainty. In this incremental, adaptive process, the planner is a pragmatist and adjuster (p. 67).

As regards uncertainty caused by lack of consensus, Christensen quotes Davidoff (1965, see Section 3.2) and Friedmann (1973), the latter for his emphasis on the interpersonal dimension of decision-making. His work is discussed in the section which follows. A second approach "derives from a more scientific tradition that tries to discover means more self-consciously. ... (It) treats uncertainty ... with conscious experimentation" (*ibid.*).

Planning for unknown technology and unknown goals (Rittel and Webber's wicked problems) presents the greatest challenge. It asks for compelling formulations so as to provide stable motivation for resolving problems. This may come from a single planner or from an interactive process. Such problem finding ... may require planners and participants to reformulate the problem: casting the problem in a new light so that people can agree that it is the right problem to tackle. To do that planners need insight both into the nature of problems and into political forces to ensure that participants agree as to what the problem is. When reformulation is successful, it reduces uncertainty about goals and simplifies conditions so that planners and participants can focus on technical aspects of how to solve the problem (p. 68).

One is reminded of Harris's disagreement with Scott and Roweis (see Section 5.4). Harris would regard this problem-finding as a political task. Be this as it may, if successful, problem-finding thrusts us into the area where only the means are uncertain.

Alternatively, problem finding may require planners and participants to sift through and articulate confused, vague goals to show how debate could focus on competing goals that already have effective technologies. This way the problem is articulated as conflict (p. 68).

This thrusts us into the area where technologies are known but consensus is lacking.

With her strategies fitting different situations, Christensen takes in effect the contingency approach referred to in Section 4.1. In attending to uncertainties she follows the line also of the "IOR School". But, neglecting uncertainties caused by the interrelatedness of various areas of choice, she does not specifically address what Friend and Jessop identify as strategic choice, or planning (see Section 6.1). Rather, her argument concerns problem-solving generally. In this book, I draw a line between problem-solving/decision-making in general and planning as attending to the interrelations between decisions.

So the parallels to the "IOR School" in the literature concern adaptations of the concept of planning, and the rejection of the rational planning model. But that model is not based (a) on the assumption of there being certain knowledge; (b) nor on that of a pre-existing consensus. Like the "IOR School", the authors quoted do not seem to appreciate this point.

They have one other thing in common. Their approach represents what Rittel and Webber (1973) have already been quoted as describing as approaches of the "second generation", relying on argumentation. Rafter (1983), quoting Wildavsky (1979) and Lindblom and Cohen (1979), describes it as a revised theory of policy analysis. It employs interactive methods (e.g. bargaining) and bases solutions on the "ordinary knowledge" of decision-makers instead of the scientific knowledge of experts. "In other words, policy relevancy, social interaction, and qualitative data are key features of the 'new theory' of public policy analysis" (p. 367). This is true also for the works discussed in the next section.

7.2 The humanistic planners

Reacting to allegedly technocratic approaches, some authors turned towards "humanistic planning". Does it pose an alternative to the rational planning model?

Humanistic planners differ from the sceptics in that, given more empathy between the participants of the planning process, they are optimistic about planning. *Retracking America* (Friedmann, 1973) represents a good example.

There are concerns which it has in common with *Planning Theory* (see Friedmann, 1974).

Friedmann describes the influences he was under whilst studying at Chicago, working at the Tennessee Valley Authority and in various countries overseas. He quotes liberally from his earlier articles (some of them referred to in Chapter 4 as shaping my own thinking). His central notion, "transactive planning", is remarkably like the views of the "IOR School". Like that school, however, in rejecting rationality, Friedmann overshoots his target. We get some inkling of this as early as in the "Preface", where Friedmann contrasts Taylorism with transactive planning. Under the former,

the individual person was treated as an instrument for the attainment of an extrinsic goal. He was reduced to complete passivity: his behavior was to be engineered to conform with the plan. The transactive planning of the future, on the other hand, is deeply rooted in face-to-face, person-centred relations within small groups. If Taylor's discipline was the ratio of resources to final product, the discipline of transactive planning is the radical openness required by dialogue. In dialogue, the object, man, disappears and is transformed into an active subject, the protagonist of history (p. xvi).

Like Webber, Friedmann regards planning as an "attitude of mind". He arrives at this conclusion after a bleak analysis of the professional role of the planner. His TVA experience taught him that planning agencies easily become bureaucratised. In "Planning, progress, and social values", he writes that, to

be truly successful, planning must become a way of life, a way of feeling, thinking, and action on all levels of the social process. ... In the broadest sense, a planning community is a community where thought at the level of planning becomes second nature to every member. It remains a pluralistic community in that it allows full freedom of expression and the pursuit of individual goals within the framework permitted by the continuing interest of the whole (quoted in Friedmann, 1973, p. 112).

Closely related is his rejection of the distinction between planning and implementation. He describes how shocked he was that the TVA did not have a plan. From this he concluded that the

exercise of planning though is infinitely more important than a neatly published book entitled: *Six Year Plan*. If we agree to accept this view, planning appears as flexible and sensitive an instrument as reason or thought itself, adaptable to any situation, capable of dealing with any contingency that may arise (Friedmann, 1969, quoted in Friedmann, 1973, p. 9).

He is opposed also to planning by experts. They should see their calling in their participation in the wider enterprise of societal self-guidance. But none of this requires rejecting the rational planning model. Like the "sceptics", Friedmann claims to give the classic decision-model an unlamented burial nevertheless.

Planning, it is said, leads to the formulation of plans; implementation is concerned with carrying them out. The intervening critical step is a decision. Planners prepare the plans and propose them to the relevant deciders who, after due deliberation, choose the alternative preferred by them and take measures that will make their choice effective. If plans fail to be implemented, it is because the deciders ignored the proposals made to them, preferring their own counsel.

The widespread notion that plans *ought* to get accepted and that, when they are not, the failure is one of communication, rests on the technocratic fallacy that planners' proposals are inherently superior to actions that result from the unaided decisions of non-planners.

(But) it is possible to assert that any action that is deliberate is also to a certain degree planned. The problem is no longer how to make decisions more "rational", but how to improve the *quality of the action* (Friedmann, 1969, p. 311, quoted in Friedmann, 1973, p. 19).

This does not concern the rational planning model, however. Rather, the issue is whether planning and implementation should be separate. Here, Friedmann overstates his case. Since Meyerson and Banfield and Davidoff and Reiner, assessments of the means of, and constraints on, implementation have always formed part of planning. Admittedly, awareness of this has not always been strong, as we have seen, and plan-making has occupied the centre of the stage in planning thought. Also, I agree that the point of planning is to improve action. That is the IOR message. Chapter 8 shows the decision-centred view, too, to focus on action taken now. But this cannot mean that we abandon plans or planning. On the contrary, the need for them will be shown to arise out of the requirements of action.

Another parallel with the "IOR School" is noteworthy. Friedmann says successful planning depends "in large measure on the planner's skill in managing interpersonal relations" (p. 20). This is at the heart of transactive planning, which is a process of mutual learning. It is a response also to the two-fold crisis of valuing and of knowing. Friedmann dwells over the disruptions which result from social change. The complexity of post-industrial society requires increasingly flexible and interactive knowledge. He suggests also that the two-fold crisis requires a learning model based on the distinction between personal and processed knowledge. The former is "limited to the experiences that one has had. Because of this, it is inadequate as an exclusive basis for action" (p. 99). The latter "is built up from symbols that stand for particular dimensions of reality, and is expressed in the form of models that can be formally communicated, critically examined, and revised on the basis of new observations" (p. 101). But it is not what many people think:

a stock of verities, solid and permanent, true knowledge of the whole, deterministic and complete, a seamless web, pressing forward into the future, an honest guide to action. If it were all these things, central guidance would be easy, and personal knowledge would be clearly revealed as an inferior form of knowing. But it is not, and we are therefore obliged to find some way of relating personal to processed knowledge on quite equal terms, using each to correct and supplement the other. And we must find a way to introduce into systems of societal guidance a mode of knowing that values the use of a diversity of models, an approach that is frankly experimental and self-correcting. ... I shall refer to the resulting process as *mutual learning* (p. 106).

The transactive style of planning is the one which is conducive to this mutual learning, based on the strength of the argument that

communication is not a matter of translating the abstract and highly symbolic language of the planner into the simpler and more experience-related vocabulary of the client. The real solution involves a restructuring of the basic relationship between planner and client.

The difficulties of relating these two methods of knowing to each other reside not only in their different foci of attention and degrees of practical relevance ..., but also in language. The planner's language is conceptual and mathematical, consciously drained of the lifeblood of human intercourse in its striving for scientific objectivity.

The language of clients lacks the formal restrictions that hedge in planning documents. It, too, employs a jargon to speed communications, but the jargon will be experience-rather than concept-related (pp. 172-3).

Transactive planning based on personal relations should overcome this. "Processed knowledge would thus be joined to action through a series of personal transactions that would bring the two worlds into conjunction. Each would thus be modified in turn." In a vein which shows Friedmann's radically humanistic stance, he exclaims.

The moral values of the planner and his client stand at the centre of this new relation, so that advice and its acceptance will be based on the degree of confidence one has in the position of the other. ... Transactive planning rests essentially on the ideas of human worth and reciprocity (pp. 111-12).

Once more Friedmann comes close to the "IOR School" where he argues that the point of looking into the future is to influence decisions in the present. This means to perceive the future, "not with the eyes of the planner, but with those of the man of action" (p. 137). This is because "men of action have in fact little interest in the future, except for a short stretch of time beyond the present" (*ibid.*).

Grabow and Heskin (1973) provide another example of the humanistic school. They propose a synthesis between abstract control implicit in rational-comprehensive planning and the spontaneous expression of individual wants. Their new paradigm is "evolutionary experimentation" (p. 111). They assert the presence also of a natural link between the individual and the evolution of organic life. It exists within and between us as an "ecological ethic" or "organic value system". Like Friedman's transactive planning, their evolutionary experimentation requires decentralisation.

A distinct school of "humanistic planners" concentrates on blockages in the planning process. Their message is that practitioners act on tacit principles which lead to ineffectiveness. Argyris and Schön (1978) distinguish between espoused theory and theory-in-use. The latter includes assumptions about interpersonal relationships which affect success in problem-solving. The common theory-in-use is defensive, assuming scarcity and the inevitability of conflict. It aims at maximising personal gain. Based on such ideas, Schön (1982, 1983) offers an understanding of how professionals think when operating with uncertain knowledge and conflicting values. It is grounded in observations of practitioners at work (see also Bolan, 1980), but is mainly a normative argument about good practice. Theories are developed through understanding particular situations. (For a critique see McDougall, 1983.)

De Neufville (1983) affirms that the notion of technical rationality based on the dominant positivistic epistemology misrepresents professional practice as the application of knowledge. This works in law and medicine, which have unambiguous goals, but not in city planning where the professional task is not so much to solve problems but to frame them so that they can be solved (see also Christensen, 1985, discussed above). It is a task of developing knowledge in action. Hypothesising and *ad-hoc* experimentation are part of this process.

Hoch (1984) shows that the rational planning model and the "humanistic planners" alike are rooted in the pragmatism of John Dewey (see also Blanco, 1985). He claims that, at rock-bottom, pragmatism represents an instrumental approach and ignores power. (See also the review of Argyris, 1982, by Baum, 1983, p. 238.) That, of course, is the essence of the "new substantivist challenge" discussed in Section 5.3. Rather than reopening that debate, the purpose of this section has been to draw parallels between Friedmann, the "IOR School", and also my planning principles (see Section 4.2) advocating open discussion and participation.

7.3 Implementation studies

A range of works distinguishes itself by focusing on implementation. Pressman and Wildavsky (1973) gave the lead with their study on how federal programmes fared in Oakland, California. Since then, implementation studies are mushrooming. A major British contribution-"unquestionably the best of the policy-implementation works" (Alexander, 1983, p. 104)-comes from the *School of Advanced Urban Studies* at the University of Bristol: *Policy & Action-Essays on the Implementation of Public Policy* (Barrett and Fudge, 1981a). How does this literature relate to the "IOR School"?

There is a remarkable convergence. There is agreement, for instance, that planning and implementation involve negotiations, and that success at the bargaining table depends upon inter-personal skills. That, of course, merely restates what the "humanistic planners" are saying.

Barrett and Fudge's work is yet another instance of academics doing less than justice to the "IOR School". There is but one reference to strategic choice in the introductory review (Barrett and Fudge, 1981b, p. 7). Associating it with the drive for administrative efficiency, it reflects inadequate appreciation of its message. The summary (Fudge and Barrett, 1981) ignores Friend *et al.* (1974) on networks. Maybe this is because, its orientation to practice notwithstanding, this is an "academic" book. Alexander (1983), for instance, has only the one criticism, that it "offers the promise of better understanding, but whether this is the kind of understanding which will enable a more successful transformation of intentions into action is still open to question" (p. 104). In the case of Barrett and Fudge, the neglect of the "IOR School" is remarkable for three reasons.

First, they advocate that implementation be studied in the manner of the "IOR School", by looking at what actually happens in practice. Like the pragmatism of that school, their perspective on implementation arises directly out of this approach:

This kind of action perspective takes "what is done" as central, focuses attention on the behaviour or actions of groups and individuals and the determination of that behaviour, and seeks to examine the degree to which action relates to policy, rather than assuming it to follow from policy. From this perspective, implementation (or action) may be regarded as a series of *responses*: to ideological commitment, to environmental pressures, or to pressures from other agencies (groups) seeking to influence or control action (pp. 12-13).

The second reason for why their neglect of the "IOR School" is astonishing is their rejection of the conventional view of implementation as "putting policy into effect"-the managerial perspective whereby

the problems of implementation are defined in terms of co-ordination, control or obtaining "compliance" with policy. Such a policy-centred or "top-down" view of the process treats implementers as "agents" for policy-makers and tends to play down issues such as power relations, conflicting interests and value systems between individuals and agencies responsible for making policy and those responsible for taking action (p. 4).

Barrett and Fudge complain that policy analysts have tended to equate policy decisions with action and point out that "policy may be a response to pressures and problems experienced on the ground. Equally, policy may be developed from specific innovations, that is, action precedes policy. Not all action relates to a specific or explicit policy" (p. 12).   —

The "IOR School", too, rejects the notion of plans imposing themselves and replaces it by a view of planning as assisting ordinary decision-making. Indeed, Barrett and Fudge use terms which might easily have been culled from that school: "If we take implementation to describe the day-by-day working of an agency . . . , then policy-making may be seen as attempts to structure this operation in a way which limits the discretionary freedom of other actors" (p. 25; on a similar view of policies as "potentialities" see Majone and Wildavsky, 1978, pp. 1080 and 114).

The third reason why the neglect of the "IOR School" is surprising is the role ascribed to negotiations:

in many instances-especially in the public policy field-those upon whom action depends are *not* in any hierarchical association with those making policy. By definition, public policy is often aimed at directing or intervening in the activities of private interests and agencies. Implementation agencies will thus, in many instances, be autonomous or semi-autonomous, with their own interests and priorities to pursue and their own policy-making role (p. 12).

They explain this with the example of a house-extension. The emphasis in the literature on "implementation capacity" (for instance: Mazmanian and Sabatier, 1981) relates to the marshalling of resources, for instance the buying of the land and obtaining the services of a builder. But "gaining acceptance (or consensus) for the proposal or avoiding conflict and resistance from the next door neighbours is quite a different matter" (p. 21). Both involve bargaining:

Without total control over resources, agencies and the whole implementation "environment", those wanting to do something may be forced to compromise their original intentions in order to get any action at all.

If implementation is defined as "putting policy into effect", that is, action in conformance with policy, then compromise will be seen as policy failure. But if implementation is regarded as "getting something done", then *performance* rather than conformance is the central objective, and compromise a means of achieving performance albeit at the expense of some original intentions. Emphasis thus shifts to the *interaction* between policy-makers and implementers, with negotiation, bargaining and compromising forming central elements in a process that might be characterised as "the art of the possible" (p. 21).

Barrett and Fudge review the literature on negotiation-as indicated, without mentioning *Public Planning-the Inter-corporate Dimension*. Of course, being aware of academic disputes, they go beyond the "IOR School". There is more attention to the structural determinants of action, especially in the final review, emphasising the need also for linking various levels of analysis in ways which remind of the proposal for a "combined paradigm of planning theory" (see Chapter 5). They raise the issue also of the effectiveness of plans and policies.

This relates to the radical implications of the "IOR School" (see Section 6.3). Implementation

may be seen either from a top-down or a bottom-up perspective. It is the former which is most frequently identified with policy-making: the setting of parameters (perhaps by means of the law) by actors at the "top", who have the power to constrain those "lower down". But we may also identify the phenomenon the other way round, when lower level actors take decisions which effectively limit hierarchical influence, pre-empt top decision-making, or alter "policies" (p. 25).

Majone and Wildavsky (1978) also distinguish two views: "policy shapes implementation" versus "implementation shapes policy". The latter is more like real-life planning. Such distinctions have been drawn also by Berman (1980), Jenkins (1978) and Stone (1980). Elmore (1979/80) develops a similar line of argument. Distinguishing two approaches to "implementation analysis"-in fact, approaches to planning-he comes to views similar to those to be presented in the next chapter:

Forward mapping is the strategy that comes most readily to mind when one thinks about how a policy-maker might try to affect the implementation process. It begins at the top of the process with as clear a statement as possible of the policy-maker's intent. ... At the bottom of the process, one states ... what a satisfactory outcome would be, measured in terms of the original statement of intent (p. 602).

This assumes that policy-makers exercise determinate control over implementation. In fact there is considerable discretion, as the analysis of zoning in Chapters 12 and 13 will also show. Backward mapping recognises this.

The logic of backward mapping is ... the opposite of forward mapping. It begins not at the top of the implementation process but at the last possible stage, the point at which administrative actions intersect private choices. It begins not with a statement of intent, but with a statement of the specific behavior at the lowest level of the implementation process that generates the need for a policy. Only after that behavior is described does the analysis presume to state an objective; the objective is first stated as a set of organizational effects, or outcomes, that will result from these operations. Having established a relatively precise target at the lowest level of the system, the analysis backs up through the structure of implementing agencies, asking at each level two questions: What is the ability of this unit to affect the behavior that is the target of the policy? And what resources does this unit require in order to have that effect? (p. 605).

Elmore points out also that success, rather than being measured in terms of compliance with the policy-maker's intent, is predicated on estimates of the ability of actors on one level to influence actors on other levels. So, there are consequences for ex-post evaluation. Ex-post evaluation studies, too, tend to take a top-down perspective, regarding lack of compliance as evidence of failure and seeing flexibility as opportunism. In suggesting that plans or policies should prevail, they keep up the spirit-thought to have passed away-of blueprint planning. The widespread interest in monitoring perhaps signals the rearguard battle of this approach.

Conclusions

There is a substantial literature which bears resemblance with the "IOR School". The consensus can be summed up as follows: (1) Planning does not proceed rationally. The real process of planning is one of bargaining amongst interest groups. (2) The planner negotiates much like everybody else. In order to be successful he or she must be able to sustain his or her position in a highly political game. In order to be really helpful to his or her clients he or she must have a special understanding of, and also empathy for, their situation. Plans have no superior claim to be implemented. They form part of an intricate web of influences on on-going decision-making. Hopefully, decision-makers become better informed by making use of them, but that is all there is to plans.

References

Alexander, E. A. (1981) "If planning isn't everything, maybe it's something", *Town Planning Review*, **52**, 131-42.

Alexander, E. A. (1983) "Review of S. Barrett, C. Fudge, 'Policy & Action: Essays on the Implementation of Public Policy' ", *Journal of the American Planning Association*, **49**, 104.

Argyris, C. (1982) *Reasoning, Learning and Action: Individual and Organizational*, Jossey-Bass, San Francisco.

Argyris, C. and Schön, D. (1978) *Organizational Learning: a Theory of Action Perspective*, Addison-Wesley, Reading, Mass.

Barrett, S. and Fudge, C. (eds) (1981a) *Policy & Action: Essays on the Implementation of Public Policy*, Methuen, London and New York.

Barrett, S. and Fudge, C. (1981b) "Introductory review: examining the policy-action relationship", in: *Policy & Action: Essays in the Implementation of Public Policy*, eds S. Barrett and C. Fudge, Methuen, London and New York, pp. 3-32.

Baum, H. S. (1983) "Review of C. Argyris, 'Reasoning, Learning and Action: Individual and Organizational' ", *Journal of the American Planning Association*, **49**, 238-9.

Berman, P. (1980) "Thinking about programmed and adaptive implementation: matching strategies to situations", in: *Why Policies Succeed or Fail*, eds H. M. Ingram and D. E. Mann, Sage Publications, Beverly Hills and London.

Blanco, H. (1985) "Pragmatism, abduction, and wicked problems", *Berkeley Planning Journal*, **1**, 93-119.

Bolan, R. S. (1980) "The practitioner as theorist: the phenomenology of the professional episode", *Journal of the American Planning Association*, **46**, 261-74.

Christensen, K. S. (1985) "Coping with uncertainty in planning", *Journal of the American Planning Association*, **51**, 63-73.

*Davidoff, P. (1965) "Advocacy and pluralism in planning", *Journal of the American Institute of Planners*, **31**, 331-8.

Elmore, R. (1979/80) "Backward mapping: implementation research and policy decisions", *Political Science Quarterly*, **94**, 601-16.

Faludi, A. (1986) *Critical Rationalism and Planning Methodology*, Pion Press, London.

Friedmann, J. (1969) "Planning and societal action", *Journal of the American Institute of Planners*, **35**, 311-18.

Friedmann, J. (1973) *Retracking America: a Theory of Transactive Planning*, Doubleday Anchor, Garden City, New York.

Friedmann, J. (1974) "Review of A. Faludi, 'Planning Theory' ", *Regional Studies*, **8**, 311.

Friend, J. K., Power, J. M. and Yewlett, C. J. L. (1974) *Public Planning: the Inter-corporate Dimension*, Tavistock, London, New York.

Fudge, C. and Barrett, S. (1981) "Reconstructing the field of analysis", in: *Policy & Action: Essays on the Implementation of Public Policy*, eds S. Barrett and C. Fudge, Methuen, London, pp. 249-78.

Grabow, S. and Heskin, A. (1973) "Foundations for a radical concept of planning", *Journal of the American Institute of Planners*, **39**, 106-16.

Gunsteren, H. R. van (1976) *The Quest for Control: a Critique of the Rational-central-rule Approach in Public Affairs*, John Wiley, New York, London, Sydney and Toronto.

Hoch, C. J. (1984) "Doing good and being right", *Journal of the American Planning Association*, **50**, 335-45.

Heywood, P. R. (1969) "Plangloss: a critique of permissive planning", *Town Planning Review*, **40**, 251-62.

Jenkins, W. I. (1978) *Policy Analysis: a Political and Organizational Perspective*, Robertson, London.

Lindblom, C. E. and Cohen, D. K. (1979) *Usable Knowledge: Social Science and Social Problem Solving*, Yale University Press, New Haven and London.

Majone, G. and Wildavsky, A. (1978) "Implementation as evolution", in *Policy Studies Review Annual*, ed. H. E. Freeman, Sage, Beverly Hills and London, pp. 103-17.

Mazmanian, D. A. and Sabatier, P. A. (eds) (1981) *Effective Policy Implementation*, Lexington Books, Lexington, Mass.

McDougall, G. (1983) "The interactional approach to organisations and planning: a critique", in: *Evaluating Urban Planning Efforts*, ed. I. Masser, Gower, Aldershot, Hants, pp. 36-53.

*Meyerson, M. M. (1956) "Building the middle-range bridge for comprehensive planning", *Journal of the American Institute of Planners*, **22**, 58-64.

Neufville, J. I. de (1983) "The doldrums of planning theory", *Journal of Planning Education and Research*, **3**, 35-45.

Popper, K. R. (1961; first published 1944/45) *The Poverty of Historicism*, Routledge & Kegan Paul, London.

Popper, K. R. (1966; 1st edition 1945) *The Open Society and its Enemies* (2 volumes), Routledge & Kegan Paul, London.

Pressman, J. L. and Wildavsky, A. (1973) *Implementation: How Great Expectations in Washington are Dashed in Oakland*, University of California Press, Berkeley, Cal.

Rafter, D. O. (1983) "Review of T. N. Clark, 'Urban Policy Analysis: Directions for Future Research' ", *Journal of the American Planning Association*, **50**, 376-68.

Reade, E. J. (1983) "If planning is anything, maybe it can be identified", *Urban Studies*, **20**, 159-71.

Rittel, H. J. W. and Webber, M. M. (1973) "Dilemmas of a general theory of planning", *Policy Sciences*, **4**, 155-69.

Schön, D. A. (1982) "Some of what a planner knows", *Journal of the American Planning Association*, **48**, 352-64.

Schön, D. A. (1983) *The Reflective Practitioner: How Professionals Think in Action*, Basic Books, New York.

Stone, C. N. (1980) "The implementation of social programs: two perspectives", *Journal of Social Issues*, **36**, 13-34.

Webber, M. M. (1963) "Order in diversity: community without propinquity", in: *Cities and Space: The Future of Urban Land*, ed. L. Wingo, Jr, Johns Hopkins University Press, Baltimore, pp. 23-54.

Webber, M. M. (1964) "The urban place and the non-place urban realm", in: *Explorations into Urban Structure*, eds M. M. Webber *et al.* University of Pennsylvania Press, Philadelphia, pp. 79-153.

Webber, M. M. (1968) "Planning in an environment of change-Part I: Beyond the industrial age", *Town Planning Review*, **39**, 179-95.

Webber, M. M. (1969) "Planning in an environment of change: Part II: Permissive planning", *Town Planning Review*, **39**, 277-95.

Webber, M. M. (1978) "A difference paradigm for planning", in: *Planning Theory in the 1980s: a Search for Future Directions*, eds R. W. Burchell and R. W. Sternlieb, Centre for Urban Policy, Rutgers University, New Jersey, pp. 151-62.

Webber, M. M. (1983) "The myth of rationality: development planning reconsidered", *Environment and Planning B: Planning and Design*, **10**, 89-99.

Wildavsky, A. (1973) "If planning is everything, maybe it's nothing", *Policy Sciences*, **4**, 127-53.

Wildavsky, A. (1979) *Speaking Truth to Power*, Little, Brown, Boston.

* Included in Faludi, A. (1973) *A Reader in Planning Theory*, Pergamon Press, Oxford.

CHAPTER 8

The Decision-centred View
of Planning

THIS chapter completes the arguments of Part One. In it I forge a link between
the "IOR School" and the mainstream literature, and in particular that
concerned with the rational planning model. More is said about the debates
to which this relates under *Background*, below. There follows the
Reconstruction of the message of the "IOR School". Under *Implications* I
review the practical, and even more so the theoretical, consequences; and, in
Doctrine in planning, the role of substantive concepts. In *Planning
methodology is the name of the Game* I argue that the main concern of
planning theory is with *methodology* of planning on *a par* with the
methodology of science. Like the "IOR School" and parallel schools of
thought, the decision-centred view will be shown to be concerned primarily
with the rationality of ongoing action. Making plans forms part of this, but
their implementation is not an issue of supreme importance.

8.1 Background

Originally the idea of bridging the gap between the "IOR School" and
academia grew out of a study of local planning at Leiden in The Netherlands
and Oxford in England (Thomas *et al.*, 1983). In Leiden we found many
departures from plans which had previously been conceived. The usual reaction
(see Section 7.3) is to blame these on "implementation". But often those plans
had failed to meet the situation. This reminded us of *Local Government and
Strategic Choice*, where it says that "the significance of any planning activity
... will depend on the guidance it can give in the selection of appropriate
courses of action to deal with current circumstances" (Friend and Jessop, 1977,
pp. 110-11; see also Friedmann, 1973, quoted in Section 7.2). This led to the
twin concept of operational and planning decisions and explorations of
flexibility, to be discussed below.

   The second stimulus came when students called for assistance on a project
on which they were working. They had tried the linear approach-then popular
in The Netherlands-such as Davidoff and Reiner have been shown to advocate.
But they had found it impossible to formulate goals without at the same time

looking at alternatives. Indeed, since Meyerson and Banfield, we know that constraints must be well-understood from the start. As Rittel and Webber (1973, p. 161) state succinctly: "The information needed to *understand* a problem depends upon one's idea for *solving* it." Unless based on an appreciation of what the planning agency in question can *do* about them, starting with problems (see Needham, 1971) can be equally ineffective. I recommended that they analyse the *decisions* which might conceivably be taken in the wake of the plan. In this I followed the strategic choice approach-which this group then applied with extraordinary acumen. Their work was to spawn a programme of action research on strategic choice in The Netherlands (see Dekker and Mastop, 1979; Faludi and Mastop, 1982; Mastop, 1983).

The third stimulus came when I prepared a new course on planning theory. I dealt with the two criticisms of procedural planning theory described in Chapter 5: suspicion that it underrated subject matter; and the Marxist-inspired "new substantivist challenge". Attempting to clarify the issues, I identified respectively an object-, control- and decision-centred "view of planning", each defining planning differently (see Faludi, 1982). The control-centred view is a credible position, but not necessarily opposed to the decision-centred one. The object-centred view, on the other hand, is to be rejected (see Chapter 5). As we shall see, the decision-centred view combines the emphasis in *Planning Theory* on rationality with the message of the "IOR School".

8.2 Reconstruction

Understandably, planners tend to overemphasise plans. So the controversy around the rational planning model has concentrated on whether *making a plan* can and should be a rational process. The decisions taken subsequently are then assumed to conform to it. But, as Barrett and Fudge (see Section 7.3) say-and as the Leiden-Oxford Study shows-departing from a plan can be as rational as following it. I agree with Healey (1983) that "plan-based action" and the use of what she calls the "rational method" are not the same. So I start with my presentation, not with plans, but with the ordinary decisions taken by actors out there in the real world-this being a major characteristic of the decision-centred view, and one that brings it close to the view emerging out of the implementation studies that action is supreme, and policy no more than one input out of several into the negotiation process.

Physical development involves a stream of decisions taken by private as well as public actors, each pursuing ends of their own. Each decision is an expression of intent entailing commitments (see also the discussion of Meyerson and Banfield, in Section 2.3). A basic classification of decisions rests on the nature of the commitments entailed by them. *Operational decisions* are those which result in definite commitment: exchanging contracts for the purchase of property, or the granting of a building permit or planning permission. The commitment to allow the development specified in the application cannot be revoked without compensation. That, then, is what definite commitment means: it cannot be reversed without incurring heavy costs.

An operational decision need not, however, entail "implementation". Rather, what commitment is entered into depends on the powers of the agency under consideration. Higher-level agencies often do not implement anything at all; they stimulate others to do so. They exercise indirect control, by approving plans, budgets, loans and the like. These are their operational decisions. For others they form an input into their decision-making.

But adopting a *plan* only entails tentative commitments. Taking a road alignment off a map may result in pressure from the automotive lobby, but there is a world of difference between this and having to revoke a contract. The fact, though, that they are tentative does not make planning decisions trivial. They are a necessary support for operational decision-making. This may include pointing out implications over a broad field of choice. That field may also present opportunities for joint action which the individual decision-maker is not aware of-indeed, does not wish to consider. There can be a qualitative difference, therefore, between what is considered during operational decision-making and planning, and the latter considerations may have to override the former. But none of this changes the fact that even the noblest plan is useless, *unless* it translates into operational decisions-which is why the latter are supreme.

Why, then, do we need plans? Because we want the decisions with which we commit ourselves to be the best possible-rational-decisions. At this point the argument could turn to whether decisions can be rational. But is this at issue? Where public decisions are concerned, rationality is already enshrined in constitutional provisions, like due process, and parliamentary rules, like question time (see Grauhan, 1969; see also Webber, 1978, 1983; Davidoff and Reiner, 1962; Davidoff, 1965). Such provisions make sure that decision-makers must be answerable for their decisions. For instance, the "certiori" power of the United States judiciary allows courts to order an official "to come forward with documents to determine whether his actions were unreasonable, arbitrary or capricious" (Rose, 1979, p12). This makes sure that decision-makers think about whether their decisions would stand up to scrutiny. Whatever deals they strike, they must be able to adduce arguments for them, therefore, that are acceptable to others. As indicated in Chapter 4, it is the arguments advanced to justify the decisions, rather than the real motives for taking them, to which rationality in planning relates.

What reasons are given for decisions? A building permit might be refused in order to preserve the open character of the area. A road proposal might be defended by the prospect of fewer traffic jams. (Opponents might point out the resulting pollution and loss of agricultural land.) So, the primary requirement is that the *consequences* of decisions are considered. Otherwise we cannot weigh the merits of a decision. It need not thereby be bad. Who knows, it may be the best of possible decisions. But unless we attend to its consequences, we shall never know.

Friend and Jessop's "operational problems" (see Section 6.1) relate also to how to establish the consequences of proposed actions (see also Friend and Hickling, 1987). Wildavsky (1973) has been shown in Section 7.1 to demand the same. The requirement that the consequences of decisions should be explored is the basis also of the rational planning model (see Faludi, 1986, Chapter 6). In view of the "proceduralist" versus "substantivist" controversy, it is worth noting that this cannot be done other than by drawing on substantive theory; which is why substantive research is so important for good planning.

But even if we desire the consequences-those which we know, of course; the others elude us-it might be that we could obtain them at less cost. Everything that we give up for desired ends counts: money, but also open space, clean air, scenic views, convenience, amenity, access, rare species, and many other "intangibles". Their scarcity hardly bears emphasis. Also, there is an endless number of worthy causes. Insisting that the relationship between ends and means, benefits and costs, should be looked into has nothing to do-as some allege-with a narrow outlook. On the contrary, it should alert us to all ramifications of our actions.

This conclusion re-emphasises what Meyerson and Banfield already said decades ago (see Section 2.3): a rational decision is one that *optimises* the ratio between ends and means. Still, the claim is merely that this is what we *mean* by a rational decision. In other words we have engaged in *conceptual* analysis, as Taylor (1984) has been shown to argue (see Section 5.4). So the argument that optimisation is not in fact feasible is not to the point.

Although expressed in terms of means-ends, and in this sense "functional" see Taylor, 1984, p. 107), rationality is not limited to considering the most efficient means leading to the achievement of fixed ends. Yet again, Meyerson and Banfield are my witnesses. They discuss how the decision-taker may come to realise that ends not immediately considered-which they term contextual-may come into play. Etzioni (1968, pp. 260-3) shows likewise how "instrumental" rationality, concerned with means to achieve given ends, changes into "comprehensive" rationality, considering alternative ends. Ultimately this results in weights being attached to various consequences. (The many ways of doing this are not a concern of this book.) Weights are one way of approaching the additional troublesome problem of the equity of the distribution of consequences over various groups (see Miller, 1985, p. 44).

So a decision is rational if it is the best out of all possible alternatives, taking into account all their consequences weighed in the light of a set of values, including, where relevant, equity. But is it possible to know all alternatives, let alone their consequences? and what about the costs involved in analysing them? I am still not tackling such questions. First, the concept of the definition of the decision situation must be introduced. Even before thinking about which is the best choice, the decision-maker must know what can be *done* about the situation, what he or she wants to *get out of it* or to *avoid*, and which *weights* must be attached to consequences. I do not mean "before" in a temporal sense, but that a definition of the decision situation containing these elements is a logical prerequisite of rational decisions.

There is no objectively rational decision. Therefore, Simon talks about "satisficing" instead of optimising (see Section 3.4). March and Simon (1958, p. 138) conclude on this basis that one "can only speak of rationality relative to a frame of reference". Later on, they amplify this as "Choice is always exercised with respect to a limited, approximate, simplified 'model' of the real situation" and call this model the chooser's "definition of the situation", adding that its elements are not given, but are the outcome of psychological and sociological processes (p. 139). Friend and Hickling (1987) rightly point out that subjectivity even extends to the appreciation of uncertainty.

So to talk about objective rationality is meaningless, and the only valid interpretation of rationality a subjective one. To come to this conclusion we only have to consult Meyerson and Banfield (see Section 2.3). "Alternatives", "constraints", "ends", all these terms refer to a specific decision-maker faced with alternatives which are uniquely *his* or *hers*. Ends are in *his* or *her* mind; constraints that apply to *him* or *her* may not apply to others. Davidoff (1965) has been shown to insist also that plan evaluation is never neutral. In strategic choice it is the same: "decision areas", "options", "option bars" and sources of uncertainty are identified from the point of view of the decision-maker.

It follows that rationality cannot be an objective criterion of the quality of decisions. Rather, it is relative to the definition of the decision situation. The questions which it raises are: whether all alternatives and all their consequences have been assessed *within* that definition, and whether the proposed decision flows from this (see Taylor and Harris, discussed in Section 5.4).

Saying that the definition of the decision situation is subjective takes care of many issues. Consider conflicting interests. Where they are irreconcilable, it is impossible to plan. Is this surprising? No! It is perfectly possible for rational people to be at cross-purposes. In claiming that rationality purports to transcend conflict, the critics of the rational planning model have simply created a straw man. In reality, applying it may make clear that there can be *no* generally acceptable "solution", because there is *no common definition of the decision situation.* (At the same time, some issues *can* be settled, and Meyerson and Banfield have indicated ways of achieving this.)

Of course, "subjective" need not mean individual, as has been pointed out when discussing Hooper's critique of my work in Section 4.3. It does not condone decision-takers letting themselves being guided by purely personal motives-like getting re-elected-either. The requirement of accountability of public decisions, and the procedural safeguards which this entails, are the best we can do to make sure that such considerations do not prevail. *Planning Theory* was shown in Section 4.2 to be greatly concerned with organisational and procedural preconditions for criticism of proposed decisions.

This view has parallels in personal construct theory (Low, 1982, see Section 4.3), the view of reality as a social construct (Berger and Luckmann, 1967; see also Barrett and Fudge, 1981; Fudge and Barrett, 1981, quoted in Section 7.3). At the same time, it is understood that, as Scott and Roweis (1977) were quoted as saying, the distribution of power pre-structures the definition of the decision-situation. This opens the way for the kind of two-pronged attack which Barrett and Fudge advocate on the problem of understanding what they call the policy-action interrelationship. It brings the decision-centred view close also to the "reconstructed pragmatism" of Hoch (1984; see Section 5.4), with the proviso that, from the point of view of the planner, it is more interesting to approach matters from the angle of the particular agency or group he or she is working for. Planning-theoretical work purporting to be of use to planners is biased, therefore, towards the "action" rather than the "structural" perspective. But obviously the more it takes account of the latter, the more enlightening as regards the constraints on planning this "action" perspective will be. This is because such a contingency approach (see Chapters 4 and 5) helps in tailoring strategy to the institutional and political situation in which the planner operates.

Limitations of the human mind and of time for preparing decisions also stop being issues. They simply form *part of* the definition of the decision situation. Any court passing a verdict asks: was it reasonable to expect the defendant to know what he was doing? Could he or she have been expected to find out? Was there time? The same goes for any other decision. (See also the critique by Dror, 1968, of Simon's satisficing.)

That definitions of decision situations are subjective is not an excuse for shortcomings. Indeed, one of the things which we expect from public decision-makers is that, limitations notwithstanding, they *plan*, thereby improving their decisions. This takes us into discussing plans as aids for decision-making.

Consider the number of decisions taken by public authorities. A medium-size town can be faced with several hundred decisions annually, concerning building permits and the like. There are investment decisions also, down to the placing of traffic signs and the planting of trees. In addition, our town may consider wooing industrialists with subsidies, as well as lobbying central government for subsidies. It is impossible to consider all the alternatives and all their consequences separately in each instance.

Imagine what this would mean. When receiving an application for a planning permission or a building permit, the officer responsible would consider all the implications of (a) granting an approval, (b) rejecting the application, or (c) granting approval under conditions. What will the effect be on neighbouring properties? On traffic generation? On retailing? Can the properties be serviced? What about schools, health and welfare services and the tax base? What other uses could the land be put to? Does the development infringe upon open space? Does it intrude on scenic views? Is it of the right type, considering community needs? Answering such questions-each of them reasonable in itself (and each likely to be raised by the press, the opposition, higher authorities and/or aggrieved parties in whatever form of inquiry, hearing or court proceeding legislation allows for)-requires research, coordination, and political decisions. In any but the most trivial cases, forming a reasoned view about the issues involved would take too long. (And what seem trivial cases might have a large cumulative impact, like allowing garages in suburban homes to be converted into granny flats which are subsequently occupied by the young, who then make new demands on services, change the lifestyle of the neighbourhood, park their vehicles in the streets, and so on, and so forth.)

So decisions cannot be considered one by one. There may be a map showing open spaces which are to be preserved. School authorities and service departments have schedules of spare capacities. There may be policies as regards the type of housing needed, or a precedent for allowing conversions of suburban homes into apartments. There are building regulations, and possibly tree preservation ordinances, sunlight ordinances, car parking ordinances, and so forth. In other words, there are various *plans* to refer to in decision-making.

What has been said above applies not only to regulatory decisions. Consider closing a street. There may be ripple-effects throughout the entire network, and these need to be considered. But the expenditure involved in placing traffic signs is trivial when compared to infrastructure, public housing, and the like. There, the question will be: what else could be done with the resources? This question-reasonable, and likely to be raised as it is-cannot be answered without reference to a capital budget, a policy statement, or some such like, in short: a plan. Plan is a generic term for any more general statement referred to in operational decision-making. The plurality of forms can hardly be over-emphasised. It should not obscure the fact, though, that operational decisions are the ones that matter. *They* make things happen, and thereby affect people's lives. It is *their* rationality which has been the starting point. Plans are merely guides referred to whenever action is called for. If they do not fulfil this purpose, then they are useless, even an impediment to action. Great effort is expended on getting around useless plans.

Of course, such views derive from the "IOR School", where it emphasises the role of plans in aiding decisions here and now. Friedmann's notion of planning as "societal action" (Friedmann, 1969) is also similar-except that he dismisses plans altogether. Barrett and Fudge were also shown to think of policy-making as the structuring of the day-by-day working of an agency. What is new is the concern for the rationality primarily of operational decisions, instead of plans, and the argument above on how the need for plans and planning arises out of it.

Not that planning decisions should not be rational. Everything that has been said above about operational decisions equally applies to them: consequences need to be considered, including the consequences of alternatives, and the choice of the plan which henceforth acts as a guide for decisions must derive logically from them. In other words, the plan-maker must have a definition of the planning situation, and planning decisions can be deemed to be rational only in the light of that definition. Again, it follows that the rationality of a plan is subjective. So, planning decisions have everything that flows from their nature as decisions in common with operational decisions; everything, also, that flows from the fact that public authorities must be able to explain themselves by demonstrating that their decisions are correct. But there are also two important differences between operational and planning decisions. First the former issue in definite commitments, the latter merely in an undertaking to use plans when taking action. As we have seen, that is how Meyerson and Banfield define a plan: a set of prospective, dated, actions which may be reversed prior to their implementation. Even so-called binding plans are nothing more, and are often departed from. The second difference is that it is more difficult to make a rational plan than to take a rational decision, simply because planning situations are more difficult to define. Doing so makes demands on scarce manpower and the attention of political decision-makers. Agendas-including those of the public at large-are crowded with problems demanding attention, making the way they are formulated into an important issue in itself (see Bachrach and Baratz, 1973). All this is quite apart from the many questions which plans raise, and which we lack the understanding-and, perhaps, the will!-to answer.

This, then, has been the reconstruction of the decision-centred view of planning. To a large extent it is implied in the work of the "IOR School".

8.3 Implications

Here I draw implications from the distinction between operational and planning decisions and introduce the concept of *decision analysis*. It aims at those operational decisions which a plan should help taking. A second concept to be introduced is *flexibility*, or the ability to match the definition of the decision situation with that of the planning situation, and vice-versa. A third concept is the *effectiveness of a plan*. It needs to be defined in terms of its performance during action and not the conformance of implementation to it. This takes us back to an issue discussed briefly in Chapter 6: the *object of planning*.

Decision analysis

I recalled above a student project stimulating the development of the decision-centred view. The popular view at that time had been to start with goals. There has always been an undercurrent of opinion against this, which held that abstract goals do not catch the attention of decision-makers (see Altshuler, 1965). Indeed, Meyerson and Banfield have already been quoted as suggesting that planning should start with the analysis of the "situation", and that action must be formulated within the area of existing opportunities. Many sceptics-above all Braybrook and Lindblom (see Section 3.4) and Wildavsky (1973; see Section 7.1) reiterate this point.

Later it was argued that problems are of more direct relevance to people, and that planning should start with those (see Needham, 1971). I am known for regarding this as a non-issue (see Faludi, 1971), and at some stage Needham seemed to agree (see Needham and Faludi, 1973), although for philosophical reasons he keeps on arguing that planning should start with those problems experienced by individual people (Needham, 1977, 1982).

I do not oppose this. The distinction in Chapter 4 between the process of formulating a plan on the one hand, and the argument on which it is based on the other, does not allow one to take a stand on this matter. The process by which an argument is formulated does not affect its validity, and one might just as well start with problems. But it is more practicable to start with the intended effect of a plan, which is to aid operational decisions. Which decisions are meant? Who is taking them? How can the planning authority influence whoever takes them? This is what decision analysis implies. Performing it, planners will discover what Fudge and Barrett (1981, p. 257) describe as an "implementation structure". It is the same as "backward mapping" (Elmore, 1979/80, p. 605; see Section 7.3).

It is worth emphasising that decision analysis encapsulates what many theorists have long argued: that planning is dependent on its context, or planning environment. This is so because it works-if indeed it does work-through a web of channels and within given constraints (see for instance, Scott and Roweis, 1977, quoted in Section 5.4). Understanding these is a precondition of good planning.

If it were not for the fact that planners do not generally perform it, the need for decision analysis would hardly bear mentioning. But planners are prone to emphasise the noble aims of plans. They forget that their plans must have an impact on operational decision-making, or else remain the products of fantasy. That is why I urge them to seek to understand the operational decisions that are on the cards. In this way they stand a better chance of changing their course, based on the unique consideration which they, and only they, can inject into decision-making. Without planners, many implications, including those over the long term, might go unnoticed. But to drive home the fact that these considerations must translate into operational decisions here and now, I recommend performing decision analysis early on, and always to formulate plans in terms of the operational decision which they are designed to guide.

Flexibility

Traditionally the issue of whether planning can-or indeed should-be rational has occupied pride of place, and Klosterman (1981) finds that the rational planning model is still universally taught at planning schools. Whilst signalling its demise, Alexander (1984) concedes also that there is little to replace it. The time may be ripe, though, for other discussions. With Taylor (1984; see Section 5.4), I see the rational model as an abstract, or formal, theory-my preference being for describing it as a methodological rule (see Section 8.5). Many problems conventionally laid at its doorstep are really problems of defining decision situations. That, rather than the rational planning model, should get most of our attention. The latter is unexceptional as far as it goes. After all, who says that decisions and/or plans should *not* be evaluated by their consequences in the light of their alternatives?

Methodological aspects of defining decision situations are discussed in *Critical Rationalism and Planning Methodology* (Faludi, 1986, pp. 90-3). The issue which gets preliminary attention here is flexibility (the main discussion taking place in Chapter 13, "Flexibility in zoning"). As we know, the Leiden-Oxford Study shows that plans are departed from, and often with good reasons. This leads us to appreciate the contradictory demands on planning. On the one hand, plans must be made *before* operational decisions, and from a *broader perspective* which, let there be no misunderstanding about this, represents a necessary, because qualitatively different, addition to the considerations of operational decision-makers. On the other hand, the longer in advance plans are made, and the farther removed plan-making is from operational decision-making, the *greater the uncertainty* surrounding planning decisions-and the greater the chance that we *must* depart from it. The reason is that the broader perspective for which planning stands may prove to be irrelevant to the real problems in operational decision-making.

Flexibility responds to this. The Leiden-Oxford study sees it as the ability to bridge the gap, in terms of time and institutional positions which they occupy, between planning and operational decision-making (see Faludi and Hamnett, 1977, p. 4). In the terminology of this work, flexibility refers to the ability of matching the definitions of the situation in planning and operational decision-making. However, sticking to a plan, even against opposition by operational decision-makers, may be entirely justified on grounds of substantive policy. What I am here concerned with is the ability to respond to new situations. I do not argue that such responses must always be at the expense of the plan.

Flexibility is a real problem. Underwood (1981, pp. 152-3) describes how development control officers in Britain are virtually left to their own devices and rely on precedents rather than on the outdated development plan. Their low status prevents them from consulting their colleagues working on new plans. Such institutional barriers stand in the way also of tailoring the plan to its real use in practice. The issue extends beyond bureaucratic squabbles. In *Critical Rationalism and Planning Methodology* (Faludi, 1986, pp. 100-2) I show that a common language is the necessary, and a shared definition of the planning situation the sufficient, condition for plans to be effective. But often, planners and operational decision-makers live in different worlds, even where, as in the United Kingdom, strategic planners and development control officers serve the same local planning authority-the most favourable situation which there is. Even there, many *other* operational decision-makers do *not* share the same offices. They far from partake in the planners' world view.

A reply might be that this is the reason why planning needs status to be able to make others toe the line. This assumes, though, that the plan represents superior wisdom. But the Leiden-Oxford Study found that many departures were reasonable responses to changing circumstances and preferences which it was impossible for the plan-makers to know beforehand. Ignorance is endemic in planning.

That is why flexibility is important. Friend and Jessop discuss it under the *robustness of plans*, meaning insensitivity to assumptions. It is desirable to make plans robust whenever outcomes are uncertain. To allow for future change is good, because all decisions "limit the future by committing the present; but inflexible decisions constrict the future by committing it as well". The same article describes robustness as an "evolutionary advantage" (O'Sullivan and Holtczlaw, 1980, p. 30).

Other ways to achieve flexibility are departures from plans, changing them, and sidestepping them altogether (see Chapter 13). These do not rely on the flexibility of plans, but of the *planning system*. Often, to the dismay of planners, that system takes account not only of "planning considerations", but others as well: due process, property rights, protection of third parties, and so forth. The fact that they are *used* by the interests which oppose plans should not deter us from recognising that appeals, hearings, variances, revisions and participation have, as their effect, that they make planning responsive.

Neither planners nor theorists of planning take kindly to flexibility. It threatens the status of plans. But there is no *prima facie* reason why plans should be adhered to. Good plans inject important considerations into decision-making and will be taken into account. But it is never self-evident that they must prevail. There can always be reasons for setting them aside. That they should be *attended to* during decision-making is all that we should insist upon.

This puts planners on the spot: they really *have* to make good plans, so that decision-makers will *want* to use them, because, in so doing, their decisions would become that much better. (The ultimate, of course, would be to have decision-makers *pay* for the plans they really want to use! Management consultants are paid handsome sums of money for their advice. So why should planners rely on statutory obligations for authorities to plan?)

Academic analysts reject flexibility for yet another reason. They see it as but another proof for the contradictions of capitalism (see Roweis, 1983, discussed in Chapter 12). But flexibility is a response to the weakness of human knowledge and foresight. The need for it exists in all conceivable social systems.

Effectiveness of plans

Following Barrett and Fudge (1981), Section 7.3 has shown that most implementation studies represent a "top-down" perspective in which the measure of effectiveness is the conformance of "implementation" to the plan. The "man in the street" would agree that a plan that is not being followed has failed. He would never dream of applying the same criterion to the one plan that he is probably using himself: his personal diary. A calendar has all the attributes of a plan. It helps in taking decisions concerning appointments, birthdays, annual holidays, and the like, chiefly by pointing out overlaps. But nobody says that it is ineffective when appointments are cancelled. Rather, in informing us about our commitments, a calendar helps to define decision situations, and that is all that we should expect of plans.

One could go further and question whether implementation studies of the "conformance" type are at all relevant. Of course, plans are departed from! So what? Let's get rid of the odour that hangs over departures. It is only by framing the analysis in terms of implementation that "conformance" becomes the criterion of success, and operational decision-makers get blamed for departures. But why should they have to answer for the failure of plans to inform them properly? Theirs is the primary activity. Operational decisions go on even without plans and planning. The, albeit important, wider considerations which planning injects are secondary. So why is the question not framed, following Barrett and Fudge, in terms of the performance of the plan during operational decision-making? That would put the onus of proof on the planners. They must prepare plans in such a way that they are useful guides in a variety of decision situations.

For investigating performance, conventional evaluation studies provide no more than a starting point. Where they signal departures we know something has happened. To find out what, requires research into how operational decision-makers make use of plans in the daily routine of dealing with "cases", negotiating with the many actors involved, trying to "get things done". Investigations of this type may be threatening to planners. They may show not only lack of conformance to plans-always attributable to stubborn operational decision-makers-but the fundamental unsuitability of plans as guides to action.

The object of planning

This has implications for the object of planning. Astonishingly little has been written about it by the "substantivists" discussed in Chapter 5. They simply assume that planning deals with some aspect of the real world, something perceived as a "problem". The sceptics discussed in Section 7.2 wondering about whether we can define-let alone resolve-problems, never challenge this assumption. (Nor is *Planning Theory* free from it, although the "technology-image", being the central element in the "model of planning agencies", would lend itself to an interpretation akin to my present view.) But is it not presumptuous to think about planning in this way? Problem-solving goes on all the time: planners have no unique claim to it. Many solutions of the past are institutionalised in regulations, policies and codes, ordinances and management practices. New problems and solutions are constantly added to the list. In terms of Chapin and Kaiser (1979), there is a "guidance system" in place which represents the sum of past efforts in problem-solving.

But problems occur in the real world. That world is not compartmentalised, as institutions are. So decisions taken with respect to one problem may conflict with those taken with respect to others. As we have seen in Chapter 6, that is where planning comes in. It relates decisions concerning various problems to each other.

That is also why we should revise our notion of the object of planning. Planning is a secondary activity grafted onto ordinary problem-solving. The latter directly concerns the real world. Planning concerns it only indirectly. Its object are decisions taken with respect to problems in the real world, and not the real world as such.

Planners will dislike this view. It forces them into a subservient role. But that should not concern us. Planning thought must be practice-oriented, but it does not have to minister to the desire of planners for a heroic self-image. So, the only relevant consideration is whether this view of the object of planning is consistent with the role of planning in practice.

Viewed in this way, the "substantivist" versus "proceduralist" controversy discussed in Chapter 5 turns out partly to concern a non-issue. What should a "substantivist" position entail? Planning has *no material object*. Planning is rearranging decisions, not intervening in the material world as such. Part Two elaborates on this view for environmental planning.

These are bold claims. But paraphrasing Daniel Burnham's dictum "Make no little plans", one might say: "Make no inconsequential claims". So I have no qualms in saying that the decision-centred view solves many problems in planning thought. Even more, it pinpoints also where the real problems lie in practice: not in the area of rationality, but in defining decision situations, including the multitude of substantive issues which the generation and evaluation of alternatives raise; in understanding flexibility; and in a properly modest view of what planning does.

8.4 Planning doctrine

Most planners do not start with decision analysis. How is it that they sometimes succeed, nevertheless? Discussing this leads to an appreciation of *planning doctrine* as an overall conception, organising our view of a field of action.

This section builds on research into the effectiveness of Dutch urban growth management (see also Faludi and de Ruijter, 1985; Faludi, 1985). Dutch central government assumes overall responsibility for guiding urban growth. Policy statements form guidelines for the spending departments and for provincial and local authorities. A National Physical Planning Agency ranking amongst the best in the world has been in existence for many decades. The object of the research was a policy statement of the late seventies relating to the pattern of growth until 1990-the third in a series of similar statements. (As was the intention, it has been revised since.) The aim was to find out how that statement had been formulated-in particular, which methods had been used-and what its effectiveness had been.

The statement foresaw a growth in designated towns which would accept an influx of many times their population, in return for subsidies. Much development in The Netherlands is subsidised anyway, but there are special grants to assist such designated areas, to cover additional infrastructure costs, the costs of social services, and overheads-like planning staffs. The reason for this policy is the desire to preserve agricultural land, especially in the "Green Heart"-the open area within the ring of towns and cities which is a characteristic of Dutch urbanisation.

This policy works: but, like the British New Towns, the growth areas drain the big cities of resources. Small towns and villages also feel threatened, because the corollary of promoting growth in one place, where it should go, is to restrict it elsewhere.

How could such a policy be successful? The planners did not perform anything like "decision analysis". In the main, the operational decisions involved concern the allocation of funds to individual projects. Also, all levels of government are locked in negotiations-in The Netherlands more so than in other countries, perhaps because proximity makes face-to-face contacts easy. So the stances taken by negotiators from the National Physical Planning Agency also count among the operational decisions taken in the wake of urbanisation policy. Making no attempt to map these decisions, and to frame urbanisation policy in terms of guidance given to them, the policy is far from being a scheme for managing the operational decisions of the authority concern. Rather, it is framed in terms of desirable patterns of urban growth at the end of the plan period.

The results seemed to vindicate the policy. Development on the ground largely conformed to it. The policy was effective even in terms of the criterion of *performance*: it did give direction to the many steering groups, working parties, planning discussions and public meetings that characterise the effectuation of something as complex as a national urban strategy. The National Physical Planning Agency made a good job of publicising the policy in the popular press and in the planning journals. Many meetings discussed the strategy, quite apart from the consultation that this, as does any statement of governmental policy on environmental matters, went through. Not the least important were the emissaries of the National Physical Planning Agency in the field-five "planning inspectors" who sit in on all meetings of provincial planning commissions. They rarely exercise their powers of control but perceive their role as that of socialising the planning fraternity into emergent policies.

This may seem a vindication of traditional approaches. The policy, it is said, owes its success to the simplicity and clarity of its substantive concepts. One does not even have to read the-convoluted-document to grasp them. The proverbial man in the street knows what is meant by the Green Heart-and is quite likely to be *for* preserving it. When the document was published, the profession had already accepted that preserving it meant to redirect urban growth. Since the beginning of the seventies, the need had been perceived also to promote alternatives to suburban sprawl. Concentrating assistance in designated areas seemed a logical step to take.

In coming to grips with this, the concept of *planning doctrine* helps. The Green Heart/growth centres idea is an overall conception of the goals of Dutch urbanisation policy, and of the types of solutions to its problems. It represents a successful instance of what Rittel and Webber (1973) and Christensen (1985) were quoted in Section 7.1 as describing as "problem- finding". There are close parallels also within the notion of a planning "ideology" as used by Foley (1960) in his rightly famous analysis of British planning. Fudge and Barrett (1981) use the term "assumptive worlds": "The function of the assumptive world is to allow the individual to cope with the events of everyday life by providing a 'map of problematic social reality'. Assumptive worlds can be seen as a hierarchically organized system of hypotheses or constraints" (pp. 265-6). They quote Young and Mills (1980):

Lower level opinions, beliefs or precepts, those through which the world is known, derive in part from and may be validated by appeal to the more fundamental aspects of culture and personality. At an intermediate level these will include the constructs with which we manage the world as it is presented to us. At a higher level of generality are the symbolic, taken-for-granted and virtually untestable represenations of the world which we might think of as the ideology of the individual (p. 266).

The policy statement was the more successful in articulating the "assumptive world" of planners, since it reflected the sentiment at the time for restraining growth in the interests of preserving the quality of life generally. As such, the Green Heart/growth centres idea has something of Kuhn's concept of a *paradigm*, that is universally recognized scientific achievements "that for a time provide model problems and solutions to a community of practitioners" (Kuhn, 1962). The benefit is to bring order into research:

(One) of the things a scientific community acquires with a paradigm is a criterion for choosing problems that, while a paradigm is taken for granted, can be assumed to have solutions. ... Other problems ... are rejected as metaphysical, as the concern of another discipline, or sometimes as just too problematic. ... A paradigm can, for that matter, even insulate the community from those socially important problems ... because they cannot be stated in terms of the conceptual and intellectual tools the paradigm supplies (Kuhn, 1962, p. 37).

Harvey (1969) rightly warns, though, that paradigms "may provide an extraordinarily efficient way of solving problems, but in general ... at the cost of sacrificing comprehensive coverage" (p. 18). He draws parallels with the concept of an image (Boulding, 1956) and extends this discussion into a consideration of language: "Part and parcel of the paradigm which a scientist accepts ... is a particular language which is restricted in the range of experience to which it can refer, but which can be used powerfully and unambiguously within that domain" (p. 22).

Kuhn also finds that "paradigm changes"-the replacement of one dominant paradigm by another-are far from the smooth transition to higher insights which is the common view of scientific progress. Rather, he describes them as revolutions in which leaders are toppled and new ones clamour for access to research funds, journals, and university posts. In the eyes of some, therefore, he has dealt a decisive blow to the prestige of science. This is why his views have evoked such a lively debate (see amongst others Lakatos and Musgrave, 1970). Be this as it may, Kuhn has a methodologically sound point, which is that scientific research never starts with a clean slate but is based on assumptions concerning its object. Because of the inflation which the term paradigm has undergone, however, Kuhn now talks in terms of research taking place within a "disciplinary matrix". He also uses the term "exemplars" (see the "Postscript to the Second Edition" in Kuhn, 1970, pp. 181-7; see also de Neufville, 1983, p. 37) showing the way in "normal science"-which he calls "puzzle-solving".

Many have taken a leaf out of Kuhn's book in interpreting approaches to planning (Galloway and Mahayni, 1977; Wormhoudt, 1981; Dyckman, 1983; de Neufville, 1983; Meier, 1985)-sometimes to herald the demise of the rational model as the predominant paradigm (Alexander, 1984). I myself have used it in distinguishing "views of planning" (see Faludi, 1982). But only rarely has it been applied to substantive content. Friedmann and Weaver (1979, p. 2; see also Chapter 5) are the exception, pointing out that there is always "a definite concept of development" underlying regional planning which they call regional planning doctrine. "Doctrine, in turn, feeds on a variety of theories in the social and environmental sciences which we designate as *substantive theories of regional planning*. Finally, both doctrine and theory are informed by certain *ideological assumptions* that change the content of regional planning and determine its outcome." They quote the emergence, after World War II, of the concept of backward regions, and of policies designed to raise their level of development to approximate the national average, as an example.

The concept of doctrine helps in interpreting Dutch urbanisation policy. The policy as such cannot be regarded as effective. For that to be the case it would have to include more specific guidance to operational decision-makers, including contingency plans. (One of the recurring complaints is that it is weak as regards financial implications-a key aspect, one would think, of a policy where most "implementation" concerns the allocation of funds.) But the underlying doctrine substitutes for the lack of guidance provided by the policy statement. It works through shaping the "assumptive worlds" of all those concerned, thereby indirectly coordinating their actions.

Methodologically speaking, there is a link between planning doctrine and the rational planning model. As in science, where many investigations are conceivable, a vast number of decisions could be taken. This variety must be reduced before we can even start making sense of situations and proceed to generating alternatives. Planning doctrine serves this purpose. It defines the problem and shows where we should look for solutions. If successful, henceforth people think about it in its terms. This is why, up to a point, planning doctrine can substitute for a well-thought-out management scheme which is specific as regards operational decision-making. That is true until persistent difficulties nibble away on the legitimacy of prevailing doctrine, and there is a "revolution".

Doctrine also carries the same danger as do paradigms in science: closure to other points of view. This is why doctrine is political; so much so that Harris (1978, p. 222; see also Section 5.4)-referring to it as normative theory-says that its development "is hardly the role of the planners themselves and not one to which questions of planning theory can be directed". So, whereas it is proper for party-political platforms to advocate a planning doctrine (and for committed planners to assist in its formulation), planners in public agencies will usually have to seek ways of reconciling *various* doctrines. And where there is consensus-as has been the case in The Netherlands for a while-too much trust can be put in the continuing validity of doctrine. Indeed, now that growth turns out to be less, and the preference is for distinctively urban lifestyles, overinvestment turns out to have taken place in areas where growth is no longer desired. That is why criticising planning doctrine is always so important. The single-minded pursuit of one line of thought is dangerous. Criticising doctrine helps to devise robust plans based on the awareness of uncertainty. (For instance, research already available at the time when Dutch urbanisation policy was made had shown a margin of uncertainty amounting to the full annual production of the building industry within the plan period of ten years. Nothing was done to take account of this uncertainty.)

This poses a challenge. It is this: how to construct planning institutions in such a way that they preserve a balance between commitment to planning doctrine on the one hand and its incessant criticism on the other? I still think that the planning principles in *Planning Theory* (see Section 4.2) represent a viable answer.

8.5 Planning methodology is the name of the game

Having come to the end of Part One, we may ask what type of discourse it represents. With deliberate vagueness, reference has been made variously to "planning thought". "Planning theory" has been used only where the literature discussed uses this term. Even where specified by adjectives such as "normative", "positive" and "empirical", it is an unsatisfactory term. (This applies to my *Planning Theory* as well.) So, what is the name of the game, and why is this an important issue? Answering these questions allows me to draw parallels between the concerns of this book and the methodology of science (see also Faludi, 1986).

Methodology of science-also referred to as the philosophy of science, the theory of method, or *The Logic of Scientific Discovery* (Popper, 1959)-concerns the claims to validity of propositions in the empirical sciences. The central concern of planning thought is similar and different at the same time. Planning results in decisions-statements expressing commitments. The similarity is that, as with scientific statements, every so often account must be given for decisions. We know now that this entails analysing their consequences, and that doing so we must draw on substantive knowledge. Only decisions which are analysed for their consequences are capable of being justified. Decisions which do not rest on such an appreciation cannot be rationally considered. They can be accepted on the authority of the decision-maker, or because his position of dominance leaves no choice, but not on rational grounds. (This, at least, is the position taken by "consequentialists". For references to the opposite "deontologist" position see Faludi, 1986, pp. 127-8; see also Kaufmann, 1981.)

In *Critical Rationalism and Planning Methodology* I compare this to Popper's "demarcation criterion" which says that scientific statements distinguish themselves from unscientific ones by the fact that observations of real-world phenomena could force one to abandon them (falsifiability). Popper gives criteria also for choosing between various scientific hypotheses-each of them by definition falsifiable. The hypothesis that has been exposed to the most rigorous testing as the one most likely to approximate truth should be chosen. Likewise, I argue in *Critical Rationalism and Planning Methodology* that the criterion of choice between alternatives is optimality. My reasons are the same as Popper's for selecting the most rigorously tested hypotheses: this way, we can at least approximate correct decisions. Besides, the very attempt enhances learning.

The difference between decisions and scientific statements is that planning methodology is concerned with justifying decisions *before* they are taken. As Rittel and Webber (1973) say:

it is a principle of science that solutions to problems are only hypotheses offered for refutation. This habit is based on the insight that there are no proofs of hypotheses, only potential refutations. ... Consequently, the scientific community does not blame its members for postulating hypotheses that are later refuted.

In the world of planning and wicked problems no such immunity is tolerated. Here the aim is not to find truth, but to improve some characteristics of the world where people live. Planners are liable for the consequences of the actions they generate; the effects can matter a great deal to those people that are touched by those actions (pp. 166-7; see also Faludi, 1986, p. 74; for a further view rejecting the analogy, frequently drawn, between the implementation of plans and scientific experiments see Alexander, 1981, p. 139).

Ultimately, the rational planning model is a means for sharing this responsibility, and this is the most important reason for advocating it, not as a prescription for how to plan, but as a yardstick against which to evaluate proposals. Planning involves risks. So there must be a way of legitimising decisions. "Legitimising" is used on purpose, and its undertone of "rationalisation after the fact" accepted. Remember that I rejected the idea of rationality as a behavioural rule. There is nothing wrong with rationalising a decision after it has been formulated, as long as the attempt is successful-as long as the decision can be shown to *be* a rational decision. Legitimacy in a legal sense also comes into play. As we have seen, a Council, an advocate, a judge, they all test decisions for their legitimacy in terms of whether they can be shown to be justified, irrespective of how they have been arrived at.

Being concerned with the justification of decisions, planning methodology, then, is the name of the game. I prefer this designation to Taylor's and Harris's "conceptual analysis". The reason is that it makes clear the analogy with the methodology of science. As with that, planning methodology is a theory of the methods of planning. It concerns the assumptions of planning and seeks to clarify its procedures, methods and its underlying logic. Over and above this, planning methodology tries to resolve issues concerning the structure, status and validity of the products of planning: plans and, ultimately, operational decisions.

There is of course more to planning thought. There are principles for bringing the rational planning model into practice-like Friend and Jessop's solutions to organisational and operational problems (see Section 6.1) and my planning principles (see Section 4.2). They are of the nature of a practice theory. The strategic choice approach, born as it is from observations of, and experiences in, practice, is another example. Lastly, there is the question of why we should engage in rational planning in the first instance. This wider justification of rational planning-rooting it in views of man and society-is the task of the philosophy of planning. So, dealing mainly with planning methodology, this work only partially covers planning thought.

Conclusions

Wherein lies the importance of the decision-centred view of planning? Merely to rescue the rational planning model by putting most problems at the doorstep of the definition of the decision situation is not enough. "Rationality" thereby becomes trivial.

But flexibility is important, both for the practice of planning, as well as for its theory. So is the understanding of the object of planning as the sum total of all decisions which a decision-taker can conceivably take. The new criterion of success in planning-performance-sheds light also on the conduct of "implementation" and "evaluation" studies. Most important is the perspective on planning which the decision-centred view offers. It extricates planning from the backrooms where rarefied analyses are undertaken, and places it where the action is: in the council chambers, around the bargaining table, indeed, everywhere where debates take place on matters of policy (where, like in the United States, the judiciary has an important role in policy-making, in court also). Never mind the many others-interested parties as well as professionals-who are also there. Never mind if they also plan. Planning is an attitude of mind, as Friedmann (1973), Friend and Jessop (1977) and Webber (1978) have been quoted as saying. There can be no monopoly on it. This does not mean to say that it does not bear any special emphasis, as Wildavsky (1973; see Section 7.1), and in his footsteps Reade (1983), argue ("if planning is everything, maybe it's nothing"). Thinking is general, too. It is useful, nevertheless, to pay attention to how it is done, what criteria to apply to its products, and how to improve upon it.

References

Alexander, E. R. (1981) "If planning isn't everything, maybe it's something", *Town Planning Review*, **52**, 131-42.

Alexander, E. R. (1984) "After rationality, what?: a review of responses to paradigm breakdown", *Journal of the American Planning Association*, **50**, 62-9.

Altshuler, A. A. (1965) *The City Planning Process*, Cornell University Press, Ithaca, New York.

Bachrach, P. and Baratz, M. S. (1973) *Power and Poverty*, Oxford University Press, New York.

Barrett, S. and Fudge, C. (1981) "Introductory review: examining the policy-action relationship", in: *Policy & Action: Essays in the Implementation of Public Policy*, eds S. Barrett and C. Fudge, Methuen, London and New York, pp. 3-32.

Berger, P. L. and Luckmann, T. (1967) *The Social Construction of Reality*, Penguin, Harmondsworth.

Boulding, K. (1956) *The Image*, University of Michigan Press, Ann Arbor, Mich.

Chapin, F. S. and Kaiser, E. J. (1979) *Urban Land Use Planning*, University of Illinois Press, Champaign, Ill.

Christensen, K. S. (1985) "Coping with uncertainty in planning", *Journal of the American Planning Association*, **51**, 63-73.

Cooke, P. N. (1983) *Theories of Planning and Spatial Development*, Hutchinson, London.

*Davidoff, P. (1965) "Advocacy and pluralism in planning", *Journal of the American Institute of Planners*, **31**, 331-8.

*Davidoff, P. and Reiner, T. A. (1962) "A choice theory of planning", *Journal of the American Institute of Planners*, **28**, 108-15.

Dekker, F. and Mastop, J. M. (1979) "Strategic choice: an application to Dutch planning practice", *Planning Outlook*, **22**, 87-96.

Dror, Y. (1968), *Public Policymaking Reexamined*, Chandler, Chicago.

Dyckman, J. W. (1983) "Reflections on planning practice in an age of reaction", *Journal of Planning Education and Research*, **3**, 5-12.

Elmore, R. (1979/80) "Backward mapping: implementation research and policy decisions", *Political Science Quarterly*, **94**, 601-16.

Etzioni, A. (1968) *The Active Society*, Collier-Macmillan, London.

Faludi, A. (1971) "Problems with problem-solving", *Journal of the Royal Town Planning Institute*, **57**, 415.

Faludi, A. (1982) "Three paradigms of planning theory", in *Planning Theory: Prospects for the 1980s*, eds P. Healey, G. McDougall and M. J. Thomas, Pergamon Press, Oxford, pp. 81-101.

Faludi, A. (1985) "A decision-centred view of environmental planning", *Landscape Planning*, **12**, 239-56.

Faludi, A. (1986) *Critical Rationalism and Planning Methodology*, Pion Press, London.

Faludi, A. and Hamnett, S. L. (1977) "Flexibility in Dutch local planning", Working Papers No. 28, Oxford Polytechnic, Department of Town Planning, Oxford.

Faludi, A. and Mastop, J. M. (1982) "The I. O. R.-School: the development of a planning methodology", *Environment and Planning B*, **9**, 241-56.

Faludi, A. and Ruijter, P. de (1985) "No match to the present crisis?: The theoretical and institutional framework of Dutch planning", in: *Public Planning in The Netherlands*, eds A. K. Dutt and F. J. Costa, Oxford University Press, Oxford, pp. 35-49.

*Foley, D. L. (1960) "British town planning: one ideology or three?", *British Journal of Sociology*, 11, 211-31.

Friedmann, J. (1969) "Planning and societal action", *Journal of the American Institute of Planners*, 35, 311-18.

Friedmann, J. (1973) *Retracking America: A Theory of Transactive Planning*, Doubleday Anchor, Garden, City, New York.

Friedmann, J. and Weaver, C. (1979) *Territory and Function: the Evolution of Regional Planning*, Edward Arnold, London.

Friend, J. K. and Hickling, A. (1987) *Planning under Pressure: the Strategic Choice Approach*, Pergamon Press, Oxford.

Friend, J. K. and Jessop, W. N. (1977; 1st edition 1969) *Local Government and Strategic Choice*, Pergamon Press, Oxford.

Fudge, C. and Barrett, S. (1981) "Reconstructing the field of analysis", in: *Policy & Action: Essays on the Implementation of Public Policy*, eds S. Barrett and C. Fudge, Methuen, London, pp. 249-78.

Galloway, T. D. and Mahayni, R. G. (1977) "Planning theory in retrospect: the process of paradigm change", *Journal of the American Institute of Planners*, 43, 62-71.

Grauhan, R. R. (1969) "Zur Struktur der planenden Verwaltung", *Stadtbauwelt*, 60, 132-7; see also "Notes on the structure of planning administration", in: A. Faludi, (ed.) (1973) *A Reader in Planning Theory*, Pergamon Press, Oxford, pp. 297-316.

Harris, B. (1978) "A vote on planning theory", *Environment and Planning A*, 10, 221-4.

Harvey, D. (1969) *Explanation in Geography,* Edward Arnold, London.

Healey, P. (1983) "Rational method as a mode of policy formation and implementation in land-use policy", *Environment and Planning B*, 10, 19-39.

Hoch, C. J. (1984) "Doing good and being right", *Journal of the American Planning Association*, 50, 335-45.

Kaufmann, J. L. (1981) "Teaching planning ethics", *Journal of Planning Education and Research*, 1, 29-35.

Klosterman, R. E. (1981) "Contemporary planning theory education: results of a course survey", *Journal of Planning Education and Research*, 1, 1-11.

Kuhn, T. S. (1962) *The Structure of Scientific Revolutions*, University of Chicago Press, Chicago.

Kuhn, T. S. (1970, 1st edition 1962) *The Structure of Scientific Revolutions*, University of Chicago Press, Chicago.

Lakatos, I. and Musgrave, A. (eds) (1970) *Criticism and the Growth of Knowledge*, Cambridge University Press, Cambridge.

Low, N. (1982) "Beyond general systems theory: a constructivist perspective", *Urban Studies*, 19, 221-33.

March, J. G. and Simon, H. A. (1958) *Organizations*, John Wiley, New York and London.

Mastop, J. M. (1983) "Co-ordination in Dutch physical planning: a case study", in *Evaluating Urban Planning Efforts*, ed. I. Masser, Gower, Aldershot, Hants, pp. 173-92.

Meier, R. (1985) "The coming paradigm for planners: community ecology", *Berkeley Planning Journal*, 1, 69-92.

Miller, D. H. (1985) "Equity and efficiency effects of investment decisions: multicriteria methods for assessing distributional implications", in: *Evaluation of Complex Policy Problems*, eds A. Faludi and H. Voogd, Delftsche Unitgevers Maatschappij, Delft, pp. 35-50.

Needham, B. (1971) "Concrete problems, not abstract goals", *Journal of the Royal Town Planning Institute*, 57, 317-19.

Needham, B. (1977) *How Cities Work*, Pergamon Press, Oxford.

Needham, B. (1982) *Choosing the Right Policy Instruments*, Gower, Aldershot, Hants.

Needham, B. and Faludi, A. (1973) "Planning and the public interest", *Journal of the Royal Town Planning Institute*, 59, 164-6.

Neufville, J. I. de (1983) "The doldrums of planning theory", *Journal of Planning Education and Research*, **3**, 35-45.

O'Sullivan, P. and Holtczlaw, G. (1980) "Transport network planning under ignorance", *Transportation Planning and Technology*, **6**, 27-32.

Popper, K. R. (1959) *The Logic of Scientific Discovery*, Hutchinson, London.

Reade, E. J. (1983) "If planning is anything, maybe it can be identified", *Urban Studies*, **20**, 159-71.

Rittel, H. J. W. and Webber, M. M. (1973) "Dilemmas of a general theory of planning", *Policy Sciences*, **4**, 155-69.

Rose, J. G. (1979) *Legal Foundations of Land Use Planning: Textbook/Casebook and Materials on Planning Law*, Center for Urban Policy Research, State University of New Jersey, New Brunswick, NJ.

Roweis, S. T. (1983) "Urban planning as professional mediation of territorial politics", *Environment and Planning D: Society and Space*, **1**, 139-62.

Scott, A. J. and Roweis, S. T. (1977) "Urban planning theory and practice: A reappraisal", *Environment and Planning A*, **9**, 1097-19.

Taylor, N. (1984) "A critique of materialist critiques of procedural planning theory", *Environment and Planning B*, **11**, 103-26.

Thomas, H. D., Minett, J. M., Hopkins, S., Hamnett, S. L., Faludi, A. and, Barrell, D. (1983) *Flexibility and Commitment in Planning*, Martinus Nijhof, The Hague, Boston and London.

Underwood, J. (1981) "Development control: a case study of discretion in action", in: *Policy & Action: Essays on the Implementation of Public Policy*, eds S. Barrett and C. Fudge, Methuen, London and New York, pp. 143-161.

Webber, M. M. (1978) "A difference paradigm for planning", in: *Planning Theory in the 1980's: A Search for Future Directions*, eds R. W. Burchell and R. W. Sternlieb, Centre for Urban Policy, Rutgers University, New Jersey, pp. 151-62.

Webber, M. M. (1983) "The myth of rationality: development planning reconsidered", *Environment and Planning B: Planning and Design*, **10**, 89-99.

Wildavsky, A. (1973) "If planning is everything, maybe it's nothing", *Policy Sciences*, **4**, 127-53.

Wormhoudt, D. T. (1981) "Paradigms and the practice of environmental planning", *Design Methods and Theories*, **12**, 141-55.

Young, K. and Mills, L. (1980) *Public Policy Research: a Review of Qualitative Methods*, Social Science Research Council, London.

* Included in Faludi, A. (ed.) (1973) *A Reader in Planning Theory*, Pergamon Press, Oxford.

Application to Environmental Planning

HAVING developed the decision-centred view of planning in Part One, I apply it in Part Two to *environmental planning*, to end the "substantivist" versus "proceduralist" controversy (see Chapter 5) by proposing a theory which *combines* an understanding of procedures and of those features of the environment that make us plan.

In discussing environmental planning, I am ignoring distinctions such as those between urban and rural planning, land use planning and environmental protection, or planning for development and conservation. A unifying concept should benefit practice and the quality of the environment generally. (On similar arguments leading him to prefer the term "development planning" see Cooke, 1983, p. 277.) As an umbrella term, environmental planning is preferable to "land use planning" which often refers to the making of statutory schemes. Such planning is rarely comprehensive. Many aspects are not touched upon, such as performance standards for the emission of pollutants, management plans for public facilities like parks, forests, coastlines or water catchments, and assessments of economic, social and environmental impacts. Measures taken under other than the land use planning acts (for instance concerning public land, environmental protection, and so forth) are nevertheless related to land use planning. For example, noise abatement legislation in The Netherlands defines zones, in terms of decibels, within which certain land uses are not permitted. Land use plans do the same when reserving buffer zones between industrial and residential uses. Land use planning needs to be complemented, therefore, by thorough awareness of other forms of intervention in the environment.

Another umbrella in Part Two is *environmental authority*. It refers to the public body intervening in the environment. Usually the prime responsibility for this lies with local authorities, but others are involved as well. So it is understood that there is more than one body fulfilling this role, with all the problems attending such arrangements.

Part Two anchors the theory of environmental planning in planning theory

139

generally. All too often that theory is confounded with the reasons for intervention. (In the terms used in Chapter 10 we should say, theories explaining the need for public environmental instruments.) Elsewhere, I have argued that there are various views of planning, each defining it differently. One of them is the control-centred view, coming in a total and a partial variant, depending on how comprehensive control is envisaged to be. The partial control-centred view, in particular, defines planning as the "identification of developments which need to be checked" by means of public intervention (Faludi, 1982, p. 88). Planning theory, according to this view, gives reasons for intervention. "Externalities", discussed in Chapter 10, is an example of a concept used in so doing. In the same paper I argue that, against this view, the decision-centred view of planning takes public powers as read, and focuses instead on ways in which they are *used*. A key concept in this decision-centred view has been shown in Chapter 8 to be that of the interrelatedness, via their consequences on each other, of operational decisions. It makes for the need for planning. So I submit in Chapter 11 that a theory of environmental *planning*-as against environmental intervention-must direct its attention to the *interrelations* between public environmental measures. This is in keeping, of course, with the view, in Part One, of planning as problem-solving "of the second order". At the same time, it means that some activities of planners-designing public housing, civic centres, attracting industries, and so forth-do not fall under this definition. This is not inherently problematic. Professional roles are hybrid. But it is still necessary to draw conceptual distinctions between their various aspects.

As will be evident, it is not my concern to assist planners clamouring for more instruments of control. Rather, I see planning as a manner of working with those public environmental instruments which already exist. So, the meaning attached to planning in Part Two is the same as that given in Part One: planning is the coordination or-to invoke a term used by Friend and Hickling (1987)-scheming of such intervention as is taking place. Of course, I recognise the possibility that persistent planning failure can point towards the need for other powers of interventions than those presently available. All I would claim here is that, when taking up this challenge, we move onto a different level of argument; that of the theory of intervention.

The spatial dimension in environmental planning-scheming-is so obviously important that it seems odd how little thought is given to what it implies. We need to spend some time on this. The most important point about space (see Downs and Stea, 1982) is that: (a) everybody and everything is located somewhere; (b) no two persons or things can occupy the same location. Therefore human cooperation implies movement in space.

To Newton space seemed a three-dimensional system of coordinates. This is the absolute theory of space. A relational theory sees space (and time) as a system of ordering relations (Popper, 1983, p.78; see also Harvey, 1969, pp. 195-7; for implications for planning see Faludi, 1973). Minimally, that is what the spatial character of environmental planning refers to: relations which we must take account of. Spatial relations will be shown to be important in environmental planning-though perhaps not quite as important as designers think. The reason is that the spatial dimension is inextricably linked to the temporal and interactive dimension, the latter referring to the relationship between various actors in development.

Chapter 9 notes common views of the environment held by authors from divergent traditions. They all: (a) conceive of the environment as, amongst others, institutionally determined in the sense of legal barriers to certain uses entering, or nuisances leaving, the areas enclosed by them forming a constitutive part of it; (b) see it as the object of both private and public decision-making; and (c) see it as the object of conflict. On this basis, Chapter 9 identifies land decision units as the foci of public and private decision-making concerning the environment. They are characterised by (a) the resources on them, (b) the channels linking them to other units, (c) the land regime providing barriers against intrusion, and (d) land titles identifying the primary decision-makers concerned. This notion of the environment goes beyond the material environment which we see, feel and smell. Sense impressions are but an outside appearance. The backcloth of those impressions-pleasurable or painful, as the case may be-is formed by the institutions of land titles and the land regime.

Chapter 10 shows that (a) public environmental measures are mostly justified by reference to externalities (effects unaccounted for in the ordinary course of individual decision-making) inequities (unjust distributional effects) of market decisions, and opportunities for creative action which would be lost without public intervention due to the short-sightedness of the actors concerned: (b) they take the form of changing one or more of the constitutive elements of sites: the resources on them, the channels linking them to other sites, the land regime, or the land title. The chapter introduces the notion also of public environmental instruments: legitimate ways of dealing with environmental problems by taking specified environmental measures. Finally, it stresses the significance of land decision units as the addresses to which public environmental measures are directed.

Areas of jurisdiction contain many land decision units, and there is much interaction between what happens on them-which is where spatial relations come into it. Public environmental measures taken with respect to different land decision units can mutually enhance each other, or they can get into each other's way. Where this occurs, Chapter 11 speaks of the externalities, inequities and opportunities of the "second order". Environmental planning stands for the preparation of environmental plans, taking account of such externalities, inequities and opportunities, so that public environmental measures are taken with full knowledge of their implications for the "public estate". This is why a theory of environmental planning must combine awareness of the element of decision-making in planning with an understanding of the externalities, inequities and opportunities of the second order arising out of the nature of public environmental measures as being addressed to land decision units with definite addresses in a spatial-temporal expanse. Chapter 11 concludes from this that the object of environmental planning-that with which environmental planners *qua* planners are, or should be, concerned-is constituted by those public environmental measures which produce externalities and inequities, and/or threaten the loss of opportunities for combining measures into creative packages. They form a subset of all public environmental measures. To isolate them planners must engage in substantive analysis, and political decisions must be taken as well. So this view results in specific questions for further research.

Chapters 12 and 13 deal with approaches to the making of environmental plans, in particular zoning. They are inspired by the Leiden-Oxford Study (see Thomas *et al.*, 1983). Practical approaches in England and Wales and The Netherlands, as well as in Australia and the United States, are reviewed. Many practices seem to run counter to established beliefs about planning. But I suggest that it is the beliefs rather than the practices that need to be changed. By arguing that we must develop flexible planning which is adapted to rapid change, these two chapters relate to a theme that has already figured prominently in Chapter 8: flexibility. It will form an important item on the agenda for future planning research.

References

Cooke, P. N. (1983 *Theories of Planning and Spatial Development*, Hutchinson, London.

Downs, R. M. and Stea, D. (1973) *Image and the Environment: Cognitive Mapping and Spatial Behavior*, Aldine, Chicago, Ill.

Faludi, A. (1973) "The systems view and planning theory", *Socio-Economic Planning Sciences*, 7, 67-77.

Faludi, A. (1982) "Three paradigms of planning theory", in *Planning Theory: Prospects for the 1980s*, eds P. Healey, G. McDougall and M. J. Thomas, Pergamon Press, Oxford, pp. 81-101.

Friend, J. and Hickling, A. (1987) *Planning under Pressure: the Strategic Choice Approach*, Pergamon Press, Oxford.

Harvey, D. (1969) *Explanation in Geography*, Edward Arnold, London.

Popper, K. R. (1983) *Realism and the Aim of Science*, Hutchinson, London, Melbourne, Sydney, Auckland and Johannesburg.

Thomas, H. D., Minett, J. M., Hopkins, S., Hamnett, S. L., Faludi, A. and Barrell, D. (1983) *Flexibility and Commitment in Planning*, Martinus Nijhoff, The Hague, Boston and London.

CHAPTER 9

The Institutional Backcloth to the Environment

As I write this, I look out on the Bay, with mountains all around and elegant bridges spanning it. The spires of San Francisco beam from a distance. An autumn sun warms the chalet. A satisfactory environment indeed?

But what do I mean by that? Something which gives me pleasure, which I am sharing with the reader? In large measure, my joy derives from the opportunity of writing unhindered by the administrative chores which are the bane of academic life. Neither is everything around me relevant to my feeling. Whilst I write, the park up on the hill does not concern me. But for planners it forms a buffer between the coast and the buoyant area further inland. And when I look down on the Bay through my planner's eyes, I see it as forming the Blue Heart of the Bay area, comparable to the unique Green Heart which characterises the West of The Netherlands. The question, then, is: What is the environment, that which gives me pleasure, or what my planner's eye sees?

The answer will be that to confuse the planner's environment with that which surrounds us is an example of misconceived concreteness. The environment which planners are concerned with can be shown to be shaped by the institutions of land titles and the land regime. These relate to sites. In the next chapter I analyse what I shall describe as public environmental measures in terms of the various attributes of sites. Therein lies the importance of the institutional view of the environment: it relates to the measures taken in environmental planning. In terms of the previous chapter, where the object of planning was identified as consisting of the operational decisions taken pursuant to a plan, this means that the institutional view of the environment predefines the object of environmental planning.

This chapter starts with *Views of the environment* by other authors. Then it introduces *An institutional view of the environment*. The last section, *Too narrow a view?*, explores whether this view can accommodate current concerns.

9.1 Views of the environment

Because of its influence on me, a German work-D. Bökemann: *The Theory of Urban and Regional Planning* (Theorie der Raumplanung, 1982)-comes first. Then works by two of my critics quoted in Chapter 5 are discussed: A. J. Scott: *The Urban Land Nexus and the State*, and S. T. Roweis: "Urban planning as professional mediation of territorial politics". Their different intellectual backgrounds notwithstanding, their views of the environment are remarkably like Bökemann's. The same is true of N. Lichfield: "Towards land policy for human survival". Between them, these views form the basis for my own, presented in the following section.

The theory of urban and regional planning

Bökemann (1982) espouses the "economic theory of democracy", saying that politicians behave as if the state apparatus was their firm, producing goods and services which they then trade for tax income and votes. In the case of environmental planning, this "firm" produces sites. I leave this concept for what it is and switch to Bökemann's view of the nature of the product of environmental planning. He says a site consists of

rights of actors to control natural resources *and* infrastructural opportunities available within certain pre-defined boundaries. *Infrastructural opportunities* are connections to inter-locational channels for obtaining *communications and supplies*.
The owners and/or users of sites ... are protected by-material as well as institutional-*barriers* which form part of inter-locational *boundary systems* (pp. 20-1; translations AF).

The power of control over sites is not vested in one person alone, but rather distributed over land owners and the various authorities in whose jurisdictions the land under consideration is located.

Bökemann discusses the value of sites also. It reflects

the number of alternative uses to which it could be put. This value-parameter, described as *locational use potential*, is determined by (1) the resources on a site ..., (2) the infrastructure providing access to markets of factors of production and of goods, and (3) by systems of barriers and boundaries (i.e. the land regime) preventing the intrusion of nuisance and other negative influences from the outside (p. 25).

In all its simplicity, this concept is basic. Sites are the building blocks of which the planner's environment consists. Everything he or she does ultimately relates to the sites within the area of jurisdiction of the environmental authority. Because all decisions in environmental planning ultimately focus on sites, I propose to call them land decision units.

The Urban Land Use Nexus and the State

The central notion in a book written by Scott (1980) in the wake of his earlier work on locational analysis and of his critique, jointly with Roweis, of mainstream planning theory (see Chapter 5), is the urban land nexus. It is a theoretical construct referring to the "process whereby urban civil society on the one hand and the urban planning system on the other combine to form an organically integrated entity" (p. 3). This nexus has a composite logic reflecting: (a) "the spontaneous decisionmaking calculus of private firms and households in urban space ... structured by the social and property relations of capitalist society" (p. 135); (b) "the rationality of collective political decisionmaking (reflecting) the global orientations, biases, and imperatives of the capitalist State as it finds itself inextricably involved in the task of managing and attempting to resolve the urban land-use problems set in motion by private decision-makers" (*ibid.*); (c) their interaction giving rise to "a field of evolving, but problematic land-use relationships in urban space" (*ibid.*). Thus, the urban land nexus "is land ... on which human beings have expended labour materialized in the form of structural and infrastructural artefacts. It is, in short, a phenomenon that is *socially produced* in a complex dynamic" (p. 136).

In this "dynamic", Scott distinguishes private and public decisions: "The combined outcomes of these two phases of the process of land development then give rise to the urban land nexus as a finished use value, that is, as a composite system of *differential location advantages" (ibid.).* This view of the environment is like Bökemann's. "Spontaneous decisionmaking by private firms and households", relates to sites. Even though he sees private interests as ultimately dominant, Scott in fact acknowledges that the right of control over sites is shared between title holders and public authorities.

"Urban planning as professional mediation of territorial politics"

Roweis (1983)—with Scott co-author of several papers criticising planning theory—argues that because land is a "seamless garment, what happens on one part of it affects other parts of it; ... because no parcel of land has on it all the necessities of its occupant(s), every occupant is, to larger or smaller extent, dependent on innumerable other occupants of innumerable other parcels of land" (p. 152). He calls this "pervasive interdependence" operating through "channels of mutual access" and "nodes of assembly": "factories, offices, shops, schools, homes, etc.". Territorial relations within these networks result from:

(a) the physical characteristics and/or the territorial configuration of the network of channels of access or of some relevant elements thereof;
(b) the type and/or intensity of use of the network of channels of access or of some relevant elements thereof; or,
(c) the types of inhabitants or users, activities, or objects available (or absent) in various nodes of assembly within the relevant territory (pp. 153-4.)

The interrelatedness which Roweis says leads to forms of territorial organisation is discussed in the following chapters. What is relevant here is again the similarity of the view of the environment as "parcels of land" covering an area of jurisdiction with Bökemann's.

"Towards land policy for human survival"

Under *resource management*, Lichfield (1983) distinguishes (non-renewable) fund or stock resources; (renewable) flow resources; and resources which are both fund and flow: biological resources, soil resources and man-made improvements attached to land. Under *land policy* he discussed land as property. Private property need not be detrimental to the wise management of land:

many a private owner, particularly of large estates ... has taken a long and wide view of his objectives and has practised resource management on lines which leave little to be desired for the community. More than that, just as for utilisation of resources it is necessary to have an owner of the landed interest (which farmer would grow crops if they were subject to legal pillage), for conservation to be implemented it is necessary to have an owner with an eye to the longer term, for otherwise no one has the interest in pursuing conservation. Tenure is a critical element in development, management and conservation (p. 5).

Therefore, Lichfield starts with the concept of a "proprietary land unit": "By definition, the management of the resource relates to that land, according to the management objectives of the proprietor, which are conditioned by his tenure" (p. 6). He adds that

long term management carries with it the concept of a plan based on the objective of optimum return over the future which is the context for the management operation, it being recognised that the return can be seen not only in financial terms but also pride of ownership, status, political power, etc. and, in these days, self-sufficiency in food, utilities and energy.

In such management the guiding principle is that the land resource can sustain man over a longer period if properly conserved (in maximum sustained use) having regard to the kind of resource in question, renewable, non-renewable, etc. (*ibid*.).

The paper ends by comparing private and public management of land. It hardly bears emphasis how much the underlying view of the environment resembles that of the other three authors discussed. It is to their common view that I turn next.

9.2 An institutional view of the environment

Do the similarities between these authors add up to one coherent view? In answering this question I give the core argument of this chapter: that the planner's environment is what Scott would call "socially produced". I prefer to describe it as institutionally determined.

The most important concept in this section is that of a *land decision unit*: an area of land forming the object of decision-making.

There are three common elements to the views summarised in the previous section.

First, all authors conceive of the environment as man-made, not only in the sense of containing man-made structures, but also of being institutionally determined. Uniquely important is the institution of property. Thus, Lichfield talks about "proprietary land units" and Bökemann sees sites as being defined by rights to control resources within their boundaries. Scott and Roweis, too, emphasise the importance of property in land.

Second, land is the object of both private and public decision-making. Scott's land nexus, as well as Roweis's territorial relations and organisation, result from the interaction between private and public decisions. Bökemann, too, shows that the right to take decisions concerning land is distributed over land owners and various levels of government. Lichfield compares private and public management of land, thereby also implying that they exist side by side.

Third, the authors agree on the environment forming the object of conflict. Scott and Roweis focus on conflict between public and private decisions. Bökemann and Lichfield are more interested in conflict, to be discussed in Chapter 10, between efficiency of land utilisation and equity of the distribution of profits from it as two opposing principles involved in environmental planning.

This is not to deny differences. Lichfield and Bökemann seem content with the present mix of public and private decision-making. Scott and Roweis emphasise the contradictory nature of state control under capitalism. But the purpose of this comparison has been to reconstruct the underlying view of the environment. It evolves around what Lichfield calls "proprietory land units", Bökemann "sites", and Roweis "parcels of land". They circumscribe areas of land which form the focus of private and public decision-making. As indicated, I call them *land decision units*. Each is characterised by the resources on it, the channels linking it with others, the land regime protecting it from instrusion, and the land title.

Man-made and natural resources

Resources refers to everything on a land decision unit that may be useful, now or in the future. This includes all the resources on land decision units as enumerated by Lichfield. Control over them is one of the benefits to be derived from land ownership. But control is shared between the title holder and the environmental authority. That is what the land regime, to be discussed below, is about.

Infrastructural channels

These are the means of moving people, goods and/or information between land decision units. They link land decision units, like the road which takes me to the library whenever I require books. The need for channels stems from what has been said about space in the Introduction to Part Two: no two things or people can be in exactly the same location. As Roweis points out, no location contains all the resources needed either. Self-sufficiency is an illusion, even for large nations, let alone for the occupants of individual land decision units. Being able to *combine* resources available in *various* locations, and to *distribute* products and waste is a condition of any higher civilisation. So there must be movement.

Channels are responsible for leakages also. Because of them, it may be impossible to contain the effects of measures. Maintaining a neighbourhood park can be difficult, simply because too many people come from far afield to use it, destroying its amenities in the process.

The land regime

The land regime is the sum total of legal barriers around a site. Contrary to the popular belief, "property rights have never been absolute in Anglo-American Law" (Wright and Webber, 1978, p. 79; on the strength of these beliefs see Popper, 1981, pp. 210-12; Strong, 1975, pp. 57-8). The land regime is based on this. It protects land decision units from intrusion by restricting movement across boundaries. The boundaries of land decision units are legal fences, therefore. They give protection against trespass and theft. But other forms of intrusion exist. Air and water can be sources of aggravation, too. At the very least, the law of nuisance gives some protection. A nuisance is "an unreasonable and substantial interference with the use and enjoyment of one's property without an actual physical entry" (Rose, 1979, p. 62)-noise, smells, smoke and fumes, dangerous and offensive conditions like garbage, insects, cesspools and septic tanks. Nuisance is an important element of the law of torts (private wrongs and injuries) and property law. If established, a court may enjoin the activities causing the nuisance. Zoning-to be discussed in more detail in Chapters 12 and 13-has developed as a generalised form of nuisance control (see Walker, 1950, pp. 54-7). Its mode of operation is the same as that of fencing an area of land. It draws boundaries. An "RI" zone under a United States zoning Ordinance is established by drawing a line around one or more areas within the jurisdiction of the environmental authority and preventing other than detached residential dwellings from being built by invoking the police power of the state. Environmental controls work similarly. They draw boundaries around sources coupled with the provision that no more than a specified quantity of pollutants must leave it. Alternatively, the maximum immissible concentration, or MIC, of certain materials may be set, requiring polluters in the vicinity to take measures designed to keep emission below that target. Sometimes, physical barriers-like the screens against noise along motorways through built-up areas-serve the same purpose, but legal barriers are far more important.

Barriers are three-dimensional. Frankel (1984, p. 339) points out that, in legal terms, "land" refers not to the surface of the earth but to "a volume of space with two of its boundary dimensions (width and length) designated with precision and the third dimension a boundless sky and bottomless depth". So the land regime concerns not only land use, but also the bulk and height of development. Cities like New York and San Francisco are developing these controls into a fine art (see Marcus and Groves, 1970; Barnett, 1974, 1982).

The land regime has yet another purpose, besides protecting activities on land decision units: to control the use of resources on them. The depletion of resources hardly bears emphasis. Many extractive activities, like gravel pits and mining, are subject to public control. These form part of the land regime. Much as with the export of some waste products which is subject to control so that other land decision units need not suffer the consequences (the chapter that follows discusses these under externalities), so with resources: their export is sometimes prevented in the interest of preserving them. This, too, is a form of barrier.

Protecting individual land decision units from intrusion and controlling the use of resources on them, the land regime defines also the involvement of the environmental authority in the management of land and resources. By implication it defines the area of freedom, too, which title holders of land enjoy. In this way it reflects the mixed public and private nature of decision-making over land. In all this I follow Bökemann, and also Roweis (who refers to this as territorial organisation).

So the land regime has two sides to it. From the angle of the individual land decision unit it is the sum total of all legal barriers protecting it from intrusion and controlling activities on it for the benefit of others. From that of the environmental authority, all land decision units within its jurisdiction form the objects of control. The next chapter introduces the notion of the public estate to describe the totality of interests in land, and of environmental planning as its management, carrying within it the notion of an overall environmental plan (much as Lichfield argues that the management of an estate carries within it the notion of a plan). In that context the land regime provides tools for the running of that estate. Environmental planning, then, is the arranging of these tools into a coherent scheme, taking into account such other measures as the environmental authority can and must undertake, in particular investments in public works.

The land title

This identifies the primary decision-maker concerning each land decision unit. Her title gives my landlady the right to enter into a rental agreement with me, ceding her view of the Golden Gate Bridge for the length of my sabbatical leave. At the same time, the land title identifies the addresses also of measures taken pursuant to the land regime.

The title holder may be a public authority, as in the case of land needed for infrastructure and utilities. The land title can pass to the public for other purposes as well: open space (like the park near to our sabbatical residence), public housing, and so forth.

Of course the primary decision-maker can contract away rights, like my landlady did. There are covenants and easements. Long-term leases on land are quite common in The Netherlands, notably in Amsterdam. In the United Kingdom the leasehold system has been used by the owners of large estates for centuries. In these cases the title holder recedes into the background, leaving most decisions to the lessee. So property in land is not an indivisible whole. Rather

the legal concept of property assumes the existence of a bundle of rights that may be exercised by the owner to use, enjoy, control and dispose of the thing, called "property". The legal concept of property includes rights that: (1) can be divided *in time*, e.g., a tenant's terms of years, a life estate, a revisionary interest; (2) can be divided *vertically*, e.g., mining rights, surface rights and air rights; (3) can be divided into *separate rights of interest or use*, e.g., joint tenancy, mortgage interests, liens, easements, development rights and deed restrictions (Rose, 1979, p. 421).

The British law of town and country planning, for instance, separates development rights from others and vests them in the public.

Between them, land titles and the land regime cover the environment with a network of boundaries. Each defines an area of land. Boundaries are specific, affecting some activities and leaving others unchanged. The network of boundaries shapes the environment in the sense of affecting its uses.

The land regime and land titles form an interlocking set of institutions. Thus, land titles would mean nothing without some land regime defining and protecting rights in land. At the same time, the land regime restricts private rights in land by defining public rights that override them.

The environment as we experience it would be inconceivable without these institutions, and public intervention always takes place against this backcloth. "Institutional backcloth" in the title of this chapter signifies the fact that the land regime, together with the land titles, mediates between (a) the set of land decision units, the resources on them and the channels linking them, and (b) the "consumers" of the environment-us as dwellers, workers, commuters and so forth.

9.3 Too narrow a view?

Compared with the sensual richness of what lies outside my window, portraying the environment as the set of land decision units within the jurisdiction of an environmental authority seems a pallid view. Also, the notion of land titles may seem to connote acceptance of private property in land, thus condemning environmental planning to tinkering. Are these valid criticisms? This section shows that the institutional view of the environment can accommodate *concerns for environmental quality* and for the *effects of private property* in land.

In referring to the concern for environmental quality, what I mean is the increasing recognition of effects of man's activities on ambient air, water, animal and plant life and non-renewable resources, including the interrelations between them. Cocks *et al.* (1978) draw attention to the fact that there are not only human but also "nature's activities"-"processes such as water purification, oxygen regeneration, 'scenery', and gene pool maintenance. While these are not usually controlled by man they are recognized as important for his continuing existence." Their concept of land functions combines both. They remind us that they "form a pattern of functions associated with discrete areas. ... (In) general it can be asserted that these areas are determined by bio-physical *and* socio-economic attributes, e.g. geology, terrain type, tenure and location" (*ibid.*, emphasis added). In a similar vein, Hite and Laurent (1972) suggest that:

our thinking can be expedited if we were ... to conceive of the environment as a bundle of useful ... natural resources, each of which is capable of producing two types of economic goods. The first of these types we may style *pecuniary goods*, meaning that they are marketable. ... The second type might be called *environmental goods*. Included ... would be such things as clean air, clean water, panoramic vistas, etc. (pp. 11-12).

Selman (1981) refers to a technocratic philosophy perceiving the environment "as merely neutral stuff from which man may profitably shape his destiny" (p. 8). Its critics

have pointed to the many spheres in which the social costs of production have now started to exceed the benefits of consumption and argue that if growth in demand is allowed to continue unchecked, an environmental catastrophe seems inevitable.

Yet by living off the *interest* of the earth rather than its *capital*, our requirements as a species could be met; our activities could complement rather than destroy the balance of nature. In an age when natural resources are becoming scarce ... it could be contended that the "ecocentric" approach-whereby we are seen as stewards of the environment conserving or enhancing its quality and productivity for the benefit of future generations-has become more relevant (*ibid.*).

All these authors raise important questions. The issue here is whether such arguments imply a view of the environment fundamentally different from the institutional one.

As regards environmental concerns, land decision units were so defined that they included all resources on the sites to which they refer (including natural resources, like the forests in the regional park near to where I write this work). Mention has been made also of air, water and other conveyors of-pleasurable or obnoxious, as the case might be-effects of activities on one land decision unit on activities on others. Although not tied to individual land decision units, from the point of view of the public estate, these are resources, too.

So the aspects of environmental quality which these and other authors feel concerned about are covered. They can provide arguments for new policies. But whatever far-reaching policy is adopted on the basis of enhanced awareness of the effects of present practices, it results always in measures aimed at the attributes of land decision units as identified above: the resources on them, the channels linking them to other units, the land regime, and/or the land titles. This is why the institutional view of the environment is not at odds with, but complements, concerns for environmental quality.

As regards any undue emphasis on property, there are those who point out that private property in land is historically quite a new, unusual and disruptive phenomenon, and who argue for holding land in public trust instead. This notion accords with the idea-popular with those concerned about the environment-of man's stewardship over nature. Land is seen as a public trust, the underlying assumption being

that people only have the right to use land in the public interest. Therefore, if land is best suited to farm or wetland use, it should be retained in this use. However, other land will be best suited to development. Equity is not served if the result of these land use decisions is that the owner of farmland can sell only at farm values whereas the owner of development land receives development value (Strong, 1981, p. 231).

The argument may be a powerful one against prevailing notions of private property in land. Indeed, ever since the beginning of this century, there has been "a revival of a concept in common currency until the spread of the belief of John Locke. This restatement of the traditional Western view that the state has fundamental ownership rights distinct from and underlying those of individual landowners has been cited frequently in cases concerned with jurisdiction over water" (Strong, 1979, p. 35). Since 1945, legal thinking increasingly echoes also "the Indian and Eskimo belief in ownership shared by members of one's society, only a few of whom are alive nowadays" (*op. cit.*, p. 36), thus giving standing to future generations. It does not seem to be beyond the ingenuity of the legal profession to give standing even to natural objects such as trees either (see Stevens, 1981, p. 24).

But none of this is an argument against the institutional view of the environment. The previous section merely talked about land titles and the land regime forming an interlocking set of institutions. It did not say anything about the distribution of responsibilities between private land owners and public authorities, nor about which concern should govern it. Property is a set of rights and obligations. It

draws a circle around the activities of each private individual and organization. Within that circle, the owner has a greater degree of freedom than without. Outside, he must justify or explain his actions, and show his authority. Within, he is master, and the state must explain and justify any interference (quote ascribed to Reich by Lefcoe, 1981, p. 460).

The notion of land decision units defined by land titles and the land regime is neutral on the issue of the types of permissible interference by the state. In some countries public authorities own much of the land. In others, "eminent domain", or compulsory purchase powers give them control at least over land coming into development, thus allowing public purposes to prevail over private interests. But, even where all land is in public ownership, in practice, authority over land decision units is vested in various title holders. Though they are not private actors, the problems are similar to those arising where private property in land exists. Even "in socialist countries with nationalized land, operational agencies in fact compete for urban land. Such agencies exercise independent and often strong influences on land use in much the same way as do large private developers" (Dunkerley, 1983, p. 32). So, land decision units still form the building blocks of the planner's environment to which he or she addresses measures. The institutional view of the environment applies irrespective of where the balance of emphasis between private and public control goes.

Conclusions

My glorious view is only the outside appearance of what we call the environment. The backcloth to it is formed by an institutional framework, preserving its pleasant character, or threatening it, as the case may be. Renting our chalet gives us the right to be in this spot, and to marvel at the sunsets over the Pacific. The bizarre towers of San Francisco are there because somebody has acquired rights to land and assembled permits and capital to build them.

The regional park is there because a park authority has acquired the land, preventing it from being built on (as developers would dearly love to do with that prize location), managing it for recreational uses instead.

This view of the environment helps in understanding public intervention. It takes effect by changing one or more of the attributes of land decision units: resources, channels, the land regime, land titles. Environmental intervention that does *not* take effect in this way is inconceivable. Public intervention is what I shall discuss next.

References

Barnett, J. (1974) *Urban Design as Public Policy: Practical Methods for Improving Cities*, Architectural Record, McGraw-Hill, New York.

Barnett, J. (1982) *An Introduction to Urban Design*, Harper & Row, New York.

Bökemann, D. (1982) *Theorie der Raumplanung*, Oldenbourg, Munich.

Cocks, K. D., Austin, M. P. and Basinski, J. J. (1978) "Conceptual framework and implementation of research program", in: *Land Use on the Coast of New South Wales*, ed. J. J. Basinski, Commonwealth Scientific and Industrial Research Organization, Australia, Canberra, pp. 12-15.

Dunkerley, H. B. (1983) "Introduction and overview", in *Urban Land Policy: Issues and Opportunities*, ed. H. B. Dunkerley, Oxford University Press, New York, pp. 3-39.

Frankel, B. H. (1984) "Three dimensional property law: the truth about air rights", *Real Estate Law Journal*, 12, 330-46.

Hite, J. C. and Laurent, E. A. (1972) *Environmental Planning: an Economic Analysis*, Praeger, New York, Washington and London.

Lefcoe, G. (1981) "California's land planning requirements: the case for deregulation", *Southern California Law Review*, 54, 447-501.

Lichfield, N. (1983) "Towards land policy for human survival", *International Centre for Land Policy Studies Newsletter*, no. 18.

Marcus, N. and Groves, M. W. (eds) (1970) *The New Zoning: Legal, Administrative and Economic Concepts and Techniques*, Praeger, New York, Washington and London.

Popper, F. J. (1981) *The Politics of Land-Use Reform*, University of Wisconsin Press, Madison, Wisc., and London.

Rose, J. G. (1979) *Legal Foundations of Land Use Planning: Textbook/Casebook and Materials on Planning Law*, Center for Urban Policy Research, State University of New Jersey, New Brunswick, NJ.

Roweis, S. T. (1983) "Urban planning as professional mediation of territorial politics", *Environment and Planning D: Society and Space*, 1, 139-62.

Scott, A. J. (1980) *The Urban Land Nexus and the State*, Pion Press, London.

Selman, P. H. (1981) *Ecology and Planning: an Introductory Study*, George Godwin, London.

Stevens, J. R. (1981) "The law and the environment: an essay", *Project Report 1980/5*, Centre for Environmental Studies, University of Tasmania, Hobart.

Strong, A. L. (1975) *Private Property and the Public Interest: the Brandywine Experience*, Johns Hopkins University Press, Baltimore and London.

Strong, A. L. (1979) *Land Banking: European Reality, American Prospect*, Johns Hopkins University Press, Baltimore and London.

Strong, A. L. (1981) "Land as a public good: an idea whose time has come again", in: *The Land Use Policy Debate in the United States*, ed. J. I. de Neufville, Plenum Press, New York and London, pp. 217-32.

Walker R. A. (1950) *The Planning Function in Urban Government*, University of Chicago Press, Chicago.

Wright, R. R. and Webber, S. (1978) *Land Use in a Nutshell*, West Publishing Co., St Paul, Minn.

CHAPTER 10

Public Environmental Measures

TRADITIONALLY, Arab-Muslim cities had an official responsible for supervising the market area. Elaborate rules existed for where particular trades could go. The basic rationale behind intervention was "to promote good and forbid evil" (Al-Hathloul, 1981, p. 133; I am grateful to Mr Khalid Alohaly for drawing my attention to this work). To this present day, the reasons for intervening in markets are the same; the assumption is that title owners on their own cannot produce a desirable environment.

Public intervention in the environment takes the form of what I describe as *public environmental measures*. These are taken by environmental authorities and relate to one or more of the attributes of land decision units: resources on them; channels between them; the land regime; the land titles.

Environmental authorities are not free to take whatever measure they like. They must make use of *public environmental instruments*, and this is the second key concept of this chapter.

The chapter starts with *Arguments in the literature*. I then expose *The theory underlying*. The next section discussed *The environment as an object of public intervention*. The last one, *Measures, instruments, addresses*, relates intervention to its location in space.

10.1 Arguments in the literature

What are the arguments in the literature for public environmental measures? This section gives an overview. The next one explores the (economic) theory underlying.

I discuss four authors: Turvey, whose article published more than three decades ago provides a lucid example of the type of reasoning involved, and also Webber, Scott and Lichfield, all of them known from previous chapters.

"What is the case for planning?"

Turvey (1955) claims that everybody is likely to agree that government has no business to interfere in what people do with their property if their use of it does not affect anybody else. But "where a decision as to land use imposes costs on other people, which are not re-imbursed, the decision taken may be antisocial, so that there is a case for interference" (p. 270). He gives the example of a glue factory. Smell is a social cost of producing glue, but not a private cost to the manufacturer. His location decision will be based primarily on his private costs. But from the overall point of view, the smell should also be considered. This constitutes a case for interference.

The same can be said of the opposite case of social benefits exceeding private ones. The general principle is:

Where social cost exceeds private cost, private interest will sometimes do what is not in the social interest and there is a case for restrictive interference. Where social benefit exceeds private benefit, private interests will sometimes not develop and thus fail to do what is in the social interest. Here there is a case for interference to encourage development. In other words, there is a case for controlling development where the developer either does not bear all the costs of the development or does not receive all the benefits.

This can be usefully restated in another manner. Planning is required for an area in many separate ownerships to do what good estate management will do if the whole area has a single owner (p. 270).

This idea will be developed into the notion-mentioned briefly in Chapter 9-of a public estate.

"Planning in an environment of change"

In his statement on the emerging planning style of the post-industrial society, Webber (1969) gives reasons also for intervention. Some invoke the concept of "public goods" which are impossible to price. Either they have the "peculiarities that (a) if they are supplied to one, they are thereby supplied to all, and (b) it costs no more to supply an additional person" (p. 282); or there are "external" (social) benefits "realized by others who do not themselves use the service, so the seller cannot charge the buyer at a price that reflects the total social value received" (*ibid.*). Webber gives a lighthouse and the treatment of communicable diseases as his respective examples. Other reasons relate to "externalities"; "dealings that result in negative external effects, that is, social costs, such that neighbours have to bear the costs of someone else's valued activity" (*ibid.*); goods which government wants to be available but which are not forthcoming simply because "some lines of business are just not feasible in the private sector, either because the scale of investment required exceeds available private funding or because the risks involved are too great" (*ibid.*); conditions in which joint action achieves superior results than individual action (non-zero sum games); and where the interests of future generations are concerned. Webber's last two reasons are preventing self-destructive and requiring healthy behaviour-like going to school-and benefit occurring not to the individual himself but to others, like in aesthetic control.

This forms part of a critique of the "civil-engineering"style of planning. Its major inventions are the technical standard and the land-use-regulation constraining locational decisions. The

innovation lay in translating the language of engineering manuals and contracts-and-specifications into government laws and regulations. The aim was basically to accomplish in the market place the sorts of deliberate outcomes that are readily accomplished in the centralized decision-setting of an engineer-client relationship or a centrally controlled government enterprise (p. 284).

But differences as against that setting are ignored:

First, market outcomes are shaped by the actions of thousands of decision-makers, whereas individual buildings are typically designed by only a few. Secondly, market outcomes represent the vector of innumerable valuations by individuals, ... in contrast to the usual consensus that makes an engineer work. And thirdly, the cumulated actions of many deciders work non-teleologically. ... In contrast, decisions on specific civil projects are typically rationalistic, aimed at accomplishing limited ends for single subsystems (*ibid.*).

Webber's critique forms the basis for proposals which have earned this article its fame. He advocates moving away from input measures to measuring output; points at the unresolved question of equity which must be dealt with in the political arena; suggests building pricing mechanisms gauging what people want into public services; and argues for incentives in lieu of regulations. Section 11.4 takes up the theme of public decision-making and the market.

The Urban Land Nexus and the State

In his work quoted in Chapter 9, Scott (1980) refers to externalities also, relating them to his "urban land nexus". It

constitutes an expanse of territory punctuated by a dense and multifarious variety of locational events. These events interact both prescriptively and negatively with another ... but their production and consumption are not structured by a market and a concomitant pricing mechanism and, as such, they represent *externalities* (p. 148).

Scott sees externalities lying "in the background of a great many urban planning interventions" (p. 149). He distinguishes between static and dynamic land-use problems. The static ones are negative spillovers, land development bottlenecks, and the "free-rider" problem. Negative spillovers refers to noise, pollution and so forth, reducing "in one way or another the satisfaction and efficaciousness of urban life, just as they tend to raise the costs of urban life" (p. 151). These problems provoke "a remarkable variety of collective responses as urban planners are called upon to counter the negative spillover effects generated in various ways at various sites in the urban land nexus" (p. 154), like zoning, pollution control, and similar devices. Land development bottlenecks refers to the assembly of land being made difficult by private ownership. So

to overcome the barriers set in their path by the institution of private land-ownership, the collectivity is inexorably drawn into the issue. Applying its prerogative of eminent domain, the State then sets about the task of breaking the power of private land ownership wherever this is essential to ensure the achievement of the overriding capitalistic goal of unhindered expansion of the bases of commodity production (p. 155).

The "free-rider" problem is yet another instance "of the failure of private and social decisionmaking to coincide with one another in a common optimal solution" (p. 158). Individuals seek to benefit free of charge from the efforts of others. The State attempts to transcend this free-rider problem. Examples are growth-pole policies and urban renewal.

The dynamic land-use problems stem from the slow convertibility of the urban land nexus, the timing and choice of land use, and the temporal myopia of private locational activity. The first refers to the longevity of investments in real-estate, so that "land-use conversions are always delayed in time as a function of the fixed capital invested in buildings and structures. This means ... that spatial inefficiencies ... become locked into the urban landscape" (p. 161).

The problem of timing and choice of land use "consists in a persistent discrepancy between privately optimal and socially optimal land-use conversion times in the twofold sense that private conversions may be premature or they may be long overdue relative to social criteria of evaluation" (p. 161).

Temporal myopia of private locational activity refers to the fact that, cumulatively, private locational decisions can generate social costs. Thus,

in pursuing their own ... interests, individual land users ... tend to block out the achievement of socially rational land-use patterns at some future point in time, and ... their own decisions tend ... to become increasingly inefficient as further private locators enter into urban space (p. 166).

Scott concludes that "the whole process underlying the growth and development of the urban land nexus is inevitably anarchical" (p. 174). Authors more in sympathy with the market, like Turvey and Webber, would debate this. The issue need not concern us here. They all agree on reasons for intervention.

—

"Towards land policy for human survival"

In saying that the legal basis of "private land policy" is a matter for government, Lichfield, in his paper quoted in Chapter 9, invokes a liberal view of the state seeing its role as that of creating and maintaining the institutions upon which the market rests. This form of *land policy* aims at the efficient utilisation of land.

Examples are the acquisition of land by government to enable current ownership patterns to be pooled; the control of the use of land without the need for government to take up part of the land; the advance purchase or banking of land to ensure that it is available for suitable development in needed quantities, appropriate sites, appropriate tenure, at the right time and at the appropriate price (Lichfield, 1983, p. 67).

Other measures aim not at efficiency of land utilisation, but at the equity of distribution of the profits from it. Yet further measures aim at minimising resource depletion and at pollution control. Lichfield calls them *land resource policies* rather than land policies. He adds *land reform* to this list of public environmental measures.

10.2 The theory underlying

Alexander (1981, p. 133) distinguishes a welfare-economics rationale for intervention "which suggests that planning is necessary for adjusting the inevitable defects of the free-market system", and a political-economy rationale proposing "the planning process as an expression of societal norms complementary to the market expression of individual decisions". But, as we have seen, authors who might be counted upon to represent a political-economy viewpoint use welfare-theoretical arguments, much as others do.

Which is the theory underlying these arguments? Answering this question gives insights into economic thinking concerning intervention in the environment. The following two sections discuss further implications for public intervention in this field.

Economists think in terms of individuals interacting freely and thereby creating markets of goods and services. Though each has his own best interest in mind, the classic argument is that, in so doing, they cannot fail but to serve the overall public interest.

This is based on the assumptions of an "ideal market" (see Lee, 1981): many buyers and sellers interacting with each other, each having good information and dealing in homogeneous products. Ways and means must be available also for excluding those unwilling to pay from services. There must be no transaction costs, and buyers and sellers must "internalise" (pay for) all consequences. Where these conditions are not met, there is *market failure*. Many expositions start at this point. Thus Lee argues that using a market failure perspective,

government could greatly reduce negative externalities in the form of pollution and land use incompatibilities, inefficiency in the provision of public services along with the attendant incentives for sprawl, as well as the costs and inequities of achieving social objectives. These results would come from designing policies to take advantage of and enhance market processes rather than replacing markets with political processes (p. 149).

Brown (1981) signals such market failures in the conversion from one land use to another. Land owners may have monopoly power, and there may be externalities involved. These failures provide grounds for intervention, but the "recommended policy should be tailored to the type of failure. If policy is to be effective, analysts must be explicit about their understanding of the nature of the problems and must design programs reflecting this understanding" (p. 147). Pierce (1983, p. 371) relates market failures to the nature of land which is unlike any other commodity because it "contains two distinct types of resource services: space, and production or consumption services. ... Whereas the former service is basically indestructible, with availability independent of past uses, the latter service is not, since it provides production/consumption functions in the form of farming, housing, recreation and transportation which alter in varying degrees the future uses to which a parcel of land can be put." Likewise, Alexander (1981, pp. 139-40) refers to the inherent indivisibility of infrastructure as a reason for public intervention.

The economic literature on these matters is vast. I do not wish to add to it, but merely summarise arguments as regards public environmental intervention under *externalities, lost opportunities, public goods* and *equity* considerations.

Externalities

Economists refer to externalities "whenever some individual's (say A's) utility function or production relationships include real (that is, nonmonetary) variables, whose values are chosen by others ... without particular attention to the effects on A's welfare" (Baumol and Wallace, 1975, p. 17). Dunkerley's (1983) less formal description says that, because uses interact

the precise use to which any plot is put affects the locational advantage and hence the value of surrounding plots. Significant differences between private and social interest can occur as a result of these interactions, or externalities which for practical or political reasons cannot be readily offset by compensating charges (pp. 29-30).

Hite and Laurent (1972) give a graphic illustration reminiscent of Turvey's example, quoted in the previous section, of the glue factory:

A landowner may choose to build a tall building on his lot and shade the neighbor's backyard swimming pool, for example. In such cases, part of the 'costs' ... are not borne by the builder, but by his neighbor ... if the builder is not liable for such damages, he is under no incentive to consider the harmful effects which the building may have on others (p. 15).

Much attention is being paid to such effects in San Francisco, of whose climate Mark Twain is reputed to have said that the coldest winter he has ever experienced was a summer there. The opposite can also happen. Facades of reflective glass can deflect heat rays into the neighbouring buildings which in tropical climates can mean an increase in the electricity bill for air-conditioning.

Hite and Laurent discuss the view also that "the creator of an externality is an offender against society and that damages are one-directional in their effect" (p. 16). They give as a counter-argument that, when somebody is prevented from doing something because of external effects, he, too, is the victim of an externality. The real question, therefore, "is not who is responsible for the damage but who should be allowed to damage whom. And the economic problem is 'to avoid the most serious harm' " (p. 16).

Pierce (1983) distinguishes offsite, intertemporal and mixed externalities. Offsite externalities occur in situations where the geographic scope of the costs is not the same as that of the decision units. Intertemporal externalities relate to the allocation of land uses over time.

Since the conversion of agricultural land to urban uses is irreversible, the intertemporal problem involves specifying a current pattern of land allocation between competing uses which will enable society to gain the maximum total benefit from both current and future consumption on its fixed land stock (p. 373).

Irreversability is frequently cited in favour of pollution control, too. Pesticides build up until, at the end of the food chain, they have disastrous effects. Acid rain threatens the forests of the northern hemisphere, and carbon dioxide may build up to such a degree as to raise the average temperature around the globe with inestimable damage due to climatic changes, the melting down of the polar ice-caps, and so forth.

Much discussion in the literature is about how to "internalise"-make decision-takers take account of-externalities. This is particularly difficult where Pierce's intertemporal externalities are concerned.

Opportunities

Other reasons for public initiatives are opportunities of better outcomes being achieved, if only somebody took an overall point of view and directed activities accordingly. Many such opportunities are realised by private enterprise through deals and mergers. But private entrepreneurs cannot always overcome the reluctance of all land owners whose plots are needed for the realisation of large-scale projects. That is what Scott means by land development bottlenecks.

Private entrepreneurs may not be able to assemble the necessary funds for large-scale projects either. For reasons of water management, new development in The Netherlands occurs in large increments. What in the United States is called planned unit development (see Chapter 13) is the norm. In the past, local authorities were the only ones who could initiate this process, which led to public-private cooperation long before the term partnership entered the public debate. (At present, developers could solve these problems, but the arrangements continue as before, simply because the institutions of Dutch planning are based on them.)

So one need not subscribe to any spurious holistic notion of the "public interest", or the common good, in order to appreciate that some projects and some developments do require government intervention so as to realise opportunities which would otherwise be missed.

Public goods

At the heart of the concept of externalities and opportunities is the interrelatedness of decisions. The concept of public goods reflects the inability, mentioned by Webber, to charge for services. Hite and Laurent (1972) quote Samuelson defining them as those "which all enjoy in common in the sense that each individual's consumption of such goods leads to no substraction from each other individual's consumption of that good" (p. 18). They themselves prefer to talk in terms of common-property resources.

Some natural resources are easily subject to exclusive appropriation under the rules of private property, as, for example, land. ... Others, including such resources as air, the oceans, and the bottom of streams, fall into the category of common property. These latter resources may be used by all who care to use them, and no single user can prevent anyone else from sharing in their exploitation.

Certain natural resources have remained common-property resources because it has not been technically possible to appropriate and defend the resource for private uses, or because ... the expected return from such private uses would not justify the cost associated with doing so (pp. 12-13).

So, environmental goods using common-property natural resources must be supplied through institutions other than the market. Pierce (1983, p. 371) ascribes public-goods characteristics to rural/agricultural land, aesthestics, wild-life habitat and a host of other environmental aspects of land use.

Baumol and Wallace (1975) relate public goods to the notion of externalities. They distinguish between depletable and undepletable externalities. The latter partake in the character of public goods (or "bads"). "Undepletable" is meant to emphasize the one characteristic of a public good that is most directly pertinent to us here: the fact that an increase in the consumption of the good by one individual does not reduce its availability to others. My breathing polluted city air can (to a reasonable degree of approximation) be taken to leave unaffected the quality of the air available to others (p. 19).

Depletable externalities, on the other hand, can be priced and distributed through the market.

Equity considerations

There are other forms of market failure as well. Brown has been quoted above as referring to monopoly power in the land market. One of the conditions of an "ideal" market is that there are many "consumers" and "producers" creating an equilibrium through their interaction. The land market is rarely of this kind. Land is not the type of commodity which classical economists had in mind either. You cannot move it around, and demand will not cause increases in production. On the contrary, it may induce land owners to withhold it from the market, hoping thereby to get a better price in the future.

Another market failure is lack of information. Klosterman (1976) identifies a school of thought in environmental planning which he describes as "adjunctive", aiming to improve market choices by providing information. He quotes Webber (1963) and also Meyerson (1956) as examples.

According to some authors a more fundamental market failure is its emphasis on efficiency:

efficiency is not the only one, albeit vital criterion for assessing the optimum spatial distribution of goods and services. Equally important is the criterion of social justice. Does the spatial distribution enhance or reduce inequality? The socially just distribution (which is equitable, giving to each according to need-but not necessarily equal or even) takes into account spatial variations in need, in positive and negative externalities, and in the distribution of environmental difficulties which must be overcome to develop a socially just society (Holcomb and Beauregard, 1981, p. 66).

These authors refer to urban revitalisation which

usually does not entail a redistribution which favors low-income people or their neighbors. Rather, it further concentrates resources in areas which are dominated by upper-and middle-class people and reinforces their control over these urban spaces. Meanwhile, the negative externalities of redevelopment are often borne disproportionately by low-income people and neighborhoods (p. 67).

The point is also emphasised in *Social Justice and the City* (Harvey, 1973). The conclusion is usually to place "social justice in land use decisions at the center of the policy, rather than subordinating equity to allocative efficiency" (Markusen, 1981, p. 107). Pierce (1983, p. 376) advances a "maximin" strategy for situations where gains and losses cannot be measured and are thus uncertain. Rather than maximising overall benefit to society as a whole, it entails minimising the costs to the least advantaged group in society. In any case, equity is another reason for public intervention-usually of a compensatory nature-in the environmental field. In addition, the distributive effects of environmental measures form an important consideration in evaluating policy (see Miller, 1985). Preservation of farmland favours the owners of existing properties in its vicinity. Their amenity remains, whereas others remain excluded. This is but one instance out of many of equity considerations entering into environmental planning.

10.3   The Environment as an Object of Public Intervention

Does market failure necessarily lead to public intervention? Which types of public intervention in the environment are there? Discussing these issues, this section introduces the key concept of this chapter: public environmental measures. It will be remembered that "public environmental measures" includes everything an environmental authority can do concerning environmental problems. "Public environmental instruments" circumscribe what that is.

Market failure need not always lead to public intervention.

Externalities which arise out of the exercise of private property rights can be handled by litigation in courts of equity. ... When private property rights are a matter of settled legal principle, a judicial system and appropriate laws of liability can function to solve many of the problems posed by externalities on the use of environmental goods (Hite and Laurent 1972, p. 15).

The reason is that the law of property does not give unrestricted control to owners. As indicated in the previous chapter, property is a bundle of rights and obligations-amongst them the obligation not to interfere with the enjoyment of property rights by others. Problems can be dealt with on a case-by-case basis having recourse to negotiations and/or to the courts.

Long before the advent of public control, large developers used restrictive covenants, easements and long leases to protect amenities. In so doing they pioneered methods of control which were later taken over by public authorities. But private controls are not easily enforceable (see Weiss, 1983). Recourse to the courts can be costly and cumbersome. So, environmental authorities are endowed with powers to control land use. They may perceive opportunities also for coordinated action which individual title holders do not appreciate or, even if they do, cannot realise. The usual reaction to externalities is to grant powers of *control* to public authorities so as to make sure that the externalities do form part of the definition of the decision situation of each private actor. The threat of opportunities for creative action being lost leads to the grant to public authorities of powers to *promote* certain developments-in particular of a public-goods character, or where equity considerations are at stake-and to *plan* them as if they were devised by one developer with one overall purpose in mind.

So, the environmental authority is given responsibility for controlling and initiating development. These powers give rise to public environmental measures, from the granting (or refusal) of building permits, to the building of public housing, irrigation schemes, roads, ports, and the like.

Various authors give attention to types of public environmental measures. Harrison (1977) lists the provision of information and taxes, subsidies, compensation payments, and lastly regulation of

where certain activities take place, how buildings should be designed, whether certain pollutants can be emitted. Although like taxes and subsidies, they set the framework within which market forces work, they do so by setting precise limits on what may or may not be done by prohibiting specific developments (p. 108).

Dunkerley (1983, p. 32) distinguishes only two types: (a) regulating initiatives of others; (b) action taken by the authority. Miller (1985, p. 35) also sees two forms of public intervention: the public supply of goods and services and the regulation of behaviour in the private sector.

Needham (1982, p. 4) draws a similar, though slightly different, distinction between physical measures acting directly upon the environment and financial measures acting upon the financial circumstances within which people make decisions regarding locations and the activities on sites. From his empirical research on employment policies at the local level he concludes that financial measures are more effective in dealing with all sorts of problems. Lee (1981), too, differentiates between "regulation of outcomes"-Needham's physical measures-and "regulation of the land market process" by the use of, for instance, effluent charges causing negative externalities to be internalised. He adds "provision of public facilities" and "regulation of other private markets" (for instance by means of lending policies). Generally, economists show a preference for market-regulation techniques over direct intervention.

My own proposal is to classify public environmental measures by the attributes which they address of land decision units identified in Chapter 9. *First*, there are changes to the *land regime* by means of public environmental measures concerning (a) resources on land decision units, for instance controls over mineral extraction, lumbering, and such-like activities, and/or (b) the barriers protecting land decision units against undesirable intrusion from outside. Most of these are legal measures. Very occasionally, barriers are physical-for instance screening against noise. *Second*, there are additions to the *infrastructure*: building dams, roads, rapid transit systems, pipelines, canals, telephone lines and similar provisions. Most of these are the result of public works programmes, but some-like telephone lines in the United States and toll roads in Italy-are privately run, though usually under some form of supervision of state authorities. *Third*, authorities can acquire *land titles* for building roads and public housing, and for providing open space and recreational facilities, thus making public works programmes possible. *Fourth*, there are *financial measures*. Where they are spatially defined (for instance: subsidies to businesses in underdeveloped regions), they act on barriers in the way of changes to land uses, like the land regime does. But they achieve their aim of shaping the definition of the decision situation of developers, not by means of prohibitions, but of incentives (for instance subsidies for restoring historic buildings in designated areas) or disincentives (for instance effluent charges).

Financial measures work indirectly. Changing the land regime and infrastructure and acquiring land titles, on the other hand, all come close to what Needham describes as physical measures, and Lee "regulation of outcomes", although with modern approaches to zoning involving, for instance, bonuses and the transfer of development rights (see Chapter 13), the distinction as against financial measures becomes somewhat blurred. The reason is that "incentive zoning" acts also upon the financial circumstances within which people make decisions. Indeed, it could be argued that the similarity goes further, and that even traditional zoning works in this way. Zoning ordinances do not require that land owners develop their land. They merely state conditions under which they can do so. It is only public works programmes (made possible by the acquisition of land titles) that directly change the environment. All other environmental measures do so indirectly-and are thus surrounded by uncertainty.

10.4   Measures, instruments, addresses

How does public intervention fit into the legal framework within which environmental authorities operate? How does it relate to space?

The most important concept in this section is that of *public environmental instruments*. They define which public environmental measures environmental authorities may take. But such measures are not to be taken in the abstract. They relate to concrete areas. Land decision units define their addresses in space.

Environmental authorities can exercise only such powers as given to them by the legislature.

Generally speaking the legislative process is too cumbersome to be invoked on a case-by-case basis. Early British planning legislation required every planning scheme to be laid before Parliament, a procedure which, obviously, proved unworkable. Only very large projects, like building a capital city, warrant special attention by the legislature. More usually, the environmental authority is an executive agency or a lower-tier authority with the power to take certain public environmental measures in certain classes of situations.

In these cases, I speak of public environmental instruments. Needham (1982, p. 3) defines an instrument as that which is available to administrations in order to influence processes around them (p. 3). Making out when and where to invoke which out of all potential public environmental measures is the principal task of the environmental authority. Mostly, its decisions are subject to appeals to higher authorities and/or to the courts. Inevitably, this arrangement gives discretion to the environmental authority and raises the issue of democratic control, which I leave aside here.

So public environmental measures result from decisions of the environmental authority to invoke one or more public environmental instrument. In terms of the previous chapter we can say they result from decisions to specify, with respect to the area of jurisdiction of an authority (or parts thereof) the land regime and other general powers to expend moneys on direct or indirect intervention. Specification is necessary because public environmental instruments are introduced on basis of only some general awareness that there might be externalities, inequities and/or opportunities for joint action which individual actors cannot grasp. Where and when this is the case must be made out in more detail. In so doing, the environmental authority pays regard to the situation on the ground: which land decision units there are, what activities go on, and what should happen. That is why an environmental authority engages in research and in political choice.

Now the significance of land decision units to environmental planners becomes clear. They are the addresses to which public environmental measures are directed. The effects of such measures are always mediated by their effects on the decision situations of title holders of land decision units. This is why many a public environmental measure has no effect: because it can not alter the decision situation of the title holder. Whether or not this is the case depends amongst other things on the address of the land decision unit. This must always be borne in mind when considering public environmental measures.

Conclusions

Public environmental measures are taken for many reasons. They add an extra dimension to the market in real estate. Their existence-and that of the environmental authority administering them-reflects the interrelatedness of activities on land decision units. Invoking a concept introduced by Turvey (see Section 10.1), we can say that, in attending to this dimension, public authorities treat their jurisdiction as if it was one public estate. Of course this is an estate with many tenants, each having jealously defended rights. But that should not distract us from the fact that they have something in common. They inhabit the same jurisdiction. That alone makes for interrelations which the planner must pay attention to. For this idea to bear fruit, public environmental measures must themselves be viewed as forming part of a scheme for managing the public estate: *they* must be *planned*. This is what the following chapter is about.

Some may think this unduly narrow. There is talk about an entirely new environmental ethics that breaks with-allegedly exploitative-Judeo-Christian attitudes. But Attfield (1983, pp. 193-4) shows that, properly conceived, that tradition encapsulates ideas like man's stewardship for nature. I, too, believe that, environmental concerns can be caught in the net of such straightforward concepts as presented in this chapter.

References

Al-Hathloul, S. A. (1981) "Tradition, continuity and change in the physical environment: the Arab-Muslim city, Ph.D, Department of Architecture, Massachussetts Institute of Technology, Cambridge, Mass.

Alexander, E. R. (1981) "If planning isn't everything, maybe it's something", *Town Planning Review*, **52**, 131-42.

Attfield, R. (1983) *The Ethics of Environmental Concern*, Basil Blackwell, Oxford.

Baumol, W. J. and Wallace, E. O. (1975) *The Theory of Environmental Policy: Externalities, Public Outlays, and the Quality of Life*, Prentice-Hall, Englewood Cliffs, NJ.

Brown, H. J. (1981) "Market failure: efficiency or equity?", in: *The Land Use Policy Debate in the United States*, ed. J. I. de Neufville, Plenum Press, New York and London, pp. 143-7.

Dunkerley, H. B. (1983) "Introduction and overview", in *Urban Land Policy: Issues and Opportunities*, ed. H. B. Dunkerley, Oxford University Press, New York, pp. 3-39.

Harrison, A. J. (1977) *Economics and Land Use Planning*, Croom Helm, London.

Harvey, D. (1973) *Social Justice and the City*, Edward Arnold, London.

Hite, J. C. and Laurent, E. A. (1972) *Environmental Planning: an Economic Analysis*, Praeger, New York, Washington and London.

Holcomb, H. B. and Beauregard, R. A. (1981) *Revitalizing Cities*, Resource Publications in Geography, Association of American Geographers, Washington, DC.

Klosterman, R. E. (1976) *"Towards a normative theory of planning"*, Cornell University, Ph.D., Urban and Regional Planning.

Lee, D. B. Jr, (1981) "Land use planning as a response to market failure", in: *The Land Use Policy Debate in the United States*, ed. J. I. de Neufville, Plenum Press, New York and London, pp. 149-64.

Lichfield, N. (1983) "Towards land policy for human survival", *International Centre for Land Policy Studies Newsletter*, no. 18.

Markusen, A. (1981) "Introduction to the political economy perspective", in: *The Land Use Policy Debate in the United States*, ed. J. I. de Neufville, Plenum Press, New York and London, pp. 193-7.

*Meyerson, M. M. (1956) "Building the middle-range bridge for comprehensive planning", *Journal of the American Institute of Planners*, **22**, 58-64.

Miller, D. H. (1985) "Equity and efficiency effects of investment decisions: multicriteria methods for assessing distributional implications", in: *Evaluation of Complex Policy Problems*, eds A. Faludi and H. Voogd, Delftsche Uitgevers Maatschappij, Delft, pp. 35-50.

Needham, B. (1982) *Choosing the Right Policy Instruments*, Gower, Aldershot, Hants.

Pierce, J. T. (1983) "Resource and economic considerations in the allocation of agricultural land in peri-urban areas: a Canadian perspective", *Landscape Planning*, **10**, 363-86.

Scott, A. J. (1980) *The Urban Land Nexus and the State*, Pion Press, London.

Turvey, R. (1955) "What is the case for planning?", *Journal of the Town Planning Institute*, **41**, 269-70.

*Webber, M. M. (1963) "Comprehensive planning and social responsibility: towards an AIP consensus on the profession's role and purpose", *Journal of the American Institute of Planners*, **29**, 232-41.

Webber, M. M. (1969) "Planning in an environment of change: Part II: Permissive planning", *Town Planning Review*, **39**, 277-95.

Weiss, M. A. (1983) "Scientific boosterism: the real estate industry and the origins of local government land-use regulation in the U.S.", Paper given at the San Francisco Conference of the Association of Collegiate Schools of Planning, Center for Urban Economic Development, School of Urban Planning and Policy, University of Illinois at Chicago, Chicago.

* Included in Faludi, A. (ed.) (1973) *A Reader in Planning Theory*, Pergamon Press, Oxford.

CHAPTER 11

The Object of Environmental Planning

CHAPTER 8 discussed the object of planning in general terms. What, then, is the object of *environmental* planning? Answering this question helps to give a realistic assessment of what planning can achieve. It shows that the object of environmental planning is constructed by selecting from among potential public environmental measures (each forming the object of operational decision-making) those which cause externalities and inequities, or offer opportunities for creative combinations, of the "second order".

By *object of environmental planning* I mean that which is planned. What is planned are the public environmental measures taken with respect to the land decision units in an area of jurisdiction. By arranging these into coherent schemes, planners seek to promote reasonable and equitable patterns of urban growth, prevent resource depletion, offer opportunities for choice, and so forth. So, it should be clear that I do not use "object of environmental planning" in the sense of "that which it is hoped to achieve", but in the sense of the "raw material" of planning.

Other key concepts are the *externalities*, *inequities* and *opportunities* of the *"second order"* referred to above. They are analoguous to similar concepts discussed in the previous chapter. The difference is that these externalities, inequities and opportunities do not relate to market failure. Rather, they stem from environmental authorities themselves failing to take account of the wider implications and potentials of their measures which rest on their inter-relatedness: spatially, because they draw on the same resource, because they depend on each other, affect each other, etc. The simple fact is that public intervention is not inherently more benign than private action. What the danger is in concrete terms depends on where measures are taken-on their locations. It matters a great deal whether a plant discharging waste is located up- or downstream from where a city draws its water supply. It also depends on when measures are taken. A school, or a clinic, opened early on during its development, can make a world of difference to the satisfaction of the residents of a new neighbourhood. The object of environmental planning has therefore a *spatial* and a *temporal* dimension. (In the following chapter I shall show that it has an interactive dimension as well.)

167

The reason why environmental authorities must attend to interrelations between measures is that their responsibility for their area of jurisdiction is indivisible. In a manner of speaking, they manage an estate. *Public estate*-the third concept introduced-alludes to an integral view of the purpose and management of public environmental measures.

The chapter starts by relating the argument of the previous two to Part One. The central notion is that of *The definition of the decision situation in environmental planning*. Section 11.2 goes on to discuss *Externalities, inequities and opportunities of the second order*. The implications of these two concepts are explored under *The object of environmental planning defined*. In the last section, *Markets of operational decisions*, I refer to public entre-preneurship in environmental planning.

11.1   The definition of the decision situation in environmental planning

Key notions in Part One were (a) that the application of the rational planning model assumes a definition of the decision situation; and (b) that the decision situation in planning should be viewed in terms of those operational decisions which might be affected by the plan under consideration. How can these notions be applied?

Chapter 9 gave an institutional view of the environment. It introduced the notions of land decision units being defined by land titles and subject to a land regime. Chapter 10 related the arguments for public environmental measures. Together, the configuration of land decision units, and the various rights conferred by land titles and the land regime profoundly influence the definitions of the decision situation of all those involved in development. More particularly, the definition of the decision situation of land owners is shaped by (a) the particular configuration of resources on, channels leading to, and boundaries surrounding, their land decision units; (b) the rights and obligations which they have acquired with their land titles; and (c) the site-specific constraints (building lines, use classifications, bulk restrictions, and so forth) imposed by the land regime. The latter obviously depend on the public environmental instruments in place: the local ordinances, plans, development control powers, environmental regulations and so forth. More is said about the problems involved in specifying these in Chapters 12 and 13. Commercial developers assess all these factors in the light of their appreciation of the marketablility of various types of development.

The definition of the decision situation of the environmental authority is not unlike that of developers. It, too, reflects the pattern of resources, channels and boundaries between the land decision units making up its area of jurisdiction. It also relates to which developers have been able to acquire which land titles. (Whether they are large national, or even international, companies or small local builders matters a great deal.) Most important are the public environmental instruments that are available to constrain and/or encourage certain forms of development in certain locations. Defining its decision situation, the environmental authority, too, assesses likely demand for various types of development. In addition, it should also have the need, based on social criteria, for certain types of development-in particular housing-in mind, and how this need can be met at prices which the users can afford. (The means vary. European authorities provide public housing. United States authorities bargain with developers about the inclusion of low- and moderate-income housing in return for density bonuses and the like.) Putting this succinctly, the definition of the decision situation of the environmental authority is shaped by its perception of (a) the resources which make up the public estate, (b) the needs of its client population, and (c) the instruments for managing the public estate, all this in the light of its appreciation of the power wielded by development interests.

The view presented here builds on Bökemann (1982) and Cocks *et al.* (1978), whose works have already been discussed in Chapter 9. Bökemann sees environmental planning as the production of sites:

Infrastructure and the land regime ... result from measures taken by territorial authorities. With every investment in infrastructure (from building roads to telephone lines) and with every territorial boundary being drawn (from subdivision to local authority boundary reform), sites are being re- or devalued or (this being in principle the same thing) new sites are being produced (p. 25).

To him this means that the "business" environment authorities are in is of producing sites. The opportunities for their users are the ultimate good they produce: for firms, the opportunities for combining on a site various means of production obtained via infrastructural channels (whilst being at the same time protected from interference by the prevailing land regime); for households, the consumption opportunities offered by their environment: a place to live, a view to enjoy, a park for jogging, a coffee shop, a pub, and so forth.

Bökemann sees sites as goods in the sense of economic theory. They can be used for certain purposes, and the right of use can be bought and sold. Additionally, in accordance with the "economic theory of democracy", as we have seen, he conceives of politicians as the owners of the state apparatus which they use for their personal ends, much as entrepreneurs would. Thus, environmental authorities act in ways similar to private firms. Their "factors of production" are land, infrastructure and the land regime. As site-producing firms, they can be characterised by their relevant constitutional powers; the ability to determine the type and quantity of the product (that is the locational potential) by means of combining the relevant factors of production; their ability to obtain the necessary factors of production and to market their products; and their production capacity, both in terms of planning and implementation (see p. 331). Sometimes, Bökemann presents a slightly different view of environmental planning: the *management* of the production of sites, rather than their production as such, stressing that it means "coordinating infrastructural and land-use control measures in such a way that ... political aims of shaping the existing urban fabric ... are achieved ...

without wasting scarce resources" (p.14). It is a small step from this to likening environmental plans to commercial production schedules:

> Any development plan enables us to have direct influence on sites by upgrading or downgrading them. We can derive from it the structure of the product in that the plan comprises:
> (1) a *spatial arrangement* of the intended infrastructural and land-use control measures ..., and
> (2) a *temporal arrangement* (phasing) of the intended infrastructural and land-use control measures in the sense of a critical path analysis.
> In a technological sense, therefore, the spatial-temporal combination (coordination) of the factors involved in the production of sites ... defines the structure of the product (p. 340).

We need not necessarily follow Bökemann in his espousal of the view of environmental authorities as firms run by politicians for their own ends to appreciate that its "factors of production" characterise environmental planning. Above, I described public environmental measures as the "raw material" of environmental planning. They, then, are its factors of production. But the distinction should be maintained-more so than Bökemann does-between production and management. Environmental planning belongs to the realm of management.

Cocks *et al.* (1978), whose work I quote for the distinction between "human" and "nature's activities" in Section 9.3, present similar views.

> Any party concerned with ... influencing land function decisions perceives a range of relevant choices (options).
> For a government to influence or proscribe land use the initial set of options is outlined by existing regulations and the possibility of modifying such regulations in the light of background policy; then comes the possibility of changing the laws behind current regulations. More specifically, government options include *legal land use controls* (e.g. zoning ordinances) and indirect measures such as the *provision of infrastructure, taxes, subsidies and bureaucratic discretion* (p. 13; emphasis added).

The options of the environmental authority are what I term public environmental measures. To be more precise, they are the measures which the environmental authority can contemplate, given (a) the public environmental instruments at its disposal; (b) the concrete situation at hand-the land decision units to which its measures might be addressed now and in the foreseeable future.

Both these views, then, are similar to my own. What I describe as the definition of the decision situation of the environmental authority are what Cocks *et al.* describe as its options and Bökemann as the stucture of its product.

Developing this further, it is possible to classify decision situations which environmental authorities face into types, depending on the kind of authority, the socio-economic make-up of the population, the prevailing power structure, and the kinds of development and developer (on the kinds of developers and how they react to regulation see Popper, 1981, pp. 186-9). In addition, legal doctrine is very important. The next chapter shows that the prevailing "proto-planning theory" of the law fundamentally influences environmental planning. Of course, attending to such differences is what the contingency approach, discussed in Chapter 5, entails.

11.2   Externalities, inequities and opportunities of the "second order"

Public environmental instruments are based on the view that public intervention is needed to ensure the proper use of the environment. Both Scott (1980) and Roweis (1983) argue thus, claiming thereby to place the root of planning in its historical context and relate it to its substance. But they merely give reasons for public intervention, and not reasons for planning. Planning arises out of what I term externalities, inequities and opportunities of the "second order". The aim of this section is to introduce these concepts, which lie at the heart of environmental planning-as distinct from public environmental measures which rest on externalities, inequities and opportunities of the first order. The section starts from the observation above that environmental authorities can cause problems similar to those caused by the free play of market forces, thus evoking similar reactions.

Environmental authorities are involved in a daily routine of decisions concerning environmental control, public works and such financial instruments as are available. As in operational decision-making generally, to take them well, preparations are needed. In Chapter 8 I described plans as aids for operational decisions, making sure that they are looked at from some overall point of view. Here I explore environmental plans as one of the many forms these frameworks take.

The previous chapter has shown that public environmental measures are always addressed to land decision units. Many of their effects (both desirable and undesirable) depend entirely on *where* the locations are and *when* the measures are taken. Taking decisions concerning public environmental measures requires insights, therefore, into the spatial as well as temporal relationships between them. So other measures (present as well as potential ones) must be explored. Together, they are the building blocks of the definition of the decision situation (the object) of the environmental authority. Now, they can greatly enhance each other, as when conservation in historic precincts combines with public investment. By the same token, they can cancel each other out, as in a case where a recreation area is located next to future sewage works. Both these, incidentally, are examples of spatial relations; but there are other relations as well, for instance via budget constraints, the depletion of natural resources, and so forth. Measures can be unjust, too, as when motorways plough through poor neighbourhoods, inconveniencing and/or displacing the people who live there for no better reason than that land there is cheap. We should insist that, whenever they decide on concrete measures, environmental authorities take such effects into account; otherwise they mismanage the public estate for which they are responsible.

However, in the ordinary course of operational decision-making, not all effects are in fact taken account of. Agencies are under pressure of time. As Popper (1981) shows, in his review of land use reform in the United States in the middle and late seventies, this pressure (due, amongst other things, to starving of agencies of the manpower necessary for the adequate discharge of their functions) is a common problem. It makes it difficult to explore any wider implications of measures.

For what it is worth, the market does not correct mistakes of public authorities, simply because the law of supply and demand does not apply here. Of course, there are budgetary controls but, like the market, they are far from perfect. So public authorities are quite capable of unwittingly producing inefficiencies and inequities, or of failing to grasp opportunities. It is these which I call externalities, inequities and opportunities of the second order. They arise out of the interrelations between public environmental measures which are not attended to by environmental authorities in the ordinary course of their work.

A possible objection to these concepts is that externalities, inequities and opportunities of the "second order" are no different from those of the first. That is true in the sense that both first- and second-order externalities, inequities and opportunities reflect interrelations in the real world on the one hand and incapability-or unwillingness-to attend fully to them on the other.

Two further points are relevant. First, externalities and inequities caused, and opportunities lost, by public authorities rather than private actors are inexcusable. It is wrong, for instance, for a school board not to take account of the likely effects of closing a school, or for a hospital board of those of relocating a hospital. To say that such boards always act as if they were private actors with their own narrow concerns in mind is an explanation, not an excuse. Authorities spend public funds and exercise public control. They are granted their powers and given their resources because of "market failures". So they are under an obligation to avoid, rather than to create, problems. Second, the institutionalisation of environmental intervention is another factor. Each public environmental instrument, or group of instruments, has been fought over in the past, until legislation was passed, manpower trained, organisations built, routines developed, and links forged with private actors forming the target of measures. Public environmental instruments do not come easily-and once they are in place they do not fall into disuse easily either. Too many interests are at stake for that to happen.

So the arguments which have led to the introduction of existing public environmental instruments-externalities, inequities and/or opportunities of the "first order"-are mostly only of academic interest. The instruments are there and used, and likely to remain so in the future, and sometimes they cause real concern because of their misuse, their inadequacy, lack of foresight, injustice, and so forth. These secondary effects are immediate and require attention. Besides, with wise management, it is-by definition-within the power of the environmental authority to take account of the effects-which, to reiterate the point, makes it imperative that it should attend to them.

Difficulties stem from: (a) complexity of the issues involved, and (b) the fact that public authorities are far from unified bodies. Concerning the former, in order to anticipate externalities and inequities and to see opportunities for creative combinations of public environmental measures, the environmental authority must have insights into the interrelations, in space and time, and via the use of resources, between present and future activities on land decision units. This includes the likely effects on these activities of public environmental measures and vice-versa. Of course, such interrelations may be indirect; that is they may result from the effects of public environmental measures on private decision-making, with adverse consequences on the purposes of other measures. For instance, some time ago the Dutch government embarked on a course of curbing commuting by means of growth management policies; but this was counteracted by a simultaneous increase in the amount deductible for the journey to work, thus making commuting less of a problem to those working some distance from where they live. Such indirect interrelations make the analysis of externalities, inequities and opportunities of the second order complicated.

The reason why all this must be taken into account is that public environmental measures must be justified in terms of their effects. Many effects materialise via the activities on land decision units. For instance, as I am writing, the proposal by the water board to invest in servicing office parks and other prestige developments in the San Ramon Valley is causing some disquiet. Berkeley and Oakland are concerned that there may not be enough water for them in the 1990s, thus inhibiting development there. Granting permission for housing on site x, refusing it on site y, and building a pipeline or a road from A to B are further examples of environmental measures which have effects on a wide range of land decision units. What exactly these effects are, depends on the particular configuration: on this general level little else can be said, other than that they are of importance in identifying the object of environmental planning in more concrete terms.

Of immediate concern to the environmental authority are the effects on the environment of its own measures. To permit housing might restrict opportunities to promote some other development in the future, might create an additional demand for schools, shopping and recreational facilities, in short, might pre-empt a whole range of future operational decisions relating to public environmental measures. It is these interrelations which give rise to the demand that public environmental measures should be *planned*, for reasons no different from those behind planning a household budget.

This not only applies to what is done here and now. The environmental authority must not be caught with its pants down. Like the two cities concerned about future water supply, it must prepare for what is coming. Housing adjacent to a future sewage plant, obnoxious industry next to a projected public park, just cannot be allowed. Following Turvey and Lichfield, the previous chapter pointed out that many public environmental measures can be justified in order to achieve what the owner of a large estate would achieve as a matter of course: coherent management, taking account of side-effects and putting together packages of measures with respect to the various areas. In so doing, an owner considers these measures from an overall, long-term point of view. That point of view is still far from comprehensive, of course. Often he fails to take social needs into consideration. But his is a more encompassing view than that of small land owners or tenants. Now the environmental authority must do the same as the owners of large estates, only more so. Its views must be broader and more long-term, in order to make good the promise on which the idea of public intervention in the environment rests, that such intervention gives better returns-in the broadest sense of the word, including equity considerations.

Having regard to the disjointed nature of public bodies, the responsibility for public environmental measures-but a fraction of all the other measures of public authorities- is usually spread over agencies who act more or less on their own. These behave much like private actors with immediate concerns in mind. Also, they are so organised that they reflect the division between various outside interests. So forestry agencies relate to the timber industry, agricultural services to farming, and so on. Often they depend on the expertise and goodwill of precisely those industries which they are supposed to regulate, making them into their mouthpieces within the administration.

So exploring interrelations between public environmental measures involves negotiations. Neither these, nor the necessary research, can be left until operational decision-making. The skills of operational decision-makers rarely concern the wider implications of decisions. Their interests are more immediate: how to build roads, pipelines, schools; how to administer controls. This is why environmental plans based on insights into externalities, inequities and opportunities of the second order are essential for the adequate discharge of their responsibilities by environmental authorities.

An additional reason for environmental planning is that some resources-which include space-are scarce and need to be preserved. There can be much argument, of course, as regards the extent to which each resource factor is scarce, and whether the pricing mechanism can adequately handle scarcity. The need to budget the use of land, for instance, depends on the concrete situation. In the Dutch case this is surely more obvious than elsewhere.

11.3 The object of environmental planning defined

Based on the notion of externalities, inequities and opportunities of the second order, how can we define the object of environmental planning? In answering this question, I summarise in this section what has been said about it so far.

As indicated, "object of environmental planning" stands for that which environmental planners are concerned with, their raw material, or that from which they start when making plans. In Section 11.1 it was agreed that, potentially, all public environmental measures are included. But from the previous section it follows that not all of these measures are always relevant.

Only those which are responsible for externalities, inequities and opportunities of the second order should be considered. This flows from the consideration that the planner's environment is shaped by the institutions of the land title and the land regime that define *land decision units* with their four attributes (resources, channels, barriers, land titles). For each land decision unit, it will be remembered, there is a *title holder*. His decisions are taken with his interests in mind (which, as Lichfield points out, can be fairly broad). Title holders operate in a market. There are also authorities which take *public environmental measures* by invoking *public environmental instruments* to obviate market failures-externalities, the danger of missed opportunities, and of an inequitable distribution of costs and benefits. These measures are designed to change the decision situations of title holders of land decision units. They do so either *directly* by changing one or more of the attributes of land decision unit, or *indirectly* by changing the context within which the title holder takes operational decisions. Authorities accomplish this by means of public works programmes, environmental control under the land regime, acquisition of land titles for public purposes and/or financial measures.

Then land decision units were described as the locations to which measures are directed. Measures influence each other, generating the externalities, inequities and opportunities of the second order discussed in the previous section (those of the first order having been considered when discussing public intervention as such in Chapter 10). Such interrelations depend on where these locations are, and when the measures are taken.

So the object of environmental planning is not the material environment around us, nor is it the activities of people making use of it. Rather, Section 11.1 has defined that object as comprising, in first approximation, of the *sum total of all operational decisions which the authority concerned could take with respect to public environmental measures addressed to land decision units (respectively to their title holders) within its area of jurisdiction*. Since public environmental measures are based on the availability of public environmental instruments, we might also say: the object of environmental planning is circumscribed by the instruments available to the environmental authority: the land regime, and the power to spend public moneys.

From this potential object, the object of environmental planning in a more concrete sense can be derived by looking at where public environmental instruments are located in space and time. This means sieving out those public environmental measures which cause externalities and inequities or create opportunities of the second order. They are the ones which form the immediate object of environmental planning, the rest being left for routine decision-making. Which ones they are depends on the configuration of land decision units, the dynamics of activities on them (creating future demand for development, or a surplus, as the case may be), and on the inherent characteristics of various forms of development. (Land which must be drained and sanded before building activities can take place, like the marshy ground in the

Western parts of The Netherlands, provides an example of measures which have to be taken in a particular sequence.) Environmental plans must arrange all these measures into coherent schemes for the management of the public estate.

Of course, none of this means that we may ignore the material environment in planning. The reason for giving the environmental authority public environmental instruments is that we wish to preserve it, enhance it even, so as to facilitate activities on land decision units. But the point is that planning affects that material environment and activities only indirectly, that is via the guidance it gives in applying public environmental instruments. The measures taken in so doing seek to influence the decision situations of the title holders of land decision units in turn. Public works and the public acquisition of land titles apart, this is the only manner in which environmental planning affects the material environment.

The above is based on the institutional view of the environment, of the concept of the environment in relation to its uses by human beings. People shape their environment in many different ways, have different needs and draw variously upon it. Institutions exist to deal with the ensuing conflicts. Land titles and the land regime are the most important and shape the environment, much as natural forces do. The powers to shape the environment via changes to land titles, together with the power to engage in public works and to offer financial incentives, define the area of concern of environmental planners.

11.4 Dealing with markets in decisions

Some environmental planners dream up desirable future environments to which their professional self-image attaches much importance. I have little patience with this, unless their planning is mediated in terms of the object of environmental planning as here defined: public environmental measures which environmental authorities might conceivably take, and in particular those which cause externalities and inequities or offer opportunities for creative action of the second order. Often, that seems too pedestrian to environmental planners. They evade their responsibility, making us believe that a precondition of successful planning is that they should be given yet more say over the environment and, with it, over our lives. But maybe much more could be achieved by the wise use of public environmental instruments which already exist. This is what they must try to do, before asking for more control. If environmental planning is seen as a public activity, where accountability of decisions is of supreme importance, there is no escape from this conclusion.

So environmental planning is the coordination of those public environmental measures that environmental authorities are involved in. To wield them together into a coherent strategy for managing the public estate is the supreme challenge.

From the point of view of environmental planning, is there much difference, then, between the operational decisions of private actors and of public authorities? Are public agencies not causing as much environmental damage as private ones? Should the environmental authority not, rather, view *all* operational decisions with respect to the environment as a whole? And should it not rely much more on influencing the decisions of private actors, rather than aiming to have a direct impact on the environment? Webber's views, discussed in Section 10.1, are clear on this. He argues for indirect action.

This takes us into discussing the concept of a *market of decisions*. Now, I did say above that the law of supply and demand does not apply to public environmental measures. Why, then, talk in terms of a market?

Over time a complex system of government intervention has developed. Many agencies use public environmental instruments, controlling development and taking intiatives to promote it. This does not replace the market, though. Markets in land, housing, industrial sites, and so forth continue. However, some actors in the market are not private any more, but are governmental agencies. Their operational decisions intermingle, so to speak, with those of private actors, and are no different from them. They entail commitments to perform certain actions. Public and private actors abide by different rules, but that is all there is to the difference between them. Estimating the effects of a plan means visualising the operational decisions of *all* the actors at which it is aimed, public as well as private. Also, one should assume that private as well as public actors are self-regarding, rather than wilful instruments of the environmental authority.

By the market of operational decisions I mean the interaction of private and public actors. The reason for describing it as a market is that, taken together, all decisions concerned have the systemic quality of mutually influencing each other. The law of supply and demand apart, this is one of the distinguishing characteristics of the concept of a market. Besides, indirectly, that law does affect public, as well as private, actors; in particular where they are providing similar or complementary services. For instance, private development bears a disproportionate share of the costs of land brought into development in The Netherlands. Thus, in fact, it subsidises public housing. When there was a slump in home construction for the private market in the early eighties, public housing projects, too, became much more difficult to finance.

Using this idea of markets of operational decisions, we can explore joint public-private enterprise, and the role of entrepreneurship in the public realm generally. Rather than sitting on the fence, and expounding the failures of the market, public authorities should enter it, in that way seeking better deals for the public. Of course, this makes public servants vulnerable. It forces them to leave the safe position of an umpire. But that role has been criticised ever since Foley (1960) identified it as one of the three ideologies of (British) town planning. Often, successful public planning has been characterised as entrepreneurial (see Bellush and Hausknecht, 1965). The concept of a "reticulist" discussed in Chapter 6 on the "IOR School" bears a strong resemblance to this. Current approaches in United States zoning (to be discussed in Chapter 13), like bonuses and the transfer of development rights, seem to be designed to require more public entrepreneurship during the negotiations which they require. (At the same time, they rely on the mechanism of supply and demand.) So, why not come out for an entrepreneurial style of planning, building coalitions around public causes and striking deals in the market of operational decisions?

Conclusions

The above view of the object of environmental planning allows us also to say what a theory of environmental planning involves. On the one hand it is theory of planning as an activity. On the other hand it must reflect the nature of its object. Now we can specify that this means externalities, inequities and opportunities for joint action of the second order which arise from public environmental measures. This is what substantive theory of environmental planning is about. With externalities, inequities and opportunities of the second order being dependent on specific spatial configurations in particular localities, environmental planning theory as such is, of course, restricted to fairly general considerations. From time to time these considerations must be expanded with local knowledge and more specific theories.

Having defined the object of environmental planning, I discuss approaches to it environmental planning in Chapter 12. Zoning reflects the spatial dimension of this object particularly well, and will form the focus of attention.

References

Bellush, J. and Hausknecht, M. (1966) "Entrepreneurs and urban renewal", *Journal of the American Institute of Planners*, **32**, 289-97.
Bökemann, D. (1982) *Theorie der Raumplanung*, Oldenbourg, Munich.
Cocks, K. D., Austin, M. P. and Basinski, J. J. (1978) "Conceptual framework and implementation of research program", in: *Land Use on the Coast of New South Wales*, ed. J. J. Basinski, Commonwealth Scientific and Industrial Research Organization, Australia, Canberra, pp. 12-15.
*Foley, D. L. (1960) "British town planning: one ideology or three?", *British Journal of Sociology*, **11**, 211-31.
Popper, F. J. (1981) *The Politics of Land-Use Reform*, University of Wisconsin Press, Madison, Wisc,. and London.
Roweis, S. T. (1983) "Urban planning as professional mediation of territorial politics", *Environment and Planning D: Society and Space*, **1**, 139-62.
Scott, A. J. (1980) *The Urban Land Nexus and the State*, Pion Press, London.

* Included in Faludi, A. (ed.) (1973) *A Reader in Planning Theory*, Pergamon Press, Oxford.

CHAPTER 12

Approaches to Environmental Planning

MANY an environmental planner forgets that he designs cities without designing individual buildings (Barnett, 1974, 1982). Whatever he proposes, the planner must consider likely reactions from others. So the potential object of environmental planning-being the sum total of all public environmental measures which an environmental authority can take-includes measures to be taken under a variety of circumstances, some of which the authority cannot know in advance. Like the option of moving closer to my place of work which was discussed in the Introduction to Part One, contingent measures are surrounded by particular uncertainty. The design tradition in planning causes spatial relations to be regarded as supreme, nevertheless. This chapter throws a different light on the matter. It points out the need for flexibility. It is a key issue in environmental planning, to be discussed in this and the following chapter.

The questions leading to such contemplations are: Which approaches to environmental planning exist? What is the nature of environmental plans? What types of statements do they comprise? How do they reflect prevailing legal philosophies? The next chapter explores how flexibility can be achieved in practice.

Key concepts are those of an environmental plan, zoning and flexibility. *Environmental plan* stands for the outcome of deliberations in environmental planning: the document, or documents, which are used in guiding operational decision-making concerning public environmental measures.

Zoning is the giving of prior notice of public environmental measures taken with respect to spatially defined classes of land decision units. Mostly it is statutory, as in the United States and on the continent of Europe. The United Kingdom is an exception in not having statutory zoning. But at heart zoning is more than a statutory instrument. It is a generic approach to analysing and regulating the use of land, and is thus an important element of every environmental plan.

Flexibility refers to the ability to bridge the gap-created by uncertainty-between planning and operational decision-making; the ability, in other words, to adapt the definition of the decision situation as we proceed from plan-making to development.

The first section, *The structure of the product of environmental planning*, shows that environmental plans are composite statements which reflect the various types of public environmental measures. *Zoning as policy* discusses how environmental authorities cope with the many operational decisions involved in environmental control by adopting policies towards certain classes of land decision units within their jurisdictions. These are expressed by delimiting the area, or areas, to which they apply on a map.

But what about subsequent departures? In many countries, departures from planning are a disgrace. This will be discussed under *Proto-planning theory A & B*. One of them is congenial to flexibility, and zoning merely indicates the intentions of the environmental authority. By regarding zoning as imperative, the other theory is inimical to flexibility. In *Taking sides* I give reasons for preferring the more flexible proto-planning theory A.

12.1 The structure of the product in environmental planning

This section picks up a point made by Bökemann about the structure of the product of environmental planning as environmental measures set out deliberately in space and time. That, then, is what an *environmental plan* is.

The concept of an environmental plan apart, the two concepts used are those of a *programme* and a *policy*: announcements of how specific measures will be taken, and how certain classes of future situations will be dealt with. Healey (1983, pp. 194-203) makes a finer distinction, and identifies eight ways in which policy can be expressed. (She claims to have found only one other attempt in the literature to classify types of policy.) However, her eight classes represent combinations of these two modes of expression relating to different problems, like activity level controls and management (maintenance) policies. Also, it should be noted that she uses the term policy in a somewhat more general sense than either Friend and Jessop or I do.

The main form of policy in the strict sense in environmental planning is zoning. (No less than three of Healey's forms of policy expression-that is area-specific policies and proposals, activity level controls, and user-oriented policies and proposals-involve zoning.)

Zoning will be discussed in more detail in the following section. It not only reflects spatial differentiation, it is a response also to the complexity of environmental action. In a jurisdiction with only a few land decision units, the environmental authority could decide upon measures as and when the occasion for them arises, taking account of the unique features of the land under consideration. This need not be the same as taking measures *ad hoc*. The number of land decision units being small, each decision could involve assessments of the likely effects throughout the area of jurisdiction of the authority-including, of course, any externalities and inequities likely to be caused, or any opportunities to be lost. In fact, under requirements for environmental impact statements, decisions concerning large projects which present unique problems are taken in this way. As we shall see shortly, in principle British planning extends case-by-case assessment to all development control decisions.

But consider the more usual case where many land decision units exist. There the occasions for considering public environmental measures are numerous. It is more difficult, then, to assess likely effects.

This applies to infrastructure programmes, land acquisition, and similar factors. But the problem is most acute in environmental control. There the environmental authority has to react to initiatives of other actors involved in shaping the environment: public, as well as private developers, the latter ranging from large companies operating perhaps on an international scale, to owner-occupiers making alterations to their homes.

Taking decisions that relate to all the measures involved in controlling initiatives by this range of actors taxes the resources of the environmental authority. As has been argued in Chapter 8, the authority will find it convenient to establish beforehand which decisions it intends to take with respect to which land decision unit, or units, in relation, amongst others, to where it plans to locate its own works. In this way it need not be merely reacting to initiatives by others, but can assess interrelations between various measures at its own pace. The environmental authority can make use of schedules of activities and/or maps to express its overall idea concerning the management of the public estate. Such a management scheme is exactly what an environmental plan is. It makes sense to inform other actors about its content.

This takes us into a discussion of statements of intent. Drawing on *Local Government and Strategic Choice* (see Chapter 6), two forms can be distinguished: that of a policy and that of a programme. A policy states which operational decisions will be taken in which classes of future situations. As Solesbury (1974, p. 50) states, policy expresses a "generic viewpoint" towards that class. So it is conditional in nature and becomes effective only if and when those situations do arise. Then, and only then, does the policy help to shape the outcome by imposing conditions and/or offering inducements. A programme, on the other hand, is a package of specific decisions. A plan regularly involves both.

It may include statements also concerning action to be taken immediately, that is operational decisions. The difference as against future decisions in a works programme is that, once taken, operational decisions cannot be changed without incurring the penalty of having to rescind some commitment, and this, of course, only where a programme as such can be changed. It is fairly common, by the way, for works to be in progress while plans (programmes and policies that is) are still under consideration, which makes it the more evident that operational decisions entailing immediate commitments are amongst the elements of a plan.

Policies allow the routinisation of operational decision-making and help also with making it more predictable and equitable. They are eminently suited for guiding environmental control. They are good also for guiding financial measures, such as subsidising the restoration of monuments, because in all these cases the first step must be taken by an outside actor. The policy merely informs him what to expect from the authority in cases where he or she does take that step. Programmes, on the other hand, concern infrastructural works, land acquisitions, and the provision of facilities, where the initiative is in the hands of the environmental authority, so that-within limits, of course-it controls their location and timing. (That is the reason also for decisions sometimes being taken even before a plan is made. Environmental authorities, like enterprises, react to opportunities as they arise.) At the same time, this is why zoning seems more problematic than works programmes are. Planning public works simply involves good housekeeping. It does not appear to raise the same legal issues as control. That is only the case where control over resources is shared as between departments and/or levels of government. Thus Healey (1983, p. 195) notes that there have, in several of the British local plans she reviewed, been difficulties with extracting commitments from public agencies. Unfortunately, most major initiatives do involve coordination of this kind, but here I shall leave those problems for what they are, and concentrate on the simple case of single authorities instead.

Environmental plans are statements, therefore, reflecting the "structure of the product" of environmental planning: a mix of public works, financial and other incentives, and environmental control measures and, sometimes, operational decisions. (Besides these, environmental planning also results in arguments used to support pleas directed to other actors to use the instruments at their disposal to conform to the plan, but, again, it would take us too far afield to explore intragovernmental relations.)

Of course, the exact mix of measures varies enormously. In some countries, "public works" refers only to infrastructure. In others, much housing is partly or wholly publicly financed. In some, land titles are very difficult to expropriate. In others (like The Netherlands) municipalities acquire land titles for green-field development with relative ease. Some planning systems exercise little in the way of environmental controls; in others the powers are manifold. Within countries, too, great variations exist, depending on the nature of activity patterns, the configuration of land titles and the style and outlooks of potential developers. Healey (1983, pp. 190-2) distinguishes five types of "land allocation policies" in the local plans which she has analysed: coordinating substantial development or redevelopment; promotion of development; social and economic revitalisation programmes; restrictive policies to protect the interests of social groups; and conservation policies. But the fact remains that an environmental plan, drawn up to guide the environmental authority in taking operational decisions concerning public environmental measures, always contains one or both categories of statements as outlined above: programmatic statements relating to public works, broadly defined (some of them to be implemented immediately, and some of them in the future), including the programmes for the acquisition of the land titles needed to implement the measures which they entail, and policy statements concerning environmental control and incentive.

Where the public works element is strong, this leads to plans differentiating spatially between areas that are the focus of attention-growth poles, action areas, development axes, and the like-and others (for instance: white areas) where no major public works take place. There are conservation areas, also, where initiatives are strongly discouraged. Dutch national planning policy even goes as far as working with two separate plans: one for development, or "urbanisation", and one for rural areas, essentially concerned with zoning the remainder in terms of various mixes of agricultural uses and preservation measures. (It is intended, though, to re-integrate them in 1988.)

Of course, there is a relation between the two types, as there is between public and private action. Thus, many public works are necessitated by private development and depend on complementary preservation measures. Also, ultimately, their viability is contingent upon whether private initiatives are in fact forthcoming. This is why public works programmes and policies concerning incentives and environmental control should form part of an integrated plan.

At the same time, it is clear that environmental plans cannot cover everything. Numerous public environmental measures are taken. This is where the notion, introduced in the previous chapter, of opportunities for creative action, and of the threat of externalities and/or inequities of the "second order", comes into its own. It offers a cogent theoretical framework for selecting those measures that need to be planned, leaving others to be decided routinely or on a case-by-case basis.

12.2 Zoning as policy

This section discusses zoning, which problem it attacks, and what it entails. The aim is to give an understanding of this vital form of expression of environmental planning.

Zoning is a generic approach to environmental planning. Early man singled out which land was suitable for planting seeds, and which could be used as burial grounds, pastures, or sources of raw materials. These were acts of zoning, reflecting the uneven distribution of resources over a spatial expanse.

Much spatial analysis does essentially the same. Thus, Cocks et al. (1978, p. 12) assert in their paper quoted in Chapter 9 that the "land functions of a region form a pattern of functions associated with discrete areas, and current land functions can be mapped by identifying these discrete areas and their associated functions". The sum total of all areas given to a function is a zone. It invites one and the same class of public environmental measures, for instance: the refusal of permissions for the conversion of areas of scientific value into agricultural, let alone urban, uses. This is what underlies the overlay map technique-sometimes also described as sieve map technique-used in environmental planning since the beginning of this century (Anjomani, 1984, p. 111). Indeed, as Selman (1981, p. 95) says, if "we are to secure the rational use of ecological resources, we must develop ... methods of survey and evaluation ... which seek to collate the most appropriate uses to units of land". When describing "ecological techniques", he explicitly refers to the creation of zones to which certain qualities can be assigned. Where it is practised, statutory zoning proceeds in exactly this way.   —

That, then, is what zoning is: an expression of policy giving prior notice of which measures are intended where, within the area of jurisdiction of the environmental authority. This involves a classification, based on spatial differentiation, of land decision units by intended measures. United States judges recognise the need for differential treatment in different areas. Constitutional requirements of equality before the courts notwithstanding, they condone treating people living in different areas differently, provided that there is a "rational basis" for it, for instance a plan based on surveys (Rose, 1979, p. 42).

Many authors entertain similar notions of zoning to mine. Bair and Bartley (1966, p. 8) see it as dividing the city into zoning districts, "and within each district limiting the height, bulk, and use of buildings and other structures, the density of population, the use to which land may be put, and other matters." Courtney (1983, p. 157) defines it as "the establishment of regulations to govern the use of the zoned land. It also includes general rules about location, bulk, height, and thus plot ratios, shape, use, and coverage of structures within each zone". Other sources are Barnett (1982, pp. 60-1), de Neufville (1981, p. 40), and Babcock (1979, p. 416). All of them leave the reader with the impression that zoning by itself would affect bulk, land use, density, and so forth. But the policy which it expresses becomes effective only if it does in fact guide the authority in its regulatory measures. This is why I stress zoning as a policy. It is here where the issue of flexibility (to be discussed in Chapter 13) arises.

There is another reason for stressing zoning as policy. British planning is said to have done away with zoning in 1947, and that is true, as far as statutory zoning is concerned. Compared with the 1932 Town and Country Planning Act, the 1947 Act does not envisage binding planning schemes. But that does not mean that there is no zoning. A "white area" or a "green belt" on a development plan does express a spatially defined policy. The only difference from most other planning systems-even those which, like the Australian, have taken their measure from earlier British planning Acts (see Faludi, 1985)-is that this policy is not binding.

In summary, then, zoning is a way of expressing environmental policies. It comes naturally when dealing with a multitude of land decision units, and underlies all approaches to environmental planning which identify areas of land, forming sub-sets of all land decision units in a jurisdiction, as members of a class. Potential surface analysis, sieve-map techniques, and land capability surveys provide examples.

The next section explores the legal issues alluded to above. They relate to the fact, emphasised at the beginning, that environmental planning operates largely indirectly, designing cities without designing buildings, as Barnett has been quoted as saying.

12.3   Proto-planning theory A and B

A zoning map portrays an imaginary spatial future. Many planners put too much emphasis on it. They forget the *temporal* and *interactive* dimensions of zoning which relate to the way in which it takes effect. These factors relate zoning to the prevailing legal and administrative philosophies.

This section compares two such philosophies, the aim being to give an understanding of different forms of environmental planning. They are the "proto-planning theory A" and "proto-planning theory B" referred to in the title of this section. The term *proto-planning theory* indicates that, without actually addressing planning issue, these philosophies pre-judge them. One (A) characterises the British system, the other (B) planning in most other countries, with The Netherlands, the United States and Australia providing examples.

Usually there is a procedure by which intending developers find out whether their intentions conform to any environmental plan, or plans, in force. It occurs at, or shortly before, the *development moment* and results in the issuing of a decree designed to shape the initiative of the developer in a way which is acceptable, from an environmental point of view. Statutory zoning involves pronouncing on this in advance, at the *plan production moment*. The two moments mark the beginning and end points of zoning, that is when the plan is made and when it comes into effect in environmental control. Proto-planning theories pre-structure the relations between the environmental plan and control measures, and also between the authorities (note the plural) and private actors.

The difference between proto-planning theory A and B becomes clear by exploring what happens when a developer applies for permission to develop land in ways *contrary* to the environmental plan. Under theory B the answer is simple. The environmental authority turns it down. But this assumes that, at the plan production moment, the authority makes up its mind once and for all-that, as they say, its plans, once adopted, are self-executing (implementable without further thought being given to the issues involved). In terms of the implementation studies discussed in Section 7.3, this theory is squarely of the "conformance" type.

But what if the environmental authority gets doubts? The developer may propose something better than what is already in the plan; or offer something which the authority dearly wants, in return for waiving some regulation. (He may be all-too-powerful to resist, anyway.) In these situations the authority must somehow bridge the gap between its definition of the situation at the plan production moment, and how that situation presents itself here and now. Naturally, that current perception is shaped by the posture of the developer as reflected in the application and/or in negotiation taking place around it. This is where the interactive dimension comes in. The question is how to interact between planning and operational decision-making.

Another way of posing it is by focusing on what is known at the plan production moment on the one hand and the development moment on the other. Self-executing planning assumes that it is possible to predict at the plan production moment the public environmental measures to be taken at the development moment. But at the plan production moment, only partial information is available about the options of developers. So the authority cannot know its own options either. The reason is that they must relate to the options which developers see for themselves. The definition of the decision situation of the environmental authority and that of developers are necessarily linked.

Thus it makes sense to allow the authority to decide cases on their merits and safeguard the rights of individuals by granting appeals. This is what theory A says. Zoning then merely expresses guidelines which the environmental authority gives to itself-for its own convenience so to speak-and from which it is at liberty to depart, like a British planning authority which is perfectly within the law in deciding to allow development in an area previously marked on the map as open space. The issue of whether this amounts to capriciousness-a key concern under proto-planning theory B-does not even arise (at least not in a legal sense). Whether an authority strictly adheres to previous guidelines, or whether it departs from them, has no bearing on appeals either. Failure to follow guidelines may be as good a reason for granting an appeal as failure to depart from them in cases of hardship, or where other consideration ought to weigh more heavily. This is because each decision must be looked at on its merits. I describe this as the *indicative theory of zoning*, because the zoning map merely gives an idea of the thinking of the environmental authority at the plan production moment. That authority does not commit itself to following it strictly when it comes to exercise its powers.

Under "proto-planning theory B", on the other hand, zoning regulations are legal enactments. In making them, the environmental authority must not pay attention to individual cases. The law usually applies not to individual instances, but to all conceivable cases covered by its terms. So, proto-planning theory B requires the principles on which decisions interfering with individuals are based to be enunciated well beforehand. Insisting that, at the development moment, plans (and the attendant regulations) drawn up in advance should be adhered to, it makes the temporal and interactive dimensions of zoning into its crux. We might call this the *imperative theory of zoning*.

The distinction between the legislative arm of government adopting general regulations and the executive arm administering them complements this theory.

As Hill (1981, p. 211) points out, it occupies an important position in democratic theory. With plans having the force of law, the executive is reduced to comparing applications with the plan, and taking its decisions strictly on that basis. At least, that is the theory.

There are points to the credit of theory B. Van Gunsteren (1976, pp. 81-4)-describing it as the "rational-central-rule-approach"-gives as its origin the struggle against arbitrary actions by authorities. The ascending bourgeoisie insisted that decisions should be based on agreed principles and universally applied to all similar cases, as against the freedom of choice enjoyed by absolute princes, and the privileged treatment granted before the law to both peers and clergy. The rule of law is held in high regard by liberal thinkers, such as Hayek (for instance: 1962; 1st edition 1944, pp. 54-65) and Popper (1966; see also Faludi, 1986, p. 68). But the evidence shows practice to work differently from the way this laudable proto-planning theory would have it work. Clearly, there is a problem here.

12.4 Taking sides

Should we opt for proto-planning theory A or B? This section reviews literature which throws light on this question. It also broaches the subject of flexibility, or the ability to bridge the gap between plan-making and operational decision-making. The next chapter pursues it in more depth.

The first study to be reviewed is the Leiden-Oxford study which first caused me to develop the decision-centred view of planning (see Chapter 8). The study found Dutch planning set great store on prior commitment to the implementation of plans, and thus epitomised the imperative theory of zoning (theory B). At the moment of development, plans are nevertheless departed from, and almost as a matter of course. British development plans, on the other hand, are not binding, but definite commitment is postponed until the development moment. Departures from plans are not against the law. Environmental planning in Britain is a rare example of a system working on the lines of proto-planning theory A in a world dedicated to upholding theory B.

The assumptions on which the imperative theory of zoning is based are simply invalid. These are:

(1) that planners can predict the nature and quantities of the community's *needs* with some precision and exactitude; (2) that planners can, with accuracy, convert the quantification of community needs into an allocation and designation of land use; (3) that the economic and political forces within the community will respond compliantly with these designations; (4) that the very act of designation of specified zones for prescribed uses will not undermine the achievement of other community goals and objectives (Rose, 1979, p. 147).

These conditions cannot be met. However hard we try, departures from plans are inevitable, and all-out commitment to environmental plans is unreasonable. But this is what proto-planning theory B requires. The sensible way out of making plans vague-and thus robust against changes in the underlying assumptions-so that one will not have to depart from them, suffers from the crucial shortcoming, from the point of view of proto-planning theory B, of not providing the certainty which it aims for.

Examples of systems that follow theory B are zoning in the United States, its Dutch counterpart. These examples are unlike British development control, and this is not surprising. Both Dutch and American planning emulate German examples of zoning under the police power (see Logan, 1976). Even more important, the United States Constitution is rooted in the same Enlightenment tradition. Wright and Webber (1978, p. 284) reject the British system, therefore, as being unsuitable for the United States. It comes "close to justifying what we refer to as spot zoning"-that is rezoning purely for the purpose of allowing a particular application to go through. The reasoning is typical for the kind of thinking under theory B: "any time the use of land is regulated on an ad hoc basis, the potential for treating one parcel differently from another increases". So, like its Dutch counterpart, the hub of the American system is the zoning ordinance which must be followed in granting or refusing approvals. As a consequence, United State zoning shares with Dutch local planning the experience of widespread departures, so much so that an eminent expert, (Babcock, 1979, p. 435) exclaims: "The name of the zoning game... is the opportunity of change".

The major difference, as against the Dutch (and German) system, is that courts can revoke zoning ordinances as being arbitrary, unreasonable or capricious, as the legal terms express it. In so doing, they get involved in policy. Indeed, it was a United States Supreme Court ruling which made zoning possible in the first instance: the famous Village of Euclid v. Amber Realty Co. case, heard in 1926. It permits excluding business and commercial uses, and also apartment buildings, from residential areas because otherwise "the residential character of the neighborhood and its desirability as a place of detached residences are utterly destroyed" (Rose, 1979, p. 80). Its significance is that councils are not liable to pay compensation, as they would have been if the Supreme Court had ruled that zoning involved "taking". (Taking away property rights under the power of "eminent domain" always involves compensation.)

The problems attending rigid zoning have long been recognised in the United States. This means that there is not so much of a need for less control as development interests are prone to argue. Rather, the need is for more effective controls to be available as and when they are needed. Although labelled a Friedmanite (after the world-famous Chicago economist, Milton Friedman, who advocates a return to market regulation) by Popper (1981, p. 23), Nelson (1977), whose critique I follow here, agrees for instance that the preference for mixed uses and for well-located high-density neighbourhoods in older central-city areas has created a demand for a fine degree of neighbourhood control. Condominium ownership-where private developers provide collective amenities-has shown the way (this, incidentally, is an example of successful packaging of measures by entrepreneurs). Another example is historic districts providing more powers and discretion at one and the same time. Their distinguishing characteristic is that whole neighbourhoods are treated as if they were large estates-which has been shown in Chapter 11 to be one of the ideas underlying planning. Indeed, Nelson argues that zoning has created collective property rights in these estates. His proposal is to allow these rights to be traded (see also Nelson, 1985).

Statutory zoning was extended gradually beyond local nuisances to whole communities. Nelson reckons that lack of discretion became

a serious limitation on the benefits of zoning to community residents. It was quite possible, on the one hand, that a particular use within an excluded use classification might actually have enhanced the community environment or, on the other, that a use in a permitted classification might prove detrimental (p. 47).

How to respond to law suits against zoning ordinances is a key problem. It is common practice to refer to the results of research:

A court should not be asked to assume that the particular zoning ordinance before it bears a reasonable or substantial relationship to the promotion of the public health and the other public benefits ... unless the ordinance really has that relationship; ... the justification of a zoning plan ... comes from the fact that those who made the plan made it purposely, and more or less scientifically and organically (Nelson, 1977, p. 58, quoting the "father of zoning", the Cincinnatti lawyer Bettman; see also Gerckens, 1982)

In the United States such research cumulates in a general, or comprehensive plan-which is why Nelson speaks of the planning theory of zoning (see also Walker, 1950, pp. 54-7). He refers also to a famous paper by Haar (1959) arguing for the need for a formal master plan that "although malleable to some degree, would constitute an 'impermanent constitution' for the zoning system" (Nelson, 1977, p. 59).

The reason why the drive towards comprehensive planning came from the legal profession was through the concern for limiting discretion by local officials likely to succumb to pressure from developers:

In the traditional legal view, planning has been an effective means of protecting against misuse of the considerable discretion that is unavoidable in zoning. The planner has been given responsibility for determining whether proposed zoning changes would serve legitimate public interest. First, in the creation of a zoning ordinance and later in comprehensive revision, legislative actions could be based on detailed land-use planning maps. In considering applications for rezoning of individual parcels, the local legislature could also refer to the land-use planning map. ... Moreover, the planning maps ... were to be more than simply advisory, because they were to be a basic resource of the courts, providing a standard for judicial review of zoning administration (pp. 62-3).

The nature of this plan as a piece of legislation, disregarding the particulars of the cases to which it might apply, becomes particularly evident in a comment by Dunham on Haar that the plan must "be adopted without knowledge of any particular case of land use" ... (quoted after Nelson, 1977, p. 63).

The planning theory of zoning underlies the Model Zoning Ordinance (Bair and Bartley, 1966) and the classic work on *The Urban General Plan* by Kent (1964). But Nelson describes comprehensive planning as "fiction". The courts have never strictly required that zoning conforms to the comprehensive plan. Rather "the actual existence of an identifiable formal plan has made it much more plausible for courts to determine that, as legally required, zoning was

'in accordance with a comprehensive plan' " (Nelson, 1977, p. 79).
Comprehensive plans

are predestined to fail, because their most essential practical purpose is not to provide the policy
principles for community land-use controls but to camouflage those principles. Overly explicit
descriptions of ... policies might endanger the planning link and the legal reasoning that sustains
the policies, and in some instances it might also be considerably at odds with the community self-
image (p. 81).

This distorts the purpose of planning. Rather than enunciating policies, plans
are hiding them. In this way, an over-ambitious theory corrupts planning.
Nelson's conclusions are like those of the Leiden-Oxford study:

The most important element of a comprehensive plan has usually been a land-use map showing
... the most desirable uses twenty or thirty years hence. ... But the critical question for local officials
has been whether to permit proposed development at a particular site now. If the development
is inconsistent with the plan, yet clearly beneficial to the community, it is almost inevitable that
the plan will be disregarded. ... After a few years ... so much development has been approved
that is inconsistent with the existing comprehensive plan that no one pays much further attention
(until a new plan is prepared) (p. 81).

Mandelker (1981) thinks that the underlying proto-planning theory is
unworkable, and flexibility inevitable. He rejects the argument also that plans
must be adhered to for the sake of fairness:

Land use allocations can never be made under precise policies, given the extreme variety in the
physical environment. Some flexibility in the application of these policies is required. Otherwise,
another kind of unfairness may evolve-the rigid application of overprecise policies (pp. 178-9).

Krasnowiecki (1974, p. 195) asks the reader whether he or she has ever heard
of a major project that has been built according to plan and describes the
underlying assumptions as nonsensical. Dunkerley (1983) points out the
inevitability of departures. Even public agencies "often fail to conform ...,
or else they stimulate changes that accommodate their own projects but are
not necessarily in the general public interest". Moreover, as pointed out before
even "in socialist countries with nationalized land, operational agencies in fact
compete for urban land. Such agencies exercise independent and often strong
influence on land use in much the same way as do large private developers"
(p. 32). Roweis (1983) concludes likewise that "standardized modes of
behaviour" cannot regulate land use: "For this reason, territorial rights and
obligations cannot be specified (or enforced) in abstraction from the *specific*
set of territorial relations they are expected to govern" (p. 154). The need to
attend to specifics leads to "recurrent pressure to change some existing social
institutions governing territorial relations ... zoning, expropriation, transfer
of development rights, taxing 'unearned land-rent increments' " (*ibid.*). In line
with his historical-materialist presuppositions, Roweis explains this as but a
reflection of inherent contradictions:

On the one hand, most social groups ... insist on preserving a minimally acceptable margin of
liberty in the private exchange and use of land. On the other hand, similarly broad pressures are
put on all levels of governments to ease ... bottlenecks. ... As a result, contemporary territorial
politics comes to rely more heavily on the making of ad hoc decisions to ease this or that bottleneck
and only minimally resorts to significant institutional change (pp. 154-5).

Rose (1979, p. 111) names two constitutional principles at work in creating this
conflict. The principle of equal protection of the laws requires comprehensiveness

and uniformity of application of zoning laws and causes rigidity. The principle of due process requires that cases should be treated on their merits to "avoid harsh or unreasonable deprivation of the use of private property".

Similar comments are directed not only at zoning-a responsibility of local government in the United States-but also at such state regulations in the field of land use as there are. Florida requires developments of regional impact-like large estates-to be approved by regional councils. Popper (1981, p. 176) reports a large developer urging "flexibility ... to allow for technological advances in planning, designing, and engineering concepts", pointing out that requirements for firm commitment, for instance as regards the type of waste treatment facility for a project to be completed 25 years from now, is unreasonable.

Such criticisms notwithstanding, if anything, the planning theory of zoning has been given a boost by the adoption, in particular on the West Coast, of a "consistency requirement". It means:

that zoning changes and subdivision approvals be "consistent" with the local general plan, and that the plan itself be internally consistent-as against previously, when they merely had to be "in accordance" with the plan, and there was no demand that plans be internally consistent (Lefcoe, 1981, p. 489).

In practice this means that the-mandatory-"land use element" of a general plan in California (being one out of a number of such elements which also includes a "housing element" and an "open space element") gives the contours of the zoning map. It means that much re-zoning requires amendments to the general plan. Besides, internal consistency requires that all parts of the municipality are treated alike. (Where boundaries criss-cross metropolitan areas, this, of course, can mean unequal treatment of adjoining areas. Also, it makes it difficult to differentiate as between standards to be applied in different areas within one and the same jurisdiction.) The result is that flexibility, traditionally allowed by the courts, has become more difficult to achieve. Lefcoe is a severe critic of the consistency requirement as it applies in California, and with it of proto-planning theory B:

Halting construction for the years it takes to adopt a general plan works great hardship. During those years of delay, some projects that were once economically feasible will become impracticable. ... For buyers priced out of the market by these delays, the loss may be irretrievable. ... Neither the courts nor the legislature seem to have understood who really pays the price when zone changes, building permits, and subdivision approvals are withheld pending the adoption of a general plan (p. 489).

Popper (1981, p. 157) indicates the range of cost increases due to delays. Developers put them at 1.5 per cent per month. Environmental economists settle for 0.5 per cent, which still means that a delay of 1 year puts up the price of homes by 6 per cent. (For a more extensive review of the cost of delays see Healy and Rosenberg, 1979, pp. 229-31.)

Worst of all, Lefcoe claims, having a general plan changes little. It is

no more than an administrative inconvenience. Some zoning changes will require plan amendments and the plan may be amended only three times a year. But these hurdles may be overcome with patience and staff effort. ... By grouping amendments, holding them in reserve for one of three

annual "amendment picnics", no zone change need occasion a fourth amendment in a single year.
... The difficulties might be worth suffering if the concept of a comprehensive plan were capable
of achieving its aspirations, which for convenience we may cluster into three groups: a rational
standard; corruption avoidance; and social engineering, comprehensive problem-solving (pp.
489-90).

In fact, none of these aims is achieved. What is achieved is the opposite of
rational standards, says Lefcoe, that is to legitimate radical changes in favour
of growth management and environmental protection. This is done by invoking
technical norms. Planning thus removes decision-making from politics.

The corruption avoidance argument is doubtful, too. Lefcoe distinguishes
two elements in it. By insisting on comprehensive planning in which, generally
speaking, people are less interested than in zoning, the consistency requirement
reduces rather than enhances public scrutiny. Also, by favouring large-lot
zoning, it increases the stakes, making corruption more, rather than less likely.
Lefcoe criticises also the

misguided belief ... that if rules and guidelines are set in advance, individual case decisions ...
will be more honest. ... This view underestimates the talents of those who would manipulate land
use controls in their own favor. Instead of waiting for their case to come forward, they will
participate in the general plan deliberations to assure that their preferred case outcomes will, indeed,
be consistent with the general plan (p. 494).

Remedying social ills is not easy either. Worse still, forcing localities to consider
everything in advance, the consistency requirement "thwarts responsible
planning that would institute a management by exception technique, targeting
for immediate treatment those problems amenable to planning solutions" (p.
496). So Lefcoe wonders "whether we would be better off if the legislature,
instead of enacting new rules each session, dedicated itself to repealing old laws.
... In land use planning ... the role of the state badly needs wholesale review"
(p. 499).

Evidence of the failings of proto-planning theory B forces us to take sides.
The need for flexibility must be recognised. Where it is neglected because of
legal requirements for too much detailed commitment early on, there these
are flouted in practice, and environmental planning gets corrupted. This need
not involve graft-though Lefcoe reminds us that it sometimes does. Corruption
of the spirit-as when environmental planners have to work strenuously to "beat
the system" in order to get anything done at all-is equally devastating. It results
in decline of public trust. A case-by-case approach as in British development
control seems more reasonable in the dual sense of allowing for (a) necessary
departures, (b) differential treatment of unlike cases.

Conclusions

Statutory zoning is both cumbersome and weak at the same time. It seems
endlessly to frustrate people and planners alike. In the United States, alternatives are discussed, like the covenants on which Houston, Texas, relies (see
Siegen, 1972). Nelson (1977, 1985) argues for zoning approvals to be traded.
Vast areas in the United States know no zoning at all anyway. Zoning is not

mandatory. Indeed, of the approximately 38,500 local jurisdictions, only 14,000 have it (see Healy and Rosenberg, 1979, p. 7). None of what is said here may be construed to justify this. What I am concerned with is not the extent of environmental control, but its sensible use, which involves both planning, and setting such plans as there are aside when needed.

Flexibility in environmental planning is important, therefore. Underlying it are assumptions concerning the relation between citizens and the state. At first sight the dividing line appears to be between those who want to give more control to public authorities, and those who trust the market. The former seem to favour statutory zoning, the latter flexibility. But, as we have seen, staunch liberals argue also that the law, once enacted, must be strictly adhered to. This is not therefore an issue between Left and Right.

References

Anjomani, A. (1984) "The overlay map technique: problems and suggested solutions", *Journal of Planning Education and Research*, **11**, 111-9.

Babcock, R. F. (1979) "Zoning", in: *The Practice of Local Government Planning*, eds. F. S. So, I. Stollman, F. Beal and D. S. Arnold, International City Managers' Association, Washington, DC, pp. 416-43.

Bair, F. H. Jr and Bartley, E. R. (1966; 3rd edition) *The Text of a Model Zoning Ordinance*, American Society of Planning Officials, Chicago.

Barnett, J. (1974) *Urban Design as Public Policy: Practical Methods for Improving Cities*, Architectural Record, McGraw-Hill, New York.

Barnett, J. (1982) *An Introduction to Urban Design*, Harper & Row, New York. —

Cocks, K. D., Austin, M. P. and Basinski, J. J. (1978) "Conceptual framework and implementation of research program", in: *Land Use on the Coast of New South Wales*, ed. J. J. Basinski, Commonwealth Scientific and Industrial Research Organization, Australia, Canberra, pp. 12-15.

Courtney, J. M. (1983) "Intervention through land use regulation", in: *Urban Land Use Policy: Issues and Opportunities*, ed. H. B. Dunkerley, Oxford University Press, New York, pp. 153-70.

Dunkerley, H. B. (1983) "Introduction and overview", in *Urban Land Policy: Issues and Opportunities*, ed. H. B. Dunkerley, Oxford University Press, New York, pp. 3-39.

Faludi, A. (1985) "Flexibility in zoning: the Australian case", *Australian Planner*, **23**, 19-24.

Faludi, A. (1986) *Critical Rationalism and Planning Methodology*, Pion Press, London.

Gerckens, L. C. (1982) "Bettmann of Cincinnati", in: *The American Planner: Biographies and Recollections*, ed. D. A. Krueckeberg, Methuen, New York and London, pp. 120-48.

Gunsteren, H. R. van (1976) *The Quest for Control: a Critique of the Rational-central-rule Approach in Public Affairs*, John Wiley, New York, London, Sydney and Toronto.

Haar, C. (1959) "The master plan: an inquiry in dialogue form", *Journal of the American Institute of Planners*, **25**, 133-42.

Hayek, F. A. (1962; 1st edition 1944) *The Road to Serfdom*, Routledge & Kegan Paul, London.

Healey, P. (1983) *Local Plans in British Land-Use Planning*, Pergamon Press, Oxford.

Healy, R. G. and Rosenberg, J. S. (1979; 1st edition 1975) *Land Use and the States*, Johns Hopkins University Press, Baltimore and London.

Hill, M. (1981) "The policy-implementation distinction: a quest for rational control?", in: *Policy & Action: Essays on the Implementation of Public Policy*, eds S. Barrett and C. Fudge, Methuen, London and New York, pp. 207-23.

Kent, T. J. Jr (1964) *The Urban General Plan*, Chandler, San Francisco.

Krasnowiecki, J. (1974) "Legal aspects of planned unit development in theory and practice", in: *Land Use Controls: Present Problems and Future Reform*, ed. D. Listokin, Center for Urban Policy Research, State University of New Jersey, New Brunswick, NJ, pp. 185-201.

194 A Decision-centred View of Environmental Planning

Lefcoe, G. (1981) "California's land planning requirements: the case for deregulation", *Southern California Law Review*, **54**, 447-501.

Logan, T. H. (1976) "The Americanization of German zoning", *Journal of the American Institute of Planners*, **42**, 377-85.

Mandelker, D. R. (1981) *Environment and Equity: a Regulatory Challenge*, McGraw-Hill, New York.

Nelson, R. H. (1977) *Zoning and Property Rights: an Analysis of the American System of Land-Use Regulation*, MIT Press, Cambridge, Mass. and London.

Nelson, R. H. (1985) "A breath of free markets in zoning", *Wall Street Journal*, 22 May.

Neufville, J. I. de (1981) "Land use policy and social policy", in: *The Land Use Policy Debate in the United States*, ed. J. I. de Neufville, Plenum Press, New York and London, pp. 31-47.

Popper, F. J. (1981) *The Politics of Land-Use Reform*, University of Wisconsin Press, Madison, Wisc. and London.

Popper, K. R. (1966; 1st edition 1945) *The Open Society and its Enemies* (2 volumes), Routledge & Kegan Paul, London.

Rose, J. G. (1979) Legal Foundations of Land Use Planning: Textbook/Casebook and Materials on Planning Law, The Center for Urban Policy Research, The State University of New Jersey, New Brunswick, NJ.

Roweis, S. T. (1983) "Urban planning as professional mediation of territorial politics", *Environment and Planning D: Society and Space*, **1**, 139-62.

Selman, P. H. (1981) *Ecology and Planning: an Introductory Study*, George Godwin, London.

Siegen, B. H. (1972) *Land Use Without Zoning*, D. C. Heath, Lexington, Mass.

Solesbury, W. (1974) *Policy in Urban Planning: Structure Plans, Programmes and Local Plans*, Pergamon Press, Oxford.

Walker, R. A. (1950) *The Planning Function in Urban Government*, University of Chicago Press, Chicago.

Wright, R. R. and Webber, S. (1978) *Land Use in a Nutshell*, West Publishing Co., St Paul, Minn.

CHAPTER 13

Flexibility in Zoning

THE British proto-planning theory A allows for flexibility. Proto-planning theory B is inimical to it. Rather than advocating a change in prevailing proto-planning theory I ask how zoning-where the problem is most acute-can be made more flexible without a fundamental revision of legal doctrine. This should help with averting frustration on the part of citizens and planners alike, without challenging basic beliefs about the function of the state.

In the first section I review *proposals in the literature*. In *Proscriptive and prescriptive zoning* I discuss ways of framing zoning regulations. In *Coping with statutory zoning: the Australian case* and *The United States experience* I discuss ways of creating areas of discretion in statutory zoning. In *Principles of flexibility* I draw general lessons.

13.1 Proposals in the Literature

In his critique of California planning, Lefcoe suggests that ongoing management of public intervention in the development of land should work "in piecemeal fashion to address the most egregious and exclusionary actions by local government" (Lefcoe, 1981, p..487). Examples are legislation that bars local government from discriminating against public housing and mobile homes, and allowing bonuses to induce developers to build housing for low- and moderate-income people. This is "far more enlightened than comprehensive planning requirements that cannot be met intelligently" (pp. 487-8). He is opposed to any visionary form of planning, saying that "communities should not be required to accept any particular theory of planning or any prescription of the ideal urban form as a precondition to their utilizing zoning or subdivision control powers" (p. 500). He even rejects the theory that plans must be internally consistent: "Since so much of land use control depends on the 'feel' of the community, it compounds the difficulties of planning without improving the product to require that all areas within a locale be subject to identical planning norms" (*ibid.*). This argument of Lefcoe's is directed against the uniformity of application of regulations within jurisdictions because it negates variety between different localities. A second reason, mentioned in the previous chapter, is that arbitrary local authority boundaries can result in anomalies between adjoining areas belonging to different jurisdictions (Lefcoe, 1985).

Lefcoe's arguments are similar to those of Popper (1981, p. 228): that the effectiveness of regulation in state planning depends on whether *differential* treatment can be given to various areas and problems because "single-purpose or single-area land use legislation tends to arouse less opposition, to be easier to pass, and to result in more demanding environmental legislation than comprehensive state laws". Popper quotes "coastal, strip mining, power plant and regional laws, but also wetland, shoreland, floodplain, industrial siting, land sales, farmland, preservation, environmental impact statement, and pollution laws", adding that "the combination of even a few such laws can easily be more effective than a comprehensive land-use law". Likewise, state-wide land-use plans have proved unsatisfactory. They are

too abstract or technical to convey much real information to the public. They also make ownership interests uneasy or rebellious by suggesting that the state has bold designs on their property and its value. Such plans apparently originate because the city planners and lawyers ... feel uncomfortable without them.

If state land-use plans are legally required or administratively necessary, they should not cover the entire state-only selected portions of it. The maps of the plans should, if possible, be mainly white space where the plans do not apply (p. 229)

It is better to identify environmentally sensitive and sturdy areas and to announce policies relating to the types of development which would be regarded as objectionable in the former and welcome in the latter (which sounds remarkably like policy statements in British development plans). Of course, in so doing, the externalities, inequities and opportunities of the second order, identified in Chapter 11 as being crucial in determining concretely the object of environmental planning, play their part.

So, arguing from experiences on different levels of planning, both authors conclude that flexible planning must take account of variety and leave as much as possible to be decided later on and/or by others than the plan-makers. But, despite Lefcoe's misgivings, decisions of environmental authorities must, in a sense, be consistent, and this would seem to apply to state land-use planning discussed by Popper as well. When measures are at cross-purposes with each other, the public complains, and rightly so. Examples are utilities which are repaired one after the other, and each time one and the same road is broken up. Likewise, if there is lack of coordination between various permitting procedures, with consequent delay and frustration (see Popper, 1981, pp. 160-5), then developers have legitimate complaints. It is the disjointed nature and understaffing of the authorities concerned which is largely responsible; but that does not mean that we may acquiesce in this situation. Public environmental measures that interfere with each other do not make sense. Even under flexible planning, consistency should remain an aim.

But it can better be sought by means of non-statutory rather than statutory plans. Many of the complaints against plans mentioned above do not apply to indicative schemes, like the ones which Popper favours. Even though non-statutory, they can act as guidelines for decisions. Dutch planning has long abandoned the attempt to make a binding National Plan, and works with policy statements instead. Provincial and municipal structure plans are indicative, too. It is only local plans which are binding, and they, above all, cause endless frustration.

A report compiled by a task force convened by the Rockefeller Brothers Fund (see Reilly, 1973) comes to the same conclusions: the pre-regulation should be replaced with case-by-case assessment of applications. Similar proposals emerge from the Leiden-Oxford Study as regards Dutch local plans. But proto-planning theory B *demands* statutory schemes. Neither the proposals of the task force, nor mine with respect to Dutch planning, left as much as a dent in this conviction. How, then, should legally binding plans be framed? The next three sections discuss this issue.

13.2 Prescriptive versus proscriptive zoning

Zoning often takes the form of legally binding schemes. Zoning which specifies what should happen is *prescriptive*. *Proscriptive* zoning merely forbids some things, and leaves to the developer the decision as to what to do. These forms exist under either the imperative or the indicative theory of zoning (see Chapter 11), but the distinction is much more important under the former.

Proscriptive and prescriptive zoning rest on different assumptions. This is illustrated by the history of zoning in the United States. Its origin lies in the law of nuisance. As we have seen in Chapter 9, that law empowers the courts to enjoin activities if they interfere with the use or enjoyment of other properties. Court decisions resulted in "judicial zoning": indications as to where particular uses would *not* be condoned. This "nuisance theory of zoning" (see Walker, 1950, pp. 54-7) led to early zoning classifications into residential, commercial and industrial uses (see Babcock, 1966, p. 5) which were cumulative in that residential uses were not barred in commercial zones, and neither residential nor commercial uses prohibited in industrial ones.

Later, the "planning theory of zoning" was superimposed. It viewed zoning as an instrument for implementing the comprehensive or master plan. The result is that zoning regulations tend to be more prescriptive. Dutch local plans, too, are prescriptive. They specify the use of every land decision unit concerned. Prescriptive zoning complements the zeal of planners to change the world into something more to their liking than the existing one (see Baer, 1977, p. 672). It complements their Utopian tradition (see Galloway and Mahayni, 1977, p. 65). Proscriptive zoning seems to restrict them to tinkering. It is often said to be negative (see Linowes and Allensworth, 1981, p. 148; Rosenbaum, 1976, p. 84). But prescriptive zoning makes planning resemble architectural design and lets planners forget that whether intentions come to fruition depends on the initiatives of others-the interactive dimension of zoning. Proscriptive zoning gives a healthy reminder that the planner's role is not that of a master designer.

It is important in this discussion to distinguish between the nature of

198 A Decision-centred View of Environmental Planning

measures and their intended *effects*. Maintaining residential property values might seem a positive effect. The point of proscriptive zoning is that it is achieved by preventing developments that would be detrimental to residential amenity-a negative measure. (In the terms used in Chapter 9 it entails the erection of barriers against the entry of threatening uses.) Of course, in effect, proscriptive zoning creates positive rights, too. Everything not proscribed can be done. Australian zoning identifies uses for each zone which can be built "as of right". In some states developers need not bother to apply for approval for such uses, and these areas are designated by reference to the permitted, rather than the proscribed, uses. The maps are similar in appearance to Dutch schemes. But they achieve their purpose differently, that is by listing prohibited uses. The designation of an area in The Netherlands for any one use automatically excludes all others because the executive, as the law has it, "can only and must" issue a permit which conforms to the plan (see Thomas *et al.*, 1983, p. 49).

The difference is more than a matter of wording. It has an effect on flexibility. Consider churches, shops, local parks and the like in residential zones. Under prescriptive zoning, the land for such accessory uses must be designated in advance. Under proscriptive zoning, unless they fall into one of the excluded categories, they can go everywhere.

Prescriptive zoning is more demanding than proscriptive zoning. It is simpler to say: you must not build on land subject to flooding, but it betrays a strong belief in planning to say what specifically *should* be done. That alone recommends prospective zoning.

Of course, where the environmental authority itself is into development, prescription can work. Dutch local authorities assemble the land for green field development. (For the admiration which this evokes see Strong, 1979, pp. 100-37). Also, much home construction is partly or wholly government-financed. So the public works element is strong, and zoning more of an adjunct to it. Even here it is interesting to observe that the promotion and control of development by environmental authorities get in each other's way. Many departures from plans take place because a local authority wishes to recoup its investment in land and infrastructure by issuing land to intending developers as fast as possible.

Often we find pro- and prescriptive zoning side by side. Public land can be zoned prescriptively by way of leases under-otherwise proscriptive-Australian planning, and prescriptive Dutch local planning knows proscriptive zoning in pursuance of noise abatement and nuisance legislation. For inner areas, where there is little scope for the large-scale projects which characterise Dutch planning, the same form of zoning has been introduced recently, albeit as a temporary measure leading up to the prescriptive plans of the preferred type. Rather than diminishing the influence of planning, as many fear, this should increase it. Finding them too demanding, so far, many towns and cities have refrained from making plans for those areas. Clearly, proscriptive zoning would be an improvement over no zoning at all.

Of course, whether framed as prescriptions or proscriptions, the imperative theory of zoning requires that regulations be adopted long before the development moment, when planners cannot know what developers really think (see Reilly, 1973, p. 183). How that problem can be tackled is the subject of the following sections.

13.3 Coping with statutory zoning: the Australian case

Australia knows a form of zoning derived from the British 1932 Town and Country Planning Act (see Faludi, 1985), based on the imperative theory of zoning. The direct means of achieving flexibility is re-zoning. It requires approval by state authorities. The ease with which it is achieved seems remarkable, as is the number of cases. In fact, re-zoning introduces British-style development control by the back door, and puts the authority in a strong bargaining position at the same time. In Queensland, for instance, many planning schemes designate most land for agricultural use until developers come up with proposals. Since re-zoning involves a council decision against which it is difficult to lodge an appeal, it is almost inevitable that developers should exercise such political influence as they can muster to obtain favourable verdicts.

As regards ways of building flexibility into zoning schemes as such, the "consent" uses demonstrate the principles particularly well. For instance, a New South Wales planning scheme defines three use categories for a residential zone: (1) purpose for which development may be carried out without development consent: dwelling house; (2) purpose for which development may be carried out only with development consent: any purpose other than those included in (1) and (3); (3) purpose for which development is prohibited: abbatoirs; advertising structures; advertisements; agriculture; amusement centres; animal boarding houses; and so forth. Terminology differs, and there are variations to this scheme which need not concern us here. We see that decisions are prestructured by defining what would and would not be permissible, without presuming that all contingencies are covered. This is because the "consent" category has the same effect as re-zoning. Rather than having to take a decision a long time in advance it allows the planning authority to make up its mind when a decision is actually needed. In other words, as regards that decision, it collapses the plan-making and the development moment into one. Also, it gives the authority a clear view of the perception of the intending developer, simply because the latter must submit an application. This is essential for taking adequate measures. There are provisions also like the United States "performance zoning" (see below), that allow planning authorities to permit development falling under the prohibited category, on condition that it conforms to certain standards. The 1984 Policy Plan and Development Plan for the Civic Centre of Canberra indicates classes of proposal that would normally be supported by the Commission, and those which would be assessed on individual merit. On other proposals the Policy Plan states that they "would normally be opposed by the Commission. However, where a proposed development or use satisfies performance criteria with respect to land use compatability, traffic generation, car parking standards and environmental impact, it will be assessed by the Commission on individual merit". The 1984 Planning Scheme for Hobart likewise allows the Council to consider proposals not in accordance with specific regulations, on condition that they are in keeping with the spirit of the entire scheme. To this end, the scheme divides Hobart into districts and precincts and states principles under which development proposals will be appraised and determined. They relate to use, density, height, landscaping and open space, parking, townscape, amenity and environment and heritage. Also, the plan sets out the desired character of every precinct. This provides the basis for the more precise Use Schedule and Density Schedule.

Another variation to the theme of consent uses is provided by The Development Plan of South Australia consolidating all plans in that state in one document. There, all development falls under the "consent" category, and "prohibited" and "as of right" classifications are the exceptions.

In various plans there are provisions that also give the planning authority discretion to raise ceilings-like those pertaining to plot ratios-subject to conditions. The Hobart plan gives the Council discretion to "approve a floor area in excess of that deemed to be approved ... provided that such a floor area does not exceed that determined by multiplying the site area by the maximum plot ratio for the Density Zone in which the development is located". Such bonuses "may be awarded in respect to development which provides specific uses, facilities and features approved or required for the benefit of the City in particular Precincts". So these approaches, too, work by postponing definite decisions until there is a real-life developer with a proposal. They are a way of saying to him: "Come back at me and we'll talk". Bringing this out into the open is better than the undercover operations which so often characterise zoning administration.

With Britain having taken a different path in 1947, it seems only natural that Australian planning should have looked to the United States. That is where we look next.

13.4 The United States experience

When he heard about my interest in flexiblity, a Californian planner commented that to him zoning was nothing *but* flexible and lacked credibility. As we approached a National Park in Tennessee, we passed through a strip of fast-food outlets, gas stations and fairgrounds, which made me curious about zoning in such a sensitive area. "The mountain men will come after you with their shotguns if you talk to them about zoning their land", was my planning host's comment. Indeed, Rosenbaum (1976, p. 24) finds "widespread resistance among conservative and rural legislators to the principle of zoning itself". Healy and Rosenberg (1979, p. 15), report that, in 1975, 39 per cent of county governments did not exercise zoning control. Besides, many hold the practice of such zoning as there is in low esteem (see Babcock, 1966, pp. 11-16; Linowes and Allensworth, 1981, p. 66). The pen itches to release the platitude, but devices discussed here can be only as effective as the community allows them to be.

But the United States presents fifty variations of zoning, all based on one and the same Supreme Court ruling certifying its constitutionality. There are thousands of local jurisdictions exercising land use control. As a field of social experimentation, United States zoning is unparalleled; and its riches should be mined by the international planning community.

The standard model

The Leiden-Oxford Study started with exploring planning at its cutting edge where the applicant meets the authority. American zoning sees this as a simple affair. The application is received and checked against the zoning ordinance, the building code and the like. If it conforms, then all that remains is for the developer to pay a fee, to build, and to await the site inspection. Upon receipt of a certificate of compliance, the new development is hooked up to the utilities. This is standard procedure in Dutch planning, too (see Thomas *et al.*, 1983, pp. 47-9). Problems are deemed to have been resolved at the plan production moment. Applicants are thought to be submissive, and third parties passively to be deriving the benefits (largely unknown to them) of zoning.

If the application does not conform, it must be turned down-which again resembles Dutch zoning. But the applicant may apply for a variance or for re-zoning. A variance is a permission in hardship cases, granted by a special Zoning Board of Appeals, to depart from the zoning ordinance. Babcock (1979, p. 433) gives yard width requirements as an example. Clearly, were they to be applied literally, lots with unusual shapes could be impossible to use. Predictably, variances are used to relax zoning regulations. But the courts hold that mere inconvenience, reduction in value, and inability to put properties to their most profitable use are insufficient grounds for variances. Rather, the problem must be caused by the ordinance, and it must be impossible to use the land "for *any purpose* for which it is reasonably adapted". In addition, ... the applicant must show, and the zoning board must ensure, that the granting of the variance will not be harmful to the public interest" (Rose, 1979, p. 114).

Re-zoning represents even more outspoken recognition of uncertainty. It is widely used, so much so that the "hallmark of zoning is the opportunity for individuals to petition for relief-to seek a change-from the general comprehensive plan" (Babcock, 1979, p. 433). Re-zoning provides the entry point for exploring the distinctive role of the judiciary. (For the amazement which the prevalence of administrative, rather than judiciary, review in Britain causes

Americans see Haar, 1984, p. 207). Even legislative decisions, like re-zoning, can be challenged subject to the rule of "presumptive validity" that "an official should be upheld as long as there is any reasonable basis for the action" (Rose, 1979, p. 12). To provide this basis, the architects of zoning, Bassett (see Krueckeberg, 1982) and Bettman (see Gerckens, 1982) argued that the zoning ordinance should be based on a comprehensive plan-the "planning theory of zoning" discussed above. It will provide the clue to the distinction between flexibility and opportunism.

As with variances, the courts aim to avoid *ad-hoc* decisions. They are hampered in this by (a) the "power of successive legislatures" principle saying that no legislature can bind its successor (thus in effect sanctioning amendments), and (b) the separation of powers preventing courts from substituting their judgement for the decisions of elected assemblies. Still, where "the court finds that the zoning amendment was adopted for the benefit of a private person and not for the welfare of the community as a whole, the amendment will be called '*spot zoning*' and held invalid" (Rose, 1979, p. 127). Some courts invoke the *mistake-change principle*; "a zoning amendment is *invalid* unless it is shown that (1) conditions in the areas have *changed*, or (2) there was a *mistake made* in the original zoning" (*ibid*.). Other state courts regard this as unduly restrictive and accept zoning amendments, as long as they are in accordance with the comprehensive plan.

Bargaining

Applicants are not always passive, as the standard model assumes them to be. Many commercial developers have expertise at their disposal and are willing and able to bargain for better deals. The new zoning (see Marcus and Groves, 1970) allows for a negotiative approach.

Conditional or *special uses* as a separate use category signal acknowledgement that a degree of review is necessary before certain, so-called accessory uses, in particular in residential neighbourhoods, can be realised (see Babcock, 1979, pp. 433-4; on special exceptions see also Rose, 1979, p. 123). This leads to a form of zoning similar to the Australian form described in the previous section. Zoning schedules list permitted and prohibited uses, as well as those uses for which a special permit is required. The latter category might be broadly defined. In Berkeley, for instance, it even includes single-family residences, so, in effect, Berkeley operates a discretionary system on British lines.

Similar reasoning led to the use of *performance zoning*; "provisions that prescribe the standards that must be met to permit a given use of the land" (Rose, 1979, p. 164; see also Hagevik *et al.*, 1974, pp. 166-7). Early experiments took place in Chicago, where standards related to noise, vibration, smoke and particulate matter, and New York City, where humidity and radiation were added to the list.

Another device is the *floating zone* for which regulations are prescribed without saying where the proposed zone would go. So the "zone is permitted to 'float' over the municipality until it is attached to a particular piece of land by application of the owner and pursuant to a prescribed procedure" (Rose, 1979, p. 147).

Cluster zoning permits smaller minimum lot sizes whilst preserving overall standards. It is used to lower the per-unit cost of street access, to encourage the separation of vehicular and pedestrian traffic, to provide recreational facilities near housing and to preserve natural features of the community. It is said to allow more efficient layout and design patterns (Linowes and Allensworth, 1981, p. 147; see also Rose, 1979, p. 176).

Incentive zoning serves to encourage developers to conform to public objectives (Rose, 1979, p. 160). In San Francisco, bonuses are given for rapid transit access and proximity, parking access, multiple building entrances, sidewalk widening, shortening walking distances, plazas, side setbacks and low coverage of upper floors, as well as for the provision of an observation deck. New York, too, developed this into a fine art, so much so that Barnett claims that New York took negotiations almost to the one-sentence zoning law: "The Planning Commission shall permit such developments as, from time to time, it considers to be appropriate" (1982, pp. 99). Of course, in essence, this is the British model, which American observers regard as capricious (see Wright and Webber, 1978, p. 284; for a balanced comparison see Haar, 1984).

Aesthetic control does not form part of the original idea of zoning. Architectural review boards flourish nevertheless because, if "the municipality stands firm the applicant will usually accede to the design requirements even though the applicant suspects there is no lawful basis to the regulation. That is known as municipal leverage" (Babcock, 1979, p. 430). A related device is the *architectural district* where resident review boards operate independently of the planning commission. Babcock says they are often biased against new development. An example of a *special district* is the theatre districts in New York (see Barnett, 1974, 1982; Weinstein, 1970). Some ordinances designate districts also for porno-shops and adult theatres (see Rose, 1979, pp. 167-8).

Mixed-use districts are used for achieving the opposite effect of traditional zoning, which is the separation of uses. An example is the revitalisation of downtown areas (Rose, 1979, p. 168). A very special case must be Disney World in Florida, where a district was created with planning powers vested in Walt Disney Corporation.

Site plan review involves an additional approval by the planning board for projects (Rose, 1979, p. 357; see also Linowes and Allensworth, 1981, pp. 144-5, who see this as a major innovation to ensure flexibility). It concerns specific site development characteristics and is similar to subdivision (the dividing of one plot of land in two or more, often involving the compulsory dedication of land for roads, open space, and so forth). Site plan review may be required for industrial parks, recreational areas and shopping centres as well as residential uses.

Linowes and Allensworth credit *contract, or conditional zoning,* with flexibility, too. Here, certain areas are zoned for unspecified or broad uses. Permits are subject to approval, so it "is assumed that detailed public control, lot by lot, tract by tract, would give way to more general and effective control. The public interest is protected, and both public and private discretion is expanded" (1981, p. 146). This is the general tendency with all these devices. Sometimes this aim is achieved by devious means. As in Australia, authorities deliberately zone for existing (mostly agricultural) uses. Every application is treated as a petition for re-zoning (see Nelson, 1977, pp. 48-9; Healy and Rosenberg, 1979, p. 267; Reilly, 1973, p. 189). The advantage of flexibility is one-sidedly with the local authority. Other than in Australila, there is no provision for state approval either.

Private planning and public control

Planned unit development (PUD) is a development of a certain size considered as an entity. As an instrument it caters for the need for control powers to be available at the development moment. Babcock (1979, p. 435) describes it as the "most pervasive device to introduce outspoken flexibility". Ordinary restrictions are waived, and compatible mixed uses encouraged. Like other devices, the PUD "shifts development determination from the ordinance to administrators. General conditions applying ... would include consistency with the community master plan, compatibility with existing and planned community facilities, and perhaps population density controls" (Linowes and Allensworth, 1981, p. 147). PUDs challenge the Euclidean rationale-so called after the Village of Euclid versus Amber Realty Supreme Court ruling, which laid the foundations of zoning in 1926. This requires uniformity of regulations, the compatibility of use districts across the board (Lefcoe's interpretation of consistency, see Chapter 12) and of the PUD district with the comprehensive plan.

Most PUDs are for residential uses and allow for mixing housing types in clusters, thus permitting the creation of open space (Rose, 1979, p. 370). It is mostly for the developer to decide whether to apply for a PUD (Babcock, 1979, p. 435). The alternative is to conform to standard zoning provisions. The incentive to go for a PUD is the possibility of building more houses; to include some small retail uses; or to design the development without being constrained by rigid yard requirements. But the most characteristic feature of a PUD is that it postpones definite decisions until the developer has made a proposal. So most PUD ordinances are short on substantive standards. "Were the standards more specific, the PUD would become just another district with a series of rigid standards, and the flexibility the PUD concept was designed to introduce would disappear" (Babcock, 1979, p. 436). Procedural rules, on the other hand, are detailed, and this was the way of persuading the courts to accept a "negotiated" approach to land-use control (Krasnowiecki, 1974,

p. 197). Rules relate to the steps in the process and to time frames. Some ordinances specify the rights which are vested at each stage "so that the developer knows that a decision once made will not be capriciously revoked" (Babcock, 1979, p. 436).

Babcock thinks that the PUD "represents a healthy departure from the old, seemingly more rigid zoning system, and PUD permits more adaptability by local ordinances to changes in the housing market. But it is necessary to remember that one person's rigidity is another persons' certainty and the very flexibility of PUD requires a high degree of sophistication and a sense of fairness that has not always been present in zoning administration" (*op. cit.*, pp. 436-7). Indeed, flexibility is not always positive. Rather, how one assesses its benefits depends on the case at hand. All that I argue in this chapter is that facilities for flexibility should exist.

New markets

The *transfer of development rights (TDR)* replaces bargaining between the authority and the developer by bargaining amongst land owners and developers, with the authority seeing to it that overall ceilings are observed. This has originated in a complaint by a New York developer that, if a community did not want development in a particular area, it should permit the land owner to sell his or her development rights (Babcock, 1979, p. 437). The precondition is, of course, that there are potential buyers. So allowing the transfer of development rights must be accompanied by down-zoning, or the reduction of overall densities, so that the primary condition of a market, scarcity, is fulfilled.

Rose (1979) describes early proposals in New York and Chicago whereby "the development rights would be transferred from landmark buildings to other lots. ... The consideration that the landmark owner receives for the sale of his excess FAR (Floor Area Ratio) ..., that is, his development rights, compensates him for preserving the landmark" (p. 470). The same author has been quoted in Chapter 9 as drawing attention to property being a bundle of rights. This is the basis of TDR programmes. They aim to preserve agricultural land and historic landmarks, to provide economic incentives for low- and moderate-income development and are even intended as a primary method of land-use regulation. Rose comments on proposals made in Fairfax County, Virginia, where every property owner receives rights, based on an assessment of needs, proportionate to the acreage of his land. Applicants must submit with their applications the requisite number of development rights acquired from other owners.

Transfer of development rights sits uneasily with constitutional doctrine. The right to develop is taken away selectively. Also, success "depends upon the proficiency of the planner and the integrity of the governing body responsible for its administration. To the extent that either group falters, the program may be jeopardized. The planner's projection of future market demand for land development must be reasonably accurate ... the governing body must withstand political pressure to modify the planner's recommendations" (Rose, 1979, p. 484). The advantages, based on Fairfax County, are: effective control of the use of land and the timing of development, compensation to owners of land whose use is restricted, and an effective mechanism for managing planned growth. The system can also save time and expense for the developers by providing certainty in the rules for determining applications. It can preserve open space and farmland. Above all, *"it can do all these things without any direct cost to government"* (*op. cit.*, p. 486; emphasis in the original).

There is a parallel between planned unit developments, the transfer of development rights, and policies relating to air pollution where global control of emission in an air basin sometimes replaces control at point sources. This way, companies which combat pollution efficiently may sell their "pollution rights" to other, less efficient, companies. It is argued that this creates an incentive for reducing pollution. The authority is relieved also of the burden of detailed control.

Most far-reaching is the proposal made in the spirit of Milton Friedman by Nelson (1977), to recognise that zoning in effect creates private collective rights, and that neighbourhoods should be allowed to sell them. Recently, neighbourhoods have indeed made deals with developers for the wholesale purchase of their properties, allowing more intensive development to take place (Nelson, 1985).

13.5 Principles of flexibility

Banfield was quoted in Section 2.3 for his distinction between a plan coordinating related prospective acts so that they form a chain of means to achieve a given end, and opportunistic decisions being made "as the event unfolds", so that they are "not mutually related as a unit having a single design". He did not address the issue raised here, which is that of planning in the face of uncertainty making it impossible to stick to a scheme drawn up beforehand. Where flexibility is asked for, is there still a distinction as against opportunism?

To answer this question we must discriminate between the two concepts. But how? A cynical answer might be that "one man's flexibility is the other man's opportunism". To advance planning, we must find a better one. Fortunately, a distinction can be made. By accepting uncertainty and applying forethought to how to cope with it, flexibility helps in achieving as much certainty as is possible in a world in flux. Opportunism, on the other hand, merely reacts to uncertainty wherever and whenever it hits. Though seemingly pragmatic, it is not a rational response to uncertainty, because erratic reactions to uncertainty form an additional source of turbulence, over and above existing uncertainties.

This being understood, tactics for postponing and/or delegating, or at least sharing, decisions discussed so far fall into place. Making sense of them is the way of constructing "grounded theory" of planning. (For the concept of grounded theory see Filstead, 1970.)

When it comes to development, as we have seen, the standard model of American zoning, although based on proto-planning theory B, recognises that not everything can be decided beforehand, thus allowing for variances and re-zoning. These create, albeit limited, areas of discretion. Australian "consent uses" and Dutch procedures for altering or waiving plan regulations (see Thomas *et al.*, 1983, p. 43) do the same. Krasnowiecki (1974, p. 186) shows that discretion can be granted either to an administrative body or the legislature. By reserving its position until a proposal has been made, the latter then exercises a quasi-administrative function. But postponing commitment is common to all forms of discretion. In practice, this shifts some of the burden of preparing decisions on to the applicant. (He or she also gets more of a chance to obtain an approval that is tailor-made for his or her needs.) Where this cannot be done, the temptation is to use devious means, like spot zoning, or to be so restrictive (like in Queensland) that every application in fact requires re-zoning, thus giving discretion after all.

In forming an opinion, remember the root cause of the problem: when they produce their schemes, planners are necessarily ignorant of the perceptions of developers. So planners can never be sure what their own definition of the decision situation at the development moment will be. Even though contravening a plan, they may discover that, overall, they like the developer's ideas better than what is in the plan.

Postponing the plan production moment until the development moment is in sight, and bringing planners, zoning administrators and developers together, are sensible. One way is to give the environmental authority discretion to vary regulations in trying to meet situations of hardship and the like. Dutch planning knows this type of discretion, as does American zoning. In both, the issue arises of what constitutes a variance, and what a change of plan. There is the issue also of who is to grant variances.

Another approach is to use broad-brush schemes which are subsequently amplified by means of in-fill plans. The problems are similar: What is within the plan, and what not? Who decides? By lumping variances and in-fill plans together, Dutch planning recognises their similarity. But in line with the prevailing proto-planning theory, it insists that they can only occur within "objective limits" defined in advance. Also, the tendency is for in-fill plans and the attendant agreements with developers to be referred to the Council.

So the devices discussed have in common that (1) definite commitments are postponed until shortly before the development moment; (2) the applicant and/or zoning administrator play a prominent part in decision-making. Flexibility therefore makes the relation between the applicant and the authority more symmetrical. In fact, two perspectives are recognised to exist, each legitimate in its own right: that of the land regime embodied in the zoning ordinance, and that which takes the particular plot of land and its potential uses as its starting point. As indicated before, in the United States, each is backed up by a separate constitutional principle: "On one hand, the principle of equal protection of the laws requires *comprehensiveness* and *uniformity of application* of zoning laws. ... On the other hand, the principle of due process requires departures from comprehensiveness and uniformity to avoid harsh or unreasonable deprivation of the use of private property" (Rose, 1979, p. 111). Flexibility brings the two perspectives closer together. As Mandelker (1970, p. 22) observes: "Unless we take the English New Town approach and place the planning, development, and management of commercial and semi-public centers in public hands, we will always need some method of accommodating the public and private interest in land development." (See also Barnett, 1982, p. 59.) In the terms of this work: lest the public works element should dominate, the two perspectives above *must* be brought together. Plans which do not allow for this will be neglected. So the effect is the opposite of what is intended: opportunism.

This gets us back to the distinction between flexibility and opportunism. This issue throws light also on that raised in Chapter 7: if it is accepted that "implementation shapes policy", what, then, is the criterion of success in planning? Departures from plans cannot be the mark of opportunism. (Many of the departures observed in Leiden, for instance, seemed reasonable.) But according to the decision-centred view, plans are anyway not so much something to be implemented, as something to be *used* when taking decisions about action (see Chapter 8). So departing from them need not necessarily entail opportunism, and British development control provides an example of how a discretionary system can be made to work.

Since departures from plans do not qualify as a distinguishing characteristic, what does? Or is this not a valid question, now that plans have been demoted from their pivotal to a more modest role? Perhaps we should follow Friedmann (see Section 7.2) and rescind the distinction between planning and implementation altogether? Surely, if that disappears, none can be drawn between flexibility and opportunism either.

There are two reasons why the distinction between plans and ordinary decision-making must be maintained. One is that, whether we like it or not, proto-planning theory B demands prior plans, and that theory is here to stay. The second is the very real need, emphasised in Chapter 8, for guidance of day-by-day action. Obviously, to fulfil their purpose of relieving decision-makers of the pressure of time, plans will continue to be made in advance. Flexibility and opportunism thus remain an issue.

Fortunately, the "change or mistake" doctrine discussed in the previous section gives a lead to distinguishing between them. United States courts accept departures on condition that the plan can be shown either to be based on eroneous assumptions or that those assumptions have become invalid. So, even though one departs from it, the plan is not lost sight of, but updated. Indeed, a flexible decision does not remain an isolated instance. Rather, it includes recognition of its wider implications for surrounding areas, future users, overall patterns of growth, resource depletion, and so forth. If only this condition applies, then there is nothing unethical about flexibility. Although ethical theory is based on "a point of view that is somehow universal" (Singer, 1979, pp. 9-10), that does not mean that particular rules must be always and necessarily applied. Circumstances alter cases. The requirement for conduct to be ethical is rather that "we go beyond our likes and dislikes. ... Ethics requires us to go beyond 'I' and 'you' to the universal law, the universalizable judgement, the standpoint of the impartial spectator or ideal observer, or whatever we choose to call it" (*op. cit.*, p. 11). This means that like cases in the future will be treated alike.

This is the same as the *stare decisis* principle which United States courts adhere to. In the interest of legal certainty courts are obliged to be guided by prior judicial decisions or precedents and "when deciding similar matters, to follow the previously established rule unless the case is distinguishable because of the facts or because the changed social, political or economic conditions" (Rose, 1979, p. 1). In planning, this principle allows plans to evolve, and ensure continuity at the same time. That, then, is the mark of flexible planning. The sense of direction which it affords must be seen as its criterion of success.

Conversely, the mark of opportunism is the failure, or unwillingness, to recognise the wider implications of decisions; to think simultaneously on the level of the overall land regime *and* the individual plot of land. Anything else is unrealistic. As Weaver and Babcock conclude, the urban land-use process is essentially political in nature, so that "long-term, comprehensive land-use planning is a virtual impossibility and land-use regulation is most basically a system designed to allow orderly change in response to specific proposals".

In the light of these facts, the goal of reform should be not a vain attempt to predict change and eliminate discretion but an attempt to assume that, when the private sector proposes a change, the discretion to grant or deny it will be exercised openly, honestly, and on the basis of as thorough and as full a participation as possible (1979, p. 260).

Also, rather than being opposed to it, as even people in Britain tend to think (see Thomas *et al.*, 1983, p. 241; Haar, 1984, p. 213), flexibility optimises certainty. It does so by (a) giving only such guidance as can be given with confidence, leaving the rest to be decided later and/or by others; (b) (as in PUDs) replacing substantive guidelines with procedural rules for how issues will be resolved when they come up; and/or (c) creating a situation in which market forces can operate freely within predefined limits.

But what type of plan would serve this purpose? The idea emerging from the Leiden-Oxford Study is that plans ought to be comprehensive and specific at the same time. The former seems like being in flat contradiction with the widespread condemnation of comprehensive plans. But what is meant is that plans must be based on comprehensive analysis of uncertainty, and include strategies for dealing with contingencies. Also, plans should be specific as regards the way they will be used in decision-making, something which many plans keep notoriously quiet about, especially where proto-planning theory B prevails. There the assumption-invalidated by the evidence-is that, being statutes, the implementation of schemes follows from their adoption. But when operational decisions entailing definite commitments are taken under the pressure of immediate circumstances, a plan can be no more than one input out of many. As with a calendar, a plan helps at best to shape the definition of the decision situation of the operational decision-maker (see Chapter 8). It is not self-executing-nor should we blame it for not having a determinate influence. Much as a calendar, a plan can fulfil its purpose by informing choice, irrespective of whether operational decisions actually conform to it.

So, the virtues of flexible plans are that they are selective in what they attend to, and that many considerations are deliberately postponed and/or delegated. Selectivity allows concentrating on urgent issues, trying to solve them as speedily as possible. Postponement and/or delegation address the problem of flexibility in a more direct manner. They allow a bridging of the gap-in temporal as well as institutional terms-between plan-making and the taking of operational decisions. The following "golden rules"-each one of them on the face of it running foul of established beliefs-apply:

Plan as little as possible!

Plan as late as possible!

Wherever possible, let others do their own planning!

Lest they should be misinterpreted as an injunction against planning, I hasten to add a fourth golden rule. It is to plan one's operational decisions as far as possible. Planners make facile assumptions, though, concerning their ability to do this. Where there is failure, they all too easily invoke a sort of conspiracy theory blaming mishaps on developers, utility companies, spending departments, short-sighted politicians, multinationals, and the like. So these rules should make them more aware of their responsibilities. Planning is not a *panacea*. It needs to be justified in every instance. Following the rules stacks the cards against planners overextending themselves, and at the same time makes uncertainty more manageable. Disobeying them, on the other hand, creates the danger of inadverted opportunism generating, as we have seen, uncertainties of its own.

Of course, if applied without integrity, the rules will do harm. But rigid plans are no remedy against lack of integrity either.

Conclusions

The need for flexibility is not universally accepted. The previous chapter recognised a liberal school of thought opposed to it. Opposition is also in evidence in the zoning literature. In the second of his two works quoted in this book, even Barnett shows some restiveness, as we have seen. In New York, negotiations seem to have gone too far, and Barnett reports the re-emergence of new types of self-executing zoning allowing no discretion at all. Popper (1981, p. 24) suggests for state land-use planning that it, too, should work with more rigorous standards. Where problems are well understood, there is nothing wrong with this. But are many problems in environmental planning of this kind?

References

Babcock, R. F. (1966) *The Zoning Game: Municipal Practices and Policies*, The University of Wisconsin Press, Madison, Wisc. and London.

Babcock, R. F. (1979) "Zoning", in: *The Practice of Local Government Planning*, eds F. S. So, I. Stollman, F. Beal and D. S. Arnold, International City Managers' Association, Washington DC, pp. 416-43.

Baer, W. C. (1977) "Urban planners: doctors or midwives?", *Public Administration Review*, 37, 671-8.

Barnett, J. (1974) *Urban Design as Public Policy: Practical Methods for Improving Cities*, Architectural Record, McGraw-Hill, New York.

Barnett, J. (1982) *An Introduction to Urban Design*, Harper & Row, New York.

Faludi, A. (1985) "Flexibility in zoning: the Australian case", *Australian Planner*, 23, 19-24.

Filstead, W. J. (1970) *Qualitative Methodology*, Markham, Chicago.

Galloway, T. D. and Mahayni, R. G. (1977) "Planning theory in retrospect: the process of paradigm change", *Journal of the American Institute of Planners*, 43, 62-71.

Gerckens, L. C. (1982) "Bettmann of Cincinnati", in: *The American Planner: Biographies and Recollections*, ed. D. A. Krueckeberg, Methuen, New York and London, pp. 120-48.

Haar, C. M. (ed.) (1984) *Cities, Law, and Social Policy: Learning from the British*, Lexington Books: D. C. Heath, Lexington, Mass. and Toronto.

Hagevik, G., Mandelker, D. R. and Brail, R. K. (1974) *Air Quality Management and Land Use Planning: Legal, Administrative, and Methodological Perspectives*, Praeger, New York, Washington and London.

Healy, R. G. and Rosenberg, J. S. (1979; 1st edition 1975) *Land Use and the States*, John Hopkins University Press, Baltimore and London.

Krasnowiecki, J. (1974) "Legal aspects of planned unit development in theory and practice", in: *Land Use Controls: Present Problems and Future Reform*, ed. D. Listokin, Center for Urban Policy Research, State University of New Jersey, New Brunswick, NJ, pp. 185-201.

Krueckeberg, D. A. (1982) "From the autobiography of Edward M. Bassett", in: *The American Planner: Biographies and Recollections*, ed. D. A. Krueckeberg, Methuen, New York and London, pp. 100-119.

Lefcoe,G. (1981) "California's land planning requirements: the case for deregulation", *Southern California Law Review*, 54, 447-501.

Lefcoe, G. (1985) Personal communication.

Linowes, R. R. and Allensworth, D. T. (1981) *The Politics of Land Use: Planning, Zoning, and the Private Developer*, Praeger, New York.

Mandelker, D. R. (1970) "The basic philosophy of zoning: incentive or restraint?", in: *The New Zoning: Legal, Administrative and Economic Concepts and Techniques*, eds N. Marcus and M. W. Groves, Praeger, New York, Washington and London, pp. 14-22.

Marcus, N. and Groves, M. W. (eds) (1970) *The New Zoning: Legal, Administrative and Economic Concepts and Techniques*, Praeger, New York, Washington and London.

Nelson, R. H. (1977) *Zoning and Property Rights: an Analysis of the American System of Land-Use Regulation*, MIT Press, Cambridge, Mass. and London.

Popper, F. J. (1981) *The Politics of Land-Use Reform*, University of Wisconsin Press, Madison, Wisc. and London.

Reilly, W. K. (ed.) (1973) *The Use of Land: a Citizen's Policy Guide to Urban Growth-A Task Force Report Sponsored by the Rockefeller Brothers Fund*, Thomas Y. Crowell, New York.

Rose, J. G. (1979) *Legal Foundations of Land Use Planning: Textbook/Casebook and Materials on Planning Law*, Center for Urban Policy Research, State University of New Jersey, New Brunswick, NJ.

Rosenbaum, N. (1976) *Land Use and the Legislatures: the Politics of State Innovation*, Urban Institute, Washington, DC.

Singer, P. (1979) *Practical Ethics*, Cambridge University Press, Cambridge.

Strong, A. L. (1979) *Land Banking: European Reality, American Prospect*, Johns Hopkins University Press, Baltimore and London.

Thomas, H. D., Minett, J. M., Hopkins, S., Hamnett, S. L., Faludi, A. and Barrell, D. (1983) *Flexibility and Commitment in Planning*, Martinus Nijhoff, The Hague, Boston and London.

Walker, R. A. (1950) *The Planning Function in Urban Government*, University of Chicago Press, Chicago.

Weaver, C. L. and Babcock, R. F. (1979) *City Zoning: the Once and Future Frontier*, Planners Press, American Planning Association, Chicago and Washington, DC.

Weinstein, R. (1970) "How New York's zoning was changed to induce the construction of legitimate theatres", in: *The New Zoning: Legal, Administrative, and Economic Concepts and Techniques*, eds N. Marcus and M. W. Groves, Praeger Publishers, New York, Washington and London, pp. 130-36.

Wright, R. R. and Webber, S. (1978) *Land Use in a Nutshell*, West Publishing Co., St Paul, Minn.

PART THREE

Summary and Implications for Planning Research

PART One has given the decision-centred view of planning which Part Two has applied to environmental planning. This part highlights the main themes in Chapter 14. Chapter 15 outlines a programme of research, both for planning methodology, as well as for environmental planning.

Many have expressed concern about the gap between theorists and practitioners in our field. The final section of Chapter 15 shows my sympathy with practitioners frustrated by theoretical debates. I propose a concordat. It is that, however fundamental and critical their stance, academics in planning should agree always to take the problems of planning practice as their frame of reference. Never should their main purpose be merely to illuminate (as some researchers have done) the nature of society by studying planning. It is this commitment, I submit, which distinguishes planning research from other forms of inquiry.

CHAPTER 14

Themes and Issues

Now that we have come to Part Three, what are the main themes and issues arising?

Naturally, they relate to the central messages of the two previous parts. Thus, *Themes concerning planning as decision-making* relate to the proposition that planning should be seen as evolving around the rational planning model in the specific and novel sense indicated in Part One. *Decision-making in environmental planning* emphasises that the decision-centred view sheds light on key issues in that field.

14.1 Themes concerning planning as decision-making

I now identify themes relating to planning as decision-making which bear special emphasis. In so doing, I hope to lay the foundations for a broad consensus in planning methodology.

The first theme in Part One is the rejection of classic planning thought evolving around "survey before plan". The reason is its lack of attention to planning method and its rootedness in a nineteenth-century view of science which has technocractic connotations. Unfortunately, many people wrongly identify the rational planning model with it.

A further theme is that planning is not simply problem-solving. Man is problem-solving anyhow, so one needs to specify the types of problems which planning addresses. They arise out of the fact that ours is an institutionalised world in which problem-solving is compartmentalised-and for good reasons. Division of labour allows for specialisation. The advantages are too obvious to be laboured. But specialisation makes for problems between problem-solvers. Their solutions do not match. Worse still, they may counteract each other. It is these problems of the "second order" which planning addresses.

Problems have been shown to be an unfortunate starting point in planning anyway. It is decisions which we should start with, and this is the next theme. Which decisions to consider depends on previous efforts to institutionalise ways of solving perceived problems. They provide the instruments of control. It is their application that we have to take decisions about. This application needs to be well-coordinated in the light of accepted goals, and it is this problem which planners should primarily be concerned with.

Of course, occasionally, existing instruments are insufficient. New problems, in particular, require our attention. An example discussed currently in environmental planning circles is the impact of new communications technology on the spatial distribution of activities. So a new round begins of searching for adequate responses and organisational and legal forms of realising them. The point is that, though often arising out of planning, the search for such solutions is not what planning is about. This search is problem-solving of the first order, requiring insight and political will to tackle perceived issues. It forms the foundation on which planning builds, let there be no misunderstanding about this; but analytically it is different from planning.

Another theme is the unconvēntional application of the rational planning model. Rather than on rationality in plan-making, the decision-centred view focuses on the rationality of individual decisions. It shows, then, that the need for plans and planning arises out of the requirements of decision-making by public authorities subject to the requirement of accountability. More particularly, it is pressure of time which requires them to draw up schemes in advance of actual decision-making.

For the rest, the review of the development of planning thought has shown how robust the rational planning model introduced by the "Chicago School" has been. Issues like uncertainty of knowledge, conflicts over goals and the need to relate decisions to each other were appreciated from the start. The review has demonstrated also that the rational planning model has been culled from sociology, economics, administrative science, operational research and so forth. Whatever the misgivings about generic planning theory, its genesis is proof for the fact that such an approach is possible.

But for some time, the rational planning model has been mistaken to represent a behavioural rule. Little wonder that many fear that it might straight-jacket creativity. The alternative view in Part One of rationality as a methodological rule is an advance. Such a rule does not have the stifling effect which many fear of rationality, but merely proposes a convention as regards the critical assessment of proposed decisions. It says what the formal requirements of their correctness are. Nothing is laid down as regards the way in which decisions should be formulated. That conventions for what to regard as correct are needed is evident. Public argument relies on them. The reason is that man is a social animal, cooperating with his fellows, and his argumentative faculty is, then, a tool which evolution has bestowed upon him. Rationality-and in its wake planning-helps with making the best use of it.

Viewing it as a rule deflects attention away from rationality to issues around the definition of the decision situation. Whose ends should be catered for? Which distribution of costs and benefits is desirable? Which alternatives are feasible? Which trade-offs are acceptable? How long into the future do we have to look? How do we take account of intangibles? How far must our awareness of ramifications of proposals reach? The entire city? The region? The nation? The world? Must the overriding concern be the achievement of an ecological balance, or sustainable development? The importance of issues such as these cannot be overestimated. But they are not planning-methodological questions.

A feature of this work which it shares with many others is its recognition that negotiations are part of decision-making and planning. The reason is not that people are too short-sighted to be able to see the superior wisdom enshrined in plans. Sometimes this seems the attitude of planners towards negotiations. They regret having to argue their case over and over again, and in many different settings. Their ideal is the making of plans so beautiful and perfect that they speak for themselves. But there is an infinite number of ways in which one can look at the world, and so the number of conceivable plans is infinite, too. The planners' plans are not intrinsically superior to others either. The various perspectives need to be adjusted to each other, and that is what negotiations are here for. They are needed, the more so, the greater the gap between planners and planned, which is why Friedmann's "transactive planning" (see Section 7.2) is a necessity.

Advocacy planning, too, arises out of the conflictual nature, not only of planning, but of various world-views. It is not opposed to rational planning-was never intended by Davidoff as such-but rather its derivative. The same goes for oppositional practices generally. The principles on which the organi-sations and procedures of planning are based must take account of them, cater for them, and regard them as sources of strength rather than as threats to the integrity of planning.

A main theme in the decision-centred view which bears special emphasis, precisely because it distinguishes this view from others, is how it handles the issue of implementation by turning its conventional formulation on its head. Until about a decade ago, planning thought has neglected implementation. This has changed, as we have seen. But normally, the problem is framed in terms of failure to get plans implemented. This has been rejected. Indeed, so radical has been the rejection of this idea that the very term implementation-suggesting a spurious *a-priori* claim of plans that they should be followed-has been banned in this work. It has been replaced by the notion of an ongoing stream of operational decisions. The reason why plans are made is to improve the taking of these decisions. So the decision-centred view has a less-than-grandiose idea about plans. Plans do not necessarily embody higher wisdom; they are mere aids for improving decisions by putting them into a wider context. How wide that context is, and how far into the future we must look, forms the topic of legitimate argument. In particular, there is no inherent reason why planning should always be concerned with the long-term future. There may be very good reasons indeed for taking a short-term view.

A further theme coming out of the "implementation literature", as well as the decision-centred view, is the revision of the commonly held notion of effectiveness in planning. Using metaphors referred to in Part One, that common notion sees plans as blueprints for construction work. So, every time a plan is departed from, people think there is a problem. But if only we started viewing plans as we view our diaries-that is as schedules of activities, not as portraits of a desired outcome-the problem would disappear. We do not blame ourselves for not sticking to our diaries. Departures from them are normal.

Planning was described also as an "attitude of mind". As such, it is not the monopoly of any profession or discipline. It may be that the discipline will disappear, once the attitude becomes widespread. But where does this leave planning students and practitioners, the readership of this book? What are their prospects at a time of retrenchment? What is the rationale for continuing to offer planning courses? Indeed, maybe the experiment at Chicago should never have taken place. Maybe everybody should have an equal share in developing the discipline of planning. The point is that, at Chicago, the Social Science Division was not interested, and Perloff (1957, p. 157) surmises why: overconcern of social scientists with their own discipline.

Even now, few programmes outside urban and regional planning address planning issues. So, let planning courses continue. Let its graduates carry on alongside with others. I believe they are well-prepared, on the whole, not only for a role in environmental planning, but in professional practice generally. "By ye fruits ye shall be known!" And, if other university departments wish to enter the planning field, they might just as well take a leaf out of the book of planning education, with its emphasis, since Chicago, on planning work in combination with scientific disciplines clustered around a core of planning theory and methods. It provides a model for education for practical effectiveness (see Faludi, 1978, pp. 182-3). Steeped in this tradition, schools of planning enter the contest with others from a base of strength.

Beyond this I believe that my modest proposals for an agreement as regards planning methodology should be acceptable to a broad range of people. This is so for the very reason that some have criticised *Planning Theory* in the past for. I mean its lack of specificity as regard substantive and political issues. It is this which makes it possible to graft various concerns onto the methodology proposed here. Part Two has given the outlines of how this could be done as regards environmental planning. The themes arising are summarised below.

14.2   Decision-making in environmental planning

Pointing out highlights of Part Two should help with bridging the gap between those who prefer to deal with planning theory *per se* ("generic" planning theory, or planning methodology, as I now think it should be called), and those who prefer that we concentrate on environmental planning. Part One has catered more to the tastes of the former; but there is no conflict between the two viewpoints.

Environmental planning has its roots in architecture and engineering. Often this heritage is blamed for the neglect of social aspects in planning. But the engineering style is not limited to those with a technical education. It is wedded to the idea of problem-solving based on substantive understanding-the "predict-and-prepare" paradigm, as Ackoff (1979, p. 100) once described it. In many instances it is a suitable approach, but it does not fit environmental planning. There, it suggests that the problem is that of designing a "better environment", based on technical specifications and standards of good design. Those harbouring such ideas have never come to terms with the fact that the environment is being designed constantly by all of us. We all make our shells according to our needs, locating and relocating ourselves as time goes by and depending on what we do. Environmental planning needs to accept that it works indirectly.

This is best discussed around the object of environmental planning. To identify that object with the material world around us has been challenged as misconceived concreteness. The environment of the planner is the world seen through institutional spectacles. His or her specific focus is formed by opportunities, externalities and inequities resulting from the actions of public authorities. To manage these actions in the interests of the public estate, to arrange them into coherent schemes, is the purpose of environmental planning. Its object-that with which environmental planning is concerned-are measures taken about resources on land decision units, the boundaries of land decision units, the channels between these units, and the titles relating to their ownership. Public environmental measures are made possible by the invocation of instruments previously granted to environmental authorities.

This may sound like an unduly narrow notion of environmental planning. But in reality it is wider than the usual conception. Often that conception is shaped by the content of whatever planning acts are in force. But the environment is not shaped by the planning acts alone. The latter are usually even among the less important influences. This need not mean conceding defeat and leaving private developers to act out their own preferences. These actors-some of them very influential in themselves-are being influenced by many measures other than those flowing from planning acts. The setting of interest rates by governments aiming to stimulate or retard economic growth is but one, very obvious, example. So this implies a broader view of the scope of environmental planning.

Such a view is needed also of the aims of environmental planning, a common theme in the planning literature these days. Next to the management of development and growth, there is also conservation and rejuvenation. They present different challenges and require new approaches, but I do not think that they require a different approach to the one taken in Part Two.

That part analysed the nature of environmental plans, too. Obviously, they reflect the "structure of the product" of environmental planning, to invoke Bökemann. The product of environmental planning is public environmental measures located in space and time, that is in the areas of jurisdiction under consideration, and within such a period of time as is deemed to be relevant. A distinction can be drawn between measures entirely within the discretion of the environmental authority, and others which merely represent the taking of a stance. I have called these the "public works" and the "policy" elements of environmental intervention respectively. The latter mostly takes the form of zoning. Zoning raises distinct problems which I discuss, albeit on the general level as is characteristic for this book. Environmental plans, then, comprise spatial and temporal arrangements of public environmental measures.

These views must be developed through applying them to concrete situations in concrete planning systems and the variety of circumstances in which environmental planning takes place. They have little in common, to be sure, except that they all involve changing boundaries, controlling resources and building channels. This is why the decision-centred view of environmental planning offers a common base for analysing all of them.

Conclusions

An aim of this work has been to settle a number of disputes. The reader must judge for himself whether I have succeeded. Meanwhile, even if it were accepted that the rational planning model is the unexceptional methodological rule invoked in the pursuit of correct decisions as which it is here presented-the business of planning theory would not thereby be finished-in particular not as regards environmental planning. There are unresolved issues requiring research and innovative action, some of a more philosophical and others of a more practical nature. The next chapter deals with such topics for research in more detail.

References

Ackoff, R. L. (1979) "The future of operational research is past", *Journal of the Operational Research Society*, **30**, 93-104.

Faludi, A. (1978) *Essays in Planning Theory and Education*, Pergamon Press, Oxford.

Perloff, H. S. (1957) *Education for Planning: City, State, & Regional*, Johns Hopkins University Press, Baltimore.

CHAPTER 15

An Agenda for Research

THE aim of giving an agenda for research is to stimulate discussion. A subsidiary aim is finally to demonstrate that my ideas do not conflict with those of others who profess to be concerned with environmental, rather than generic, planning theory. Often they seem to think that attention to generic theory detracts us from the problems that really matter, whereas in actual fact our research agendas overlap.

As with the themes and issues in the previous chapter, some items on this agenda are general in nature, and others relate to the further development of environmental planning theory.

15.1 Generic planning theory

With the claim that the rational planning model is uncontroversial, is there still much to be done in planning methodology as here conceived? Or can we close the books on generic planning theory?

In Section 8.5 I indicated three areas in planning-theoretical thought: philosophy of planning, planning methodology proper, and practice theory: ways of rendering methodology practicable.

The importance of philosophy of planning, which this book barely touches upon, is evident. The current crisis of planning is a philosophical one. The challenges against it are equally philosophical. Work in this area must intensify.

For instance, traditionally, planning has been wedded to a strong role of the state, and theorists of environmental planning are expected to be supportive of it. But critics from the Left and Right are questioning now whether the state is benign, and there are similarities in their characterising state intervention as stifling initiatives. Obviously, their analyses as to the reasons differ, but there is agreement on the problematic nature of state intervention.

Planners should pay attention to such issues. As Dyckman (1961) once said: "When the planner can clearly see that the consequences of a development will violate the goals of a community, it is his professional responsibility to point out this divergence" (in Faludi, 1973, p. 249). This also applies to the consequences of too much planning. Opinion on whether we have reached this stage obviously differs, and this is an area of legitimate argument. Amongst the authors discussed in this work, Webber and Friedmann belong to the more

220

outspoken, the former defending the virtues of pluralism, and the latter arguing for new Utopian ventures.

Decentralisation, devolution of power, privatisation and deregulation have a bearing on this. They must be taken seriously. Deregulation, in particular, is something too precious to be left to those on the right of the political spectrum. After all, many planning strategies discussed in the literature rely on just that. Deregulation has positive aspects, therefore. It can free energies for making a better job of planning.

So what is needed are dispassionate analyses of the work of thinkers who, even though on the face of it are opponents of planning, nevertheless represent serious and concerned viewpoints. The article by Sorensen and Day (1981) on "Libertarian planning", drawing amongst others on Hayek, is a welcome example.

Rigorous evaluations are needed also of existing planning institutions: the philosophies behind them, the view of plans and of planning on which they are based, their performance as aids to decision-making. There is a great deal to be learned also from doing this comparatively. Planning ideas have moved around the world. Their uncritical acceptance does more harm than good. Resources for the type of evaluation which is envisaged are scarce, and various countries might just as well pool them.

Methodology of planning itself requires further attention. This is despite the fact that there has been a degree of closure, of finalisation of planning thought. We know what the rational model entails, and a definite formulation of that model is available, together with a solid understanding of its nature, limitations and applications. But there is a more fundamental level on which this discussion must continue. As my parallel work (Faludi, 1986) tries to demonstrate, the decision-centred view of planning accords well with critical rationalism. There I argue also for comparable inquiries as regards the planning-methodological implications of other schools of thought in the theory of science and in ethics.

But if, for the time being anyway, we accept my planning methodology and agree to move on, where shall we go? One direction is that of exploring the concept that has been shown to flow from the rational model: the definition of the decision situation. What are the general issues involved in defining decision situations? What are the practical problems encountered per field and issue? In the work quoted above I explore the former, and what Popperian philosophy can contribute to their solution. As regards the latter, they depend very much on the concrete problems at hand. For environmental planning these will be discussed in the section that follows.

There are other issues: for instance a firmer understanding of how plans are used in practice. Their value largely depends on whether they are flexible enough to adapt to changing circumstances. This has repercussions for plan-making, as well as for the whole planning system. They relate to the root cause of the need for flexibility, which is uncertainty, and thus an issue in the theory of knowledge. Flexibility also relates to the role of language and the social construction of the concepts which we use. The social sciences seem to be groping towards a better understanding of these issues, and planning must partake in this.

There is a need also to relate planning methods-by now quite well developed-to the concrete situations in which they are being applied. I foresee a kind of "contextual planning methodology" matching decision situations with methods to be used. Environmental planning provides an ideal testing ground, both for the study of flexibility, as well as for the development of contextual planning methodology.

Neither can be developed without empirical research. Part One bears evidence of the importance which such research-mostly in the form of case studies-has had on the development of planning thought ever since *Politics, Planning, and the Public Interest*. Indeed, the rigorous and comprehensive evaluation of the institutions of planning which I ask for must of course be based on empirical evidence.

It seems that practice theory as such needs the least of our attention. In the work of the "IOR School" we find a reasonably well-developed approach to the key problems in planning. Their most recent work, *Planning under Pressure* (Friend and Hickling, 1987), gives a comprehensive account. The approaches are not ready-made tools but need to be adapted and supplemented in the sense discussed under contextual planning methodology above. The chief need is for practitioners to *apply* this practice theory, and above all to accept the fundamental attitudes towards planning that go with it. These are the ones embodied in the decision-centred view of planning.

Issues of more immediate relevance to environmental planning are discussed in the next section.

15.2   Research for environmental planning

What, then, are the research themes worth tackling so as to improve our conduct of environmental planning?

Environmental planning concerns the ordering, as we have seen, of public environmental measures into coherent schemes for the management of the public estate. Particular attention should be paid to the opportunities for creatively combining these measures, as well as to the threat of externalities and inequities of the "second order"-those side-effects resulting from measures taken by public authorities, rather than private actors. Which configurations of public environmental measures offer opportunities, and which help in avoiding harm? Much of what planners have traditionally been concerned with in terms of planning concepts and standards relates to these questions. This does not mean to say that they are less important, or that sufficient answers have been found in the past. Also, what will the activity patterns of the future be, which should the responses be in terms of public environmental measures, and which public environmental instruments are needed to make them possible? These are important themes in environmental planning.

What this amounts to is a plea for continuous evaluation of, and research into, the adequacy of existing planning doctrine. My argument has never been against tackling such issues, not even against giving them a prominent place on the agenda for research. My only concern has been that planners often seem to think that research and innovation concerning how to deal with them is all that there is to planning. My plea in the past has been to recognise the methodological dimension in planning, not to neglect any of the others.

So the point of environmental planning is to guide environmental authorities in taking their measures. The ultimate aims are improvements to the public estate. But it transpires in Part Two that there are a number of intermediate steps between adopting a plan and its ultimate effects: from the plan to the taking of operational decisions concerning public environmental measures (1); from these decisions to the measures themselves (2); from the decisions and/or measures of the environmental authority to the decision situations of other actors, like title holders of land decision units, developers, entrepreneurs, people looking for housing, and so forth (3); from their decisions to actual changes in the material environment (4); from such changes to activity patterns, at least to the extent that they are relevant to the public estate (5). The length of this cause-and-effect chain means considerable uncertainty concerning the effects of adopting environmental plans. It is as well for planners to realise this.

Each step above forms an area of research. Do operational decision-makers use plans? If so, how? If not, why not? Are the plans suitable as guides to operational decision-making? Have the plan-makers foreseen the problems which operational decision-makers are faced with? What would operational decision-makers like to see included in plans so as to give them optimal guidance? How should plans be framed to give firm directions whilst at the same time leaving open the possibility of change? These questions relate to step number one, from plans to decisions.

Operational decisions have been so defined as to entail firm commitments. Reversing such a decision entails costs; but obviously, sometimes commitments *are* reversed. Worse still, apparently firm commitments turn out to be weak in practice, such as when authorities neglect the policing of environmental measures. Enforcement then becomes a grey area where policy issues re-emerge under cover, so to speak. The question as to where to enforce, and why, becomes important. At the same time, policy relating to enforcement-if any-becomes difficult to control. We need not necessarily think about weak systems of government. It is difficult to think of a country with a more highly developed system than The Netherlands. But in vast areas of the country, no-statutorily required-plans exist, and where they do, many of the requirements written into them are never enforced, and where enforcement takes place, there is little follow-up. Research into such issues relates to step two, from decisions to measures.

It throws light also on the third step concerning the response to actions of environmental authorities. This area is reasonably well-researched. There are studies of migration patterns, industrial and office location, the take-up rate of subsidies, transport facilities, and the like. Still, planners wanting to predict the consequences of proposed measures find they are notoriously short of knowledge. Obviously, more research is needed.

There is a further problem which is in some way similar to that of enforcement. Once outside actors are sufficiently moved by public measures to take a favourable decision, the question still remains whether they can implement it. Some firms go broke whilst engaged in development. Some subsidies go down the drain. Some people put their names on lists as willing to move to new towns but never arrive there. Some such leakages may be avoidable, and some at least predictable, given more knowledge of the real processes involved.

Besides, it is not enough to know whether, and to what degree, for instance, commercial developers avail themselves of the opportunity offered by new office parks. Before being able to predict whether providing them will have an effect on local unemployment, we need to know where they will draw their labour force from, whether they will compete with existing businesses to such an extent as to force them out of the market, thus causing rather than mitigating unemployment, and so forth. This relates to the fifth step as indicated above-that is the ultimate effect of environmental measures on activity patterns, and the public estate generally.

Having outlined my current agenda for research on environmental planning, I hope finally to have put the minds of my critics to rest. If there is still conflict between "generic" planning theory and the theory of environmental planning, between a "procedural" approach associated with my past work, and "substantive" research, then I fail to see it.

Conclusions: Theory and practice in environmental planning

My final comment is on the academic enterprise of planning thought. These days, who dares to project a bright future for it? As far as pessimism is concerned, I am no exception: support for planning education and research may wane still further. Priorities are likely to be on "practical" issues. But laudable "practice-orientation" all too easily translates into single-minded concentration on the issues of the day as perceived by practitioners in positions of power. Planning academics need to reaffirm the importance of fundamental research.

On the other hand, one cannot help but sympathise with practitioners who are sceptical about academic research. The temptation is great to blame this on one's theoretical adversaries and to claim supreme relevance to the real issues in practice for one's own line of thought. Let me say only this, therefore: there needs to be a concordat between the institutions of practice and academia, an understanding that-however independent and fundamental-planning research will always take the problems of planners in practice as its frame of reference. Whatever issues are addressed, research should be framed in these terms. That is what distinguishes planning research, and that is the deal which should be struck. Beyond this, academics must be able to interpret freely what "relevance to practice" means-subject, of course, to the general requirement that they make themselves explicit and are prepared to answer criticisms, as regards the relevance of their research to practice, much as on any other point.

What distinguishes this book, or so I hope, from *Planning Theory*, is indeed the more than ten years of, albeit indirect, exposure to practice during case studies and action research, mainly in The Netherlands. Reference has been made to the Leiden-Oxford Study which laid the foundation to my programme of work. Now that this book has come to an end, it seems apposite to return to it.

It was during that study that I came to view development as a process of ongoing decision-making. One of the first decisions which I came across in the Leiden municipal archives related to a shopping centre. One day the Council passed the motion to build a number of shops with flats above and garages at the rear forming phases 2 and 3 of the development of that centre. The Council voted funds also for the making of the necessary detailed plans and empowered the Burgomaster and Aldermen (the executive of a Dutch municipality) to apply for, and accept, government grants for the housing in this development. They explicitly refer to the shopping centre as forming part of a statutory plan adopted previously.

This very ordinary example of a decision concerning development encapsulates the elements of my approach to environmental planning. It states the commitments of the Council as the environmental authority concerned, all of them perfectly within its powers. In lieu of a full analysis of the pros and cons of the decisions, the motion refers to a previous plan forming the framework within which the Council acts. That plan has had as an important consequence that the municipality, armed with the compulsory purchase powers available in such cases, has been able to acquire the land titles in the area. Such is the degree of control over land which Dutch local authorities enjoy. So, it has most-but not all!-the means needed for implementing the shopping centre development at its disposal. Not the least important are government subsidies available on the strength of the argument that housing is a social good. Still, such developments are built and managed by private companies. As a result of the changing perception of the profitability of the proposed development on the part of the developer, eventually only phase 2 was built according to plan, and phase 3 changed beyond recognition during the many years over which the completion of this shopping centre extended-and not necessarily to the worse for that.

It is clear that such decision-making and planning requires a great deal of knowledge. Some of it is immediately available, and some of it requires research. When one of the grand masters of modern Dutch architecture and urban design, Berlage, presented his plan for areas in the South of Amsterdam-one of the first to be adopted under the new Housing Act of 1901-a Council member asked whether the plan met the requirements, in terms of housing types and costs, of Amsterdam. Much planning research arises out of reasonable and concrete questions such as this. Many items on my agenda above are of this kind, too. Sometimes, answering them requires fundamental reflection, as we have seen. The introduction of the term "proto-planning theory" in Chapter 12 to understand something as apparently mundane as flexibility in zoning forms an example.

Innovation in the field of planning also has its roots in practical problems. When, at the beginning of this century, the municipalities of the province of North Holland started submitting, as the law required, their new plans to the provincial executive for approval, it found it had a problem. Some plans conflicted with those of neighbouring authorities, sometimes in obvious ways, and sometimes in more subtle ways. How could such issues be resolved? From modest beginnings of trying to answer this question, strategic planning developed. Needless to say, a great deal of thinking was needed to sort out the problems of inter-governmental relations which it causes. (Again, a sort of proto-planning theory comes into this.) Whether planners find it frustrating or not, solving such issues forms an integral part of environmental planning.

Now that many countries have fully grown planning systems (some of them systems of the "second generation" based on subtle ideas of the role of plans and including several levels of planning), there is still no room for complacency. They work inadequately, bringing planning into discredit. The frustration with existing planning is evidence for this. A hard look is needed at current practices, and at the use which is made of plans against the background of planning thought, planning doctrine, and the legal and administrative philosophies on which planning is based. Such comprehensive inquiries, country by country, individually, as well as comparatively, are what is needed to advance planning.

References

*Dyckman, J. W. (1961) "What makes planners plan?", *Journal of the American Institute of Planners*, 27, 164-7.
Faludi, A. (1986) *Critical Rationalism and Planning Methodology*, Pion Press, London.
Friend, J. K. and Hickling, A. (1987) *Planning under Pressure: the Strategic Choice Approach*, Pergamon Press, Oxford.
Sorensen, A. D. and Day, R. A. (1981) "Libertarian planning", *Town Planning Review*, 52, 390-402.

* Included in Faludi, A. (ed.) (1973) *A Reader in Planning Theory*, Pergamon Press, Oxford.

INDEX

3

Index   235

Other titles in the series

239

FAGENCE, M.
Citizen Participation and Planning (Volume 19)

FALUDI, A. K. F.
Essays on Planning Theory and Education (Volume 20)

BLOWERS, A.
The Limits of Power: The Politics of Local Planning Policy (Volume 21)

McAUSLAN, J. P.
The Ideologies of Planning Law (Volume 22)

MASSAM, B. H.
Spatial Search: Applications to Planning Problems in the Public Sector (Volume 23)

HOYLE, B. S. & PINDER, D. A.
Cityport Industrialisation and Regional Development (Volume 24)

TAYLOR, J. L. & WILLIAMS, D. G.
Urban Planning Practice in Developing Countries (Volume 25)

SPENCE, N. et al.
British Cities: An Analysis of Urban Change (Volume 26)

PARIS, C.
Critical Readings in Planning Theory (Volume 27)

STARKIE, D.
The Motorway Age (Volume 28)

HEALEY, P. et al.
Planning Theory: Prospects for the 1980s (Volume 29)

O'RIORDAN, T. & TURNER, R. K.
An Annotated Reader in Environmental Planning and Management (Volume 30)

HEALEY, P.
Local Plans in British Land-Use Planning (Volume 31)

COPE, D. et al.
Energy Policy and Land Use Planning: An International Perspective (Volume 32)

BANDMAN, M.
Regional Development in the USSR: Modelling the Formation of Soviet Territorial Production Complexes (Volume 33)

BROMLEY, R.
Planning for Small Enterprises in Third World Cities (Volume 34)

DE BOER, E.
Transport Sociology: Social Aspects of Transport Planning (Volume 35)

CHADWICK, G.
Models of Urban & Regional Systems in Developing Countries: Some Theories and their Application in Physical Planning (Volume 36)

FRIEND, J. & HICKLING, A.
Planning under Pressure: The Strategic Choice Approach (Volume 37)